GHOST STORIES

AND

Tales of Mystery.

WITH ILLUSTRATIONS BY "PHIZ."

DUBLIN

JAMES M'GLASHAN, 50 UPPER SACKVILLE-STREET.

WILLIAM S. ORR AND CO., AMEN-CORNER, LONDON,
AND LIVERPOOL.

MDCCCLI.

Strange Bedfellows

CONTENTS.

———◆———

ILLUSTRATIONS.

———◆———

GHOST STORIES.

The Watcher.

IT is now more than fifty years since the occurrences
which I am about to relate caused a strange sensation
in the gay society of Dublin. The fashionable world,
however, is no recorder of traditions; the memory of
selfishness seldom reaches far; and the events which
occasionally disturb the polite monotony of its pleasant
and heartless progress, however stamped with the characters of misery and horror, scarcely ever outlive the
gossip of a season; and, except perhaps in the remembrance of a few more directly interested in the consequences of the catastrophe, are in a little time lost to
the recollection of all. The appetite for scandal, or for
horror, has been sated; the incident can yield no more
of interest or of novelty; curiosity, frustrated by impenetrable mystery, gives over the pursuit in despair;
the tale has ceased to be new, grows stale and flat; and
so, in a few years, inquiry subsides into indifference,
and all is forgotten.

B

Somewhere about the year 1794, the younger brother of a certain baronet, whom I shall call Sir James Barton, returned to Dublin. He had served in the navy with some distinction, having commanded one of his Majesty's frigates during the greater part of the American war. Captain Barton was now apparently some two or three-and-forty years of age. He was an intelligent and agreeable companion, when he chose it, though generally reserved, and occasionally even moody. In society, however, he deported himself as a man of the world, and a gentleman. He had not contracted any of the noisy brusqueness sometimes acquired at sea; on the contrary, his manners were remarkably easy, quiet, and even polished. He was in person about the middle size, and somewhat strongly formed; his countenance was marked with the lines of thought, and on the whole wore an expression of gravity and even of melancholy; being however, as we have said, a man of perfect breeding, as well as of affluent circumstances and good family, he had, of course, ready access to the best society of the metropolis, without the necessity of any other credentials. In his personal habits Mr. Barton was unexpensive. He occupied lodgings in one of the *then* fashionable streets in the south side of the town, kept but one horse and one servant, and though a reputed free-thinker, yet lived an orderly and moral life, indulging neither in gaming, drinking, nor any other vicious pursuit, living very much to himself, without forming any intimacies, or choosing any companions, and appearing to mix in gay society rather for the sake of its bustle and distraction, than for any opportunities which it offered of interchanging either thoughts or feelings

with its votaries. Barton was therefore pronounced a
saving, prudent, unsocial sort of a fellow, who bid fair
to maintain his celibacy alike against stratagem and assault, and was likely to live to a good old age, die rich,
and leave his money to an hospital.

It was soon apparent, however, that the nature of Mr.
Barton's plans had been totally misconceived. A young
lady, whom we shall call Miss Montague, was at this
time introduced into the gay world of Dublin, by her
aunt, the Dowager Lady Rochdale. Miss Montague
was decidedly pretty and accomplished, and having some
natural cleverness, and a great deal of gaiety, became for
a while a reigning toast. Her popularity, however,
gained her, for a time, nothing more than that unsubstantial admiration which, however pleasant as an incense
to vanity, is by no means necessarily antecedent to ma-
trimony; for, unhappily for the young lady in question,
it was an understood thing, that, beyond her personal
attractions, she had no kind of earthly provision. Such
being the state of affairs, it will readily be believed that
no little surprise was consequent upon the appearance of
Captain Barton as the avowed lover of the penniless
Miss Montague.

His suit prospered, as might have been expected, and
in a short time it was confidentially communicated by old
Lady Rochdale to each of her hundred-and-fifty particular
friends in succession, that Captain Barton had actually
tendered proposals of marriage, with her approbation, to
her niece, Miss Montague, who had, moreover, accepted
the offer of his hand, conditionally upon the consent of
her father, who was then upon his homeward voyage
from India, and expected in two or three months at

furthest. About his consent there could be no doubt. The delay, therefore, was one merely of form ; they were looked upon as absolutely engaged, and Lady Rochdale, with a rigour of old-fashioned decorum with which her niece would, no doubt, gladly have dispensed, withdrew her thenceforward from all further participation in the gaieties of the town. Captain Barton was a constant visiter, as well as a frequent guest at the house, and was permitted all the privileges of intimacy which a betrothed suitor is usually accorded. Such was the relation of parties, when the mysterious circumstances, which darken this narrative with inexplicable melancholy, first began to unfold themselves.

Lady Rochdale resided in a handsome mansion at the north side of Dublin, and Captain Barton's lodgings, as we have already said, were situated at the south. The distance intervening was considerable, and it was Captain Barton's habit generally to walk home without an attendant, as often as he passed the evening with the old lady and her fair charge. His shortest way in such nocturnal walks lay, for a considerable space, through a line of street which had as yet been merely laid out, and little more than the foundations of the houses constructed. One night, shortly after his engagement with Miss Montague had commenced, he happened to remain unusually late, in company only with her and Lady Rochdale. The conversation had turned upon the evidences of revelation, which he had disputed with the callous scepticism of a confirmed infidel. What were called "French principles" had, in those days, found their way a good deal into fashionable society, especially that portion of it which professed allegiance to Whiggism, and neither

the old lady nor her charge were so perfectly free from
the taint as to look upon Mr. Barton's views as any serious objection to the proposed union. The discussion
had degenerated into one upon the supernatural and the
marvellous, in which he had pursued precisely the same
line of argument and ridicule. In all this, it is but truth
to state, Captain Barton was guilty of no affectation ;
the doctrines upon which he insisted were, in reality,
but too truly the basis of his own fixed belief, if so it
might be called ; and perhaps not the least strange of
the many strange circumstances connected with this
narrative, was the fact that the subject of the fearful influences we are about to describe was himself, from the
deliberate conviction of years, an utter disbeliever in
what are usually termed preternatural agencies.

It was considerably past midnight when Mr. Barton
took his leave, and set out upon his solitary walk homeward. He had now reached the lonely road, with its
unfinished dwarf walls tracing the foundations of the
projected rows of houses on either side. The moon was
shining mistily, and its imperfect light made the road he
trod but additionally dreary ; that utter silence, which
has in it something indefinably exciting, reigned there,
and made the sound of his steps, which alone broke it,
unnaturally loud and distinct. He had proceeded thus
some way, when he on a sudden heard other footsteps,
pattering at a measured pace, and, as it seemed,
about two score steps behind him. The suspicion of
being dogged is at all times unpleasant ; it is, however,
especially so in a spot so desolate and lonely : and this
suspicion became so strong in the mind of Captain Barton, that he abruptly turned about to confront his pur-

suers, but, though there was quite sufficient moonlight
to disclose any object upon the road he had traversed,
no form of any kind was visible there.

The steps he had heard could not have been the rever-
beration of his own, for he stamped his foot upon the
ground, and walked briskly up and down, in the vain
attempt to awake an echo; though by no means a fanci-
ful person, therefore, he was at last fain to charge the
sounds upon his imagination, and treat them as an illusion.
Thus satisfying himself, he resumed his walk, and before
he had proceeded a dozen paces, the mysterious footfalls
were again audible from behind, and this time, as if with
the special design of showing that the sounds were not
the responses of an echo, the steps sometimes slackened
nearly to a halt, and sometimes hurried for six or eight
strides to a run, and again abated to a walk.

Captain Barton, as before, turned suddenly round, and
with the same result; no object was visible above the
deserted level of the road. He walked back over the
same ground, determined that, whatever might have
been the cause of the sounds which had so disconcerted
him, it should not escape his search; the endeavour,
however, was unrewarded. In spite of all his scepticism,
he felt something like a superstitious fear stealing fast
upon him, and, with these unwonted and uncomfortable
sensations, he once more turned and pursued his way.
There was no repetition of these haunting sounds, until
he had reached the point where he had last stopped to
retrace his steps. Here they were resumed, and with
sudden starts of running, which threatened to bring
the unseen pursuer close up to the alarmed pedestrian.
Captain Barton arrested his course as formerly; the un-

accountable nature of the occurrence filled him with vague and almost horrible sensations; and, yielding to the excitement he felt gaining upon him, he shouted, sternly—

"Who goes there?"

The sound of one's own voice, thus exerted, in utter solitude, and followed by total silence, has in it something unpleasantly exciting, and he felt a degree of nervousness which, perhaps, from no cause had he ever known before. To the very end of this solitary street the steps pursued him, and it required a strong effort of stubborn pride on his part to resist the impulse that prompted him every moment to run for safety at the top of his speed. It was not until he had reached his lodging, and sate by his own fireside, that he felt sufficiently reassured to arrange and reconsider in his own mind the occurrences which had so discomposed him: so little a matter, after all, is sufficient to upset the pride of scepticism, and vindicate the old simple laws of nature within us.

Mr. Barton was next morning sitting at a late breakfast, reflecting upon the incidents of the previous night, with more of inquisitiveness than awe, so speedily do gloomy impressions upon the fancy disappear under the cheerful influences of day, when a letter just delivered by the postman was placed upon the table before him. There was nothing remarkable in the address of this missive, except that it was written in a hand which he did not know—perhaps it was disguised—for the tall narrow characters were sloped backward; and with the self-inflicted suspense which we so often see practised in such cases, he puzzled over the inscription for a full

minute before he broke the seal. When he did so, he
read the following words, written in the same hand :—

"Mr. Barton, late Captain of the ' Dolphin,' is
warned of DANGER. He will do wisely to avoid ——
street—[here the locality of his last night's adventure
was named]—if he walks there as usual he will meet
with something bad. Let him take warning, once for
all, for he has good reason to dread
                                    "THE WATCHER."

Captain Barton read and re-read this strange effusion ;
in every light and in every direction he turned it over
and over. He examined the paper on which it was
written, and closely scrutinized the handwriting. Defeated here, he turned to the seal ; it was nothing but a
patch of wax, upon which the accidental impression of a
coarse thumb was imperfectly visible. There was not the
slightest mark, no clue or indication of any kind, to lead
him to even a guess as to its possible origin. The
writer's object seemed a friendly one, and yet he subscribed himself as one whom he had " good reason to
dread." Altogether, the letter, its author, and its real
purpose, were to him an inexplicable puzzle, and one,
moreover, unpleasantly suggestive, in his mind, of associations connected with the last night's adventure.

In obedience to some feeling—perhaps of pride—Mr.
Barton did not communicate, even to his intended bride,
the occurrences which we have just detailed. Trifling
as they might appear, they had in reality most disagreeably affected his imagination, and he cared not to disclose, even to the young lady in question, what she might
possibly look upon as evidences of weakness. The letter

might very well be but a hoax, and the mysterious foot-
fall but a delusion of his fancy. But although he affected
to treat the whole affair as unworthy of a thought, it
yet haunted him pertinaciously, tormenting him with
perplexing doubts, and depressing him with undefined
apprehensions. Certain it is, that for a considerable
time afterwards he carefully avoided the street indicated
in the letter as the scene of danger.

It was not until about a week after the receipt of the
letter which I have transcribed, that anything further
occurred to remind Captain Barton of its contents, or
to counteract the gradual disappearance from his mind
of the disagreeable impressions which he had then received. He was returning one night, after the interval
I have stated, from the theatre, which was then situated
in Crow-street, and having there handed Miss Montague
and Lady Rochdale into their carriage, he loitered for
some time with two or three acquaintances. With
these, however, he parted close to the College, and pursued his way alone. It was now fully one o'clock, and
the streets were quite deserted. During the whole of his
walk with the companions from whom he had just
parted, he had been at times painfully aware of the
sound of steps, as it seemed, dogging them on their
way. Once or twice he had looked back, in the uneasy
anticipation that he was again about to experience the
same mysterious annoyances which had so much disconcerted him a week before, and earnestly hoping that he
might *see* some form from whom the sounds might
naturally proceed. But the street was deserted; no
form was visible. Proceeding now quite alone upon his
homeward way, he grew really nervous and uncomfort-

able, as he became sensible, with increased distinctness, of the well-known and now absolutely dreaded sounds.

By the side of the dead wall which bounded the College Park, the sounds followed, recommencing almost simultaneously with his own steps. The same unequal pace—sometimes slow, sometimes, for a score yards or so, quickened to a run—was audible from behind him. Again and again he turned; quickly and stealthily he glanced over his shoulder, almost at every half-dozen steps; but no one was visible. The horrors of this intangible and unseen persecution became gradually all but intolerable; and when at last he reached his home, his nerves were strung to such a pitch of excitement that he could not rest, and did not attempt even to lie down until after the day-light had broken.

He was awakened by a knock at his chamber-door, and his servant entering, handed him several letters which had just been received by the penny post. One among them instantly arrested his attention; a single glance at the direction aroused him thoroughly. He at once recognised its character, and read as follows:—

" You may as well think, Captain Barton, to escape from your own shadow as from me; do what you may, I will see you as often as I please, and you shall see me, for I do not want to hide myself, as you fancy. Do not let it trouble your rest, Captain Barton; for, with a *good conscience*, what need you fear from the eye of

"THE WATCHER."

It is scarcely necessary to dwell upon the feelings elicited by a perusal of this strange communication. Captain Barton was observed to be unusually absent and

out of spirits for several days afterwards; but no one
divined the cause. Whatever he might think as to
the phantom steps which followed him, there could be
no possible illusion about the letters he had received;
and, to say the least of it, their immediate sequence upon
the mysterious sounds which had haunted him was an
odd coincidence. The whole circumstance was, in his
own mind, vaguely and instinctively connected with
certain passages in his past life, which, of all others, he
hated to remember.

It happened, however, that in addition to his own
approaching nuptials, Captain Barton had just then—
fortunately, perhaps, for himself—some business of an
engrossing kind connected with the adjustment of a large
and long-litigated claim upon certain properties. The
hurry and excitement of business had its natural effect
in gradually dispelling the marked gloom which had for
a time occasionally oppressed him, and in a little while
his spirits had entirely resumed their accustomed tone.

During all this time, however, he was occasionally
dismayed by indistinct and half-heard repetitions of the
same annoyance, and that in lonely places, in the day-
time as well as after nightfall. These renewals of the
strange impressions from which he had suffered so much
were, however, desultory and faint, insomuch that often
he really could not, to his own satisfaction, distinguish
between them and the mere suggestions of an excited
imagination. One evening he walked down to the House
of Commons with a Mr. Norcott, a member. As they
walked down together, he was observed to become absent
and silent, and to a degree so marked as scarcely to consist with good breeding; and this, in one who was ob-

viously, in all his habits, so perfectly a gentleman, seemed to argue the pressure of some urgent and absorbing
anxiety.   It was afterwards known that, during the
whole of that walk, he had heard the well-known footsteps dogging him as he proceeded. This, however, was
the last time he suffered from this phase of the persecution, of which he was already the anxious victim.   A
new and a very different one was about to be presented.

Of the new series of impressions which were afterwards gradually to work out his destiny, that evening
disclosed the first ; and but for its relation to the train
of events which followed, the incident would scarcely
have been remembered by any one. As they were walking in at the passage, a man, of whom his friend could
afterwards remember only that he was short in stature,
looked like a foreigner, and wore a kind of travelling-cap,
walked very rapidly, and as if under some fierce excitement, directly towards them, muttering to himself fast
and vehemently the while.   This odd-looking person
walked straight toward Barton, who was foremost, and
halted, regarding him for a moment or two with a look
of menace and fury almost maniacal ; and then turning
about as abruptly, he walked before them at the same
agitated pace, and disappeared by a side passage.   Norcott distinctly remembered being a good deal shocked at
the countenance and bearing of this man, which indeed irresistibly impressed him with an undefined sense
of danger, such as he never felt before or since from the
presence of anything human ; but these sensations were
far from amounting to anything so disconcerting as to
flurry or excite him—he had seen only a singularly
evil countenance, agitated, as it seemed, with the ex-

citement of madness. He was absolutely astonished, however, at the effect of this apparition upon Captain Barton. He knew him to be a man of proved courage and coolness in real danger, a circumstance which made his conduct upon this occasion the more conspicuously odd. He recoiled a step or two as the stranger advanced, and clutched his companion's arm in silence, with a spasm of agony or terror; and then, as the figure disappeared, shoving him roughly back, he followed it for a few paces, stopped in great disorder, and sat down upon a form. A countenance more ghastly and haggard it was impossible to fancy.

"For God's sake, Barton, what is the matter?" said Norcott, really alarmed at his appearance. "You're not hurt, are you?—nor unwell? What is it?"

"What did he say?—I did not hear it—what was it?" asked Barton, wholly disregarding the question.

"Tut, tut—nonsense," said Norcott, greatly surprised; "who cares what the fellow said. You are unwell, Barton—decidedly unwell; let me call a coach."

"Unwell! Yes—no—not exactly unwell," he said, evidently making an effort to recover his self-possession; "but to say the truth, I am fatigued—a little overworked—and perhaps over anxious. You know I have been in Chancery, and the winding up of a suit is always a nervous affair. I have felt uncomfortable all this evening; but I am better now. Come, come; shall we go on?"

"No, no. Take my advice, Barton, and go home; you really do need rest; you are looking absolutely ill. I really do insist on your allowing me to see you home," replied his friend.

It was obvious that Barton was not himself disinclined to be persuaded. He accordingly took his leave, politely declining his friend's offered escort. Notwithstanding the few commonplace regrets which Norcott had expressed, it was plain that he was just as little deceived as Barton himself by the extempore plea of illness with which he had accounted for the strange exhibition, and that he even then suspected some lurking mystery in the matter.

Norcott called next day at Barton's lodgings, to inquire for him, and learned from the servant that he had not left his room since his return the night before; but that he was not seriously indisposed, and hoped to be out again in a few days. That evening he sent for Doctor Richards, then in large and fashionable practice in Dublin, and their interview was, it is said, an odd one.

He entered into a detail of his own symptoms in an abstracted and desultory kind of way, which seemed to argue a strange want of interest in his own cure, and, at all events, made it manifest that there was some topic engaging his mind of more engrossing importance than his present ailment. He complained of occasional palpitations, and headach. Doctor Richards asked him, among other questions, whether there was any irritating circumstance or anxiety to account for it. This he denied quickly and almost peevishly; and the physician thereupon declared his opinion, that there was nothing amiss except some slight derangement of the digestion, for which he accordingly wrote a prescription, and was about to withdraw, when Mr. Barton, with the air of a man who suddenly recollects a topic which had nearly escaped him, recalled him.

" I beg your pardon, doctor, but I had really almost forgot; will you permit me to ask you two or three medical questions—rather odd ones, perhaps, but as a wager depends upon their solution, you will, I hope, excuse my unreasonableness."

The physician readily undertook to satisfy the inquirer.

Barton seemed to have some difficulty about opening the proposed interrogatories, for he was silent for a minute, then walked to his book-case, and returned as he had gone; at last he sat down, and said —

" You'll think them very childish questions, but I can't recover my wager without a decision ; so I must put them. I want to know first about lock-jaw. If a man actually has had that complaint, and appears to have died of it—so much so, that a physician of average skill pronounces him actually dead—may he, after all, recover ?"

The physician smiled, and shook his head.

" But—but a blunder may be made," resumed Barton. " Suppose an ignorant pretender to medical skill ; may *he* be so deceived by any stage of the complaint, as to mistake what is only a part of the progress of the disease, for death itself?"

" No one who had ever seen death," answered he, " could mistake it in a case of lock-jaw."

Barton mused for a few minutes. " I am going to ask you a question, perhaps still more childish; but first tell me, are not the regulations of foreign hospitals, such as those of, let us say, Lisbon, very lax and bungling? May not all kinds of blunders and slips occur in their entries of names, and soforth ?"

Doctor Richards professed his inability to answer that query.

"Well, then, doctor, here is the last of my questions. You will, probably, laugh at it; but it must out, nevertheless. Is there any disease, in all the range of human maladies, which would have the effect of perceptibly contracting the stature, and the whole frame—causing the man to shrink in all his proportions, and yet to preserve his exact resemblance to himself in every particular—with the one exception, his height and bulk; *any* disease, mark, no matter how rare, how little believed in, generally, which could possibly result in producing such an effect?"

The physician replied with a smile, and a very decided negative.

"Tell me, then," said Barton, abruptly, "if a man be in reasonable fear of assault from a lunatic who is at large, can he not procure a warrant for his arrest and detention?"

"Really, that is more a lawyer's question than one in my way," replied Doctor Richards; "but I believe, on applying to a magistrate, such a course would be directed."

The physician then took his leave; but, just as he reached the hall-door, remembered that he had left his cane up stairs, and returned. His reappearance was awkward, for a piece of paper, which he recognized as his own prescription, was slowly burning upon the fire, and Barton sitting close by with an expression of settled gloom and dismay. Doctor Richards had too much tact to appear to observe what presented itself; but he had seen quite enough to assure him that the mind, and not the body, of Captain Barton was in reality the seat of his sufferings.

A few days afterwards, the following advertisement appeared in the Dublin newspapers :—

"If Sylvester Yelland, formerly a foremast-man on board his Majesty's frigate Dolphin, or his nearest of kin, will apply to Mr. Robert Smith, solicitor, at his office, Dame-street, he or they may hear of something greatly to his or their advantage. Admission may be had at any hour up to twelve o'clock at night, for the next fortnight, should parties desire to avoid observation; and the strictest secrecy, as to all communications intended to be confidential, shall be honourably observed."

The Dolphin, as we have mentioned, was the vessel which Captain Barton had commanded; and this circumstance, connected with the extraordinary exertions made by the circulation of hand-bills, &c., as well as by repeated advertisements, to secure for this strange notice the utmost possible publicity, suggested to Doctor Richards the idea that Captain Barton's extreme uneasiness was somehow connected with the individual to whom the advertisement was addressed, and he himself the author of it. This, however, it is needless to add, was no more than a conjecture. No information whatsoever, as to the real purpose of the advertisement itself, was divulged by the agent, nor yet any hint as to who his employer might be.

Mr. Barton, although he had latterly begun to earn for himself the character of a hypochondriac, was yet very far from deserving it. Though by no means lively,

c

he had yet, naturally, what are termed "even spirits,"
and was not subject to undue depressions. He soon,
therefore, began to return to his former habits; and
one of the earliest symptoms of this healthier tone of
spirits was, his appearing at a grand dinner of the Free-
masons, of which worthy fraternity he was himself a
brother. Barton, who had been at first gloomy and
abstracted, drank much more freely than was his wont—
possibly with the purpose of dispelling his own secret
anxieties—and under the influence of good wine, and
pleasant company, became gradually (unlike his usual
self) talkative, and even noisy. It was under this unwonted excitement that he left his company at about
half-past ten o'clock; and as conviviality is a strong
incentive to gallantry, it occurred to him to proceed
forthwith to Lady Rochdale's, and pass the remainder
of the evening with her and his destined bride.

Accordingly, he was soon at ——— street, and chatting gaily with the ladies. It is not to be supposed that
Captain Barton had exceeded the limits which propriety
prescribes to good fellowship; he had merely taken
enough of wine to raise his spirits, without, however, in
the least degree unsteadying his mind, or affecting his
manners. With this undue elevation of spirits had supervened an entire oblivion or contempt of those undefined apprehensions which had for so long weighed
upon his mind, and to a certain extent estranged him
from society; but as the night wore away, and his
artificial gaiety began to flag, these painful feelings gradually intruded themselves again, and he grew abstracted
and anxious as heretofore. He took his leave at length,
with an unpleasant foreboding of some coming mischief,

and with a mind haunted with a thousand mysterious apprehensions, such as, even while he acutely felt their pressure, he, nevertheless, inwardly strove, or affected to contemn.

It was his proud defiance of what he considered to be his own weakness, which prompted him upon this occasion to the course which brought about the adventure which we are now about to relate. Mr. Barton might have easily called a coach, but he was conscious that his strong inclination to do so proceeded from no cause other than what he desperately persisted in representing to himself to be his own superstitious tremors. He might also have returned home by a route different from that against which he had been warned by his mysterious correspondent; but for the same reason he dismissed this idea also, and with a dogged and half desperate resolution to force matters to a crisis of some kind, if there were any reality in the causes of his former suffering, and if not, satisfactorily to bring their delusiveness to the proof, he determined to follow precisely the course which he had trodden upon the night so painfully memorable in his own mind as that on which his strange persecution had commenced. Though, sooth to say, the pilot who for the first time steers his vessel under the muzzles of a hostile battery, never felt his resolution more severely tasked than did Captain Barton, as he breathlessly pursued this solitary path—a path which, spite of every effort of scepticism and reason, he felt to be, as respected *him*, infested by a malignant influence.

He pursued his way steadily and rapidly, scarcely breathing from intensity of suspense; he, however, was

troubled by no renewal of the dreaded footsteps, and
was beginning to feel a return of confidence, as, more
than three-fourths of the way being accomplished with
impunity, he approached the long line of twinkling oil
lamps which indicated the frequented streets.   This
feeling of self-gratulation was, however, but momentary.
The report of a musket at some two hundred yards behind him, and the whistle of a bullet close to his head,
disagreeably and startlingly dispelled it.   His first impulse was to retrace his steps in pursuit of the assassin;
but the road on either side was, as we have said, embarrassed by the foundations of a street, beyond which
extended waste fields, full of rubbish and neglected lime
and brick kilns, and all now as utterly silent as though
no sound had ever disturbed their dark and unsightly
solitude.   The futility of, single-handed, attempting,
under such circumstances, a search for the murderer,
was apparent, especially as no sound whatever was
audible to direct his pursuit.

With the tumultuous sensations of one whose life has
just been exposed to a murderous attempt, and whose
escape has been the narrowest possible, Captain Barton
turned, and without, however, quickening his pace actually to a run, hurriedly pursued his way. He had
turned, as we have said, after a pause of a few seconds,
and had just commenced his rapid retreat, when on a
sudden he met the well-remembered little man in the
fur cap.   The encounter was but momentary.   The
figure was walking at the same exaggerated pace, and
with the same strange air of menace as before ; and as
it passed him, he thought he heard it say, in a furious
whisper, " Still alive—still alive ! "

The state of Mr. Barton's spirits began now to work a corresponding alteration in his health and looks, and to such a degree that it was impossible that the change should escape general remark. For some reasons, known but to himself, he took no step whatsoever to bring the attempt upon his life, which he had so narrowly escaped, under the notice of the authorities; on the contrary, he kept it jealously to himself; and it was not for many weeks after the occurrence that he mentioned it, and then in strict confidence, to a gentleman, whom the torments of his mind at last compelled him to consult.

Spite of his blue devils, however, poor Barton, having no satisfactory reason to render to the public for any undue remissness in the attentions which his relation to Miss Montague required, was obliged to exert himself, and present to the world a confident and cheerful bearing. The true source of his sufferings, and every circumstance connected with them, he guarded with a reserve so jealous, that it seemed dictated by at least a suspicion, that the origin of his strange persecution was known to himself, and that it was of a nature which, upon his own account, he could not or dared not disclose.

The mind thus turned in upon itself, and constantly occupied with a haunting anxiety which it dared not reveal, or confide to any human breast, became daily more excited, and, of course, more vividly impressible, by a system of attack which operated through the nervous system; and in this state he was destined to sustain, with increasing frequency, the stealthy visitations of that apparition, which from the first had seemed to possess so unearthly and terrible a hold upon his imagination.

*   *   *   *   *   *   *

It was about this time that Captain Barton called upon the then celebrated preacher, Doctor Macklin, with whom he had a slight acquaintance, and an extraordinary conversation ensued.   The divine was seated in his chambers in college, surrounded with works upon his favourite pursuit, and deep in theology, when Barton was announced.   There was something at once embarrassed and excited in his manner, which, along with his wan and haggard countenance, impressed the student with the unpleasant consciousness that his visiter must have recéntly suffered terribly indeed, to account for an alteration so striking, almost shocking.

After the usual interchange of polite greeting, and a few common-place remarks, Captain Barton, who obviously perceived the surprise which his visit had excited, and which Doctor Macklin was unable wholly to conceal, interrupted a brief pause by remarking :—

"This is a strange call, Doctor Macklin, perhaps scarcely warranted by an acquaintance so slight as mine with you.   I should not, under ordinary circumstances, have ventured to disturb you; but my visit is neither an idle nor impertinent intrusion.   I am sure you will not so account it, when——"

Doctor Macklin interrupted him with assurances, such as good breeding suggested, and Barton resumed :—

"I am come to task your patience by asking your advice.   When I say your patience, I might, indeed, say more ; I might have said your humanity, your compassion ; for I have been, and am a great sufferer."

"My dear sir," replied the churchman, "it will, indeed, afford me infinite gratification if I can give you comfort in any distress of mind ; but—but——"

"I know what you would say," resumed Barton, quickly ; "I am an unbeliever, and, therefore, incapable of deriving help from religion ; but don't take that for granted. At least you must not assume that, however unsettled my convictions may be, I do not feel a deep, a very deep, interest in the subject. Circumstances have lately forced it upon my attention, in such a way as to compel me to review the whole question in a more candid and teachable spirit, I believe, than I ever studied it in before."

"Your difficulties, I take it for granted, refer to the evidences of revelation," suggested the clergyman.

"Why—no—yes; in fact I am ashamed to say I have not considered even my objections sufficiently to state them connectedly; but—but there is one subject on which I feel a peculiar interest."

He paused again, and Doctor Macklin pressed him to proceed.

"The fact is," said Barton, "whatever may be my uncertainty as to the authenticity of what we are taught to call revelation, of one fact I am deeply and horribly convinced, that there does exist beyond this a spiritual world—a system whose workings are generally in mercy hidden from us—a system which may be, and which is sometimes, partially and terribly revealed. I am sure, I *know*," continued Barton, with increasing excitement, "there is a God—a dreadful God—and that retribution follows guilt. In ways, the most mysterious and stupendous ; by agencies, the most inexplicable and terrific;

there is a spiritual system—great God, how frightfully
I have been convinced!—a system malignant, and inex-
orable, and omnipotent, under whose persecutions I am,
and have been, suffering the torments of the damned!
—yes, sir—yes—the fires and frenzy of hell!"

As Barton spoke, his agitation became so vehement
that the divine was shocked, and even alarmed. The
wild and excited rapidity with which he spoke, and,
above all, the indefinable horror which stamped his features, afforded a contrast to his ordinary cool and un-
impassioned self-possession striking and painful in the
last degree.

"My dear sir," said Doctor Macklin, after a brief
pause, "I fear you have been suffering much, indeed;
but I venture to predict that the depression under which
you labour will be found to originate in purely physical
causes; and that with a change of air, and the aid of
a few tonics, your spirits will return, and the tone of
your mind be once more cheerful and tranquil as heretofore. There was, after all, more truth than we are
quite willing to admit in the classic theories which assigned the undue predominance of any one affection of
the mind, to the undue action or torpidity of one or
other of our bodily organs. Believe me, that a little
attention to diet, exercise, and the other essentials of
health, under competent direction, will make you as
much yourself as you can wish."

"Doctor Macklin," said Barton, with something like
a shudder, "I *cannot* delude myself with such a hope.
I have no hope to cling to but one, and that is, that by
some other spiritual agency more potent than that which
tortures me, *it* may be combated, and I delivered. If
this may not be, I am lost—now and for ever lost."

"But, Mr. Barton, you must remember," urged his companion, "that others have suffered as you have done, and ——"

"No, no, no," interrupted he with irritability; "no, sir, I am not a credulous—far from a superstitious man. I have been, perhaps, too much the reverse—too sceptical, too slow of belief; but unless I were one whom no amount of evidence could convince, unless I were to contemn the repeated, the *perpetual* evidence of my own senses, I am now—now at last constrained to believe— I have no escape from the conviction, the overwhelming certainty, that I am haunted and dogged, go where I may, by—by a DEMON."

There was an almost preternatural energy of horror in Barton's face, as, with its damp and deathlike lineaments turned towards his companion, he thus delivered himself.

"God help you, my poor friend," said Doctor Macklin, much shocked, "God help you; for, indeed, you *are* a sufferer, however your sufferings may have been caused."

"Ay, ay, God help me," echoed Barton sternly; "but *will* he help me? will he help me?"

"Pray to him; pray in an humble and trusting spirit," said he.

"Pray, pray," echoed he again; "I can't pray; I could as easily move a mountain by an effort of my will. I have not belief enough to pray; there is something within me that will not pray. You prescribe impossibilities—literal impossibilities."

"You will not find it so, if you will but try," said Doctor Macklin.

"Try! I *have* tried, and the attempt only fills me with confusion and terror; I have tried in vain, and more than in vain. The awful, unutterable idea of eternity and infinity oppresses and maddens my brain, whenever my mind approaches the contemplation of the Creator; I recoil from the effort, scared, confounded, terrified. I tell you, Doctor Macklin, if I am to be saved, it must be by other means. The idea of the Creator is to me intolerable; my mind cannot support it."

"Say, then, my dear sir," urged he; "say how you would have me serve you; what you would learn of me; what can I do or say to relieve you?"

"Listen to me first," replied Captain Barton, with a subdued air, and an evident effort to suppress his excitement; "listen to me while I detail the circumstances of the terrible persecution under which my life has become all but intolerable—a persecution which has made me fear *death* and the world beyond the grave as much as I have grown to hate existence."

Barton then proceeded to relate the circumstances which we have already detailed, and then continued:—

"This has now become habitual—an accustomed thing. I do not mean the actual seeing him in the flesh —thank God, *that* at least is not permitted daily. Thank God, from the unutterable horrors of that visitation I have been mercifully allowed intervals of repose, though none of security; but from the consciousness that a malignant spirit is following and watching me wherever I go, I have never, for a single instant, a temporary respite. I am pursued with blasphemies, cries of despair, and appalling hatred. I hear those dreadful sounds called after me as I turn the corners of streets; they come

in the night-time, while I sit in my chamber alone; they
haunt me everywhere, charging me with hideous crimes,
and—great God!—threatening me with coming vengeance and eternal misery. Hush!—do you hear *that!*"
he cried with a horrible smile of triumph; " there—
there, will that convince you?"

The clergyman felt the chillness of horror irresistibly
steal over him, while, during the wail of a sudden gust of
wind, he heard, or fancied he heard, the half articulate
sounds of rage and derision mingling in their sough.

"Well, what do you think of *that!*" at length Barton
cried, drawing a long breath through his teeth.

" I heard the wind," said Doctor Macklin; " what
should I think of it? what is there remarkable about
it?"

" The prince of the powers of the air," muttered Barton, with a shudder.

"Tut, tut! my dear sir,"said the student, with an effort to reassure himself; for though it was broad day-
light, there was nevertheless something disagreeably
contagious in the nervous excitement under which his
visiter so obviously suffered. " You must not give way
to those wild fancies; you must resist those impulses of
the imagination."

"Ay, ay; 'resist the devil and he will flee from
thee,'" said Barton in the same tone; "but *how* resist
him? ay, there it is; there is the rub. What—*what*
am I to do? what *can* I do?"

" My dear sir, this is fancy," said the man of folios;
"you are your own tormonter."

" No, no, sir; fancy has no part in it," answered Barton, somewhat sternly. "Fancy, forsooth! Was it that

made you, as well as me, hear, but this moment, those
appalling accents of hell? Fancy, indeed! No, no."

" But you have seen this person frequently," said the
ecclesiastic; "why have you not accosted or secured him?
Is it not somewhat precipitate, to say no more, to assume,
as you have done, the existence of preternatural agency,
when, after all, everything may be easily accountable, if
only proper means were taken to sift the matter."

" There are circumstances connected with this—this
appearance," said Barton, "which it were needless to
disclose, but which to *me* are proofs of its horrible and
unearthly nature. I know that the being who haunts
me is not *man*. I say I *know* this; I could prove it to
your own conviction." He paused for a minute, and then
added,—" And as to accosting it, I dare not, I could not.
When I see it I am powerless; I stand in the gaze of
death, in the triumphant presence of preter-human power
and malignity. My strength, and faculties, and memory
all forsake me. O God! I fear, sir, you know not what
you speak of. Mercy, mercy! heaven have pity on me!"

He leaned his elbow on the table, and passed his hand
across his eyes, as if to exclude some image of horror,
muttering the last words of the sentence he had just
concluded, again and again.

" Doctor Macklin," he said, abruptly raising himself,
and looking full upon the clergyman with an imploring
eye, " I know you will do for me whatever may be done.
You know now fully the circumstances and the nature of
the mysterious agency of which I am the victim. I tell
you I cannot help myself; I cannot hope to escape; I am
utterly passive. I conjure you, then, to weigh my case
well, and if anything may be done for me by vicarious

supplication, by the intercession of the good, or by any aid or influence whatsoever, I implore of you, I adjure you in the name of the Most High, give me the benefit of that influence, deliver me from the body of this death. Strive for me, pity me; I know you will ; you cannot refuse this ; it is the purpose and object of my visit. Send me away with some hope, however little, some faint hope of ultimate deliverance, and I will nerve myself to endure, from hour to hour, the hideous dream into which my existence is transformed."

Doctor Macklin assured him that all he could do was to pray earnestly for him, and that so much he would not fail to do. They parted with a hurried and melancholy valediction. Barton hastened to the carriage, which awaited him at the door, drew the blinds, and drove away, while Dr. Macklin returned to his chamber, to ruminate at leisure upon the strange interview which had just interrupted his studies.

It was not to be expected that Captain Barton's changed and eccentric habits should long escape remark and discussion. Various were the theories suggested to account for it. Some attributed the alteration to the pressure of secret pecuniary embarrassments; others to a repugnance to fulfil an engagement into which he was presumed to have too precipitately entered ; and others, again, to the supposed incipiency of mental disease, which latter, indeed, was the most plausible, as well as the most generally received, of the hypotheses circulated in the gossip of the day.

From the very commencement of this change, at first so gradual in its advances, Miss Montague had of course been aware of it. The intimacy involved in their peculiar relation, as well as the near interest which it inspired, afforded, in her case, alike opportunity and motive for the successful exercise of that keen and penetrating observation peculiar to the sex. His visits became, at length, so interrupted, and his manner, while they lasted, so abstracted, strange, and agitated, that Lady Rochdale, after hinting her anxiety and her suspicions more than once, at length distinctly stated her anxiety, and pressed for an explanation. The explanation was given, and although its nature at first relieved the worse solicitudes of the old lady and her niece, yet the circumstances which attended it, and the really dreadful consequences which it obviously threatened as regarded the spirits and indeed the reason of the now wretched man who made the strange declaration, were enough, upon a little reflection, to fill their minds with perturbation and alarm.

General Montague, the young lady's father, at length arrived. He had himself slightly known Barton, some ten or twelve years previously, and being aware of his fortune and connexions, was disposed to regard him as an unexceptionable and indeed a most desirable match for his daughter. He laughed at the story of Barton's supernatural visitations, and lost not a moment in calling upon his intended son-in-law.

"My dear Barton," he continued, gaily, after a little conversation, "my sister tells me that you are a victim to blue devils, in quite a new and original shape."

Barton changed countenance, and sighed profoundly.

"Come, come; I protest this will never do," continued the general; "you are more like a man on his way to the gallows than to the altar. These devils have made quite a saint of you."

Barton made an effort to change the conversation.

"No, no, it won't do," said his visiter laughing; "I am resolved to say out what I have to say upon this magnificent mock mystery of yours. Come, you must not be angry; but really it is too bad to see you, at your time of life, absolutely frightened into good behaviour, like a naughty child, by a bugaboo, and, as far as I can learn, a very particularly contemptible one. Seriously, though, my dear Barton, I have been a good deal annoyed at what they tell me; but, at the same time, thoroughly convinced that there is nothing in the matter that may not be cleared up, with just a little attention and management, within a week at furthest."

"Ah, general, you do not know ——" he began.

"Yes, but I do know quite enough to warrant my confidence," interrupted the soldier. "I know that all your annoyance proceeds from the occasional appearance of a certain little man in a cap and great coat, with a red vest and a bad countenance, who follows you about, and pops upon you at the corners of lanes, and throws you into ague fits. Now, my dear fellow, I'll make it my business to *catch* this mischievous little mountebank, and either beat him into a jelly with my own hands, or have him whipped through the town at the cart's-tail."

"If *you* knew what *I* know," said Barton, with gloomy agitation, "you would speak very differently. Don't imagine that I am so weak and foolish as to assume, without proof the most overwhelming, the conclusion to which I have been forced. The proofs are here, locked up here." As he spoke he tapped upon his breast, and with an anxious sigh continued to walk up and down the room.

" Well, well, Barton," said his visiter, " I'll wager a
rump and dozen I collar the ghost, and convince yourself before many days are over."

He was running on in the same strain when he was
suddenly arrested, and not a little shocked, by observing
Barton, who had approached the window, stagger slowly
back, like one who had received a stunning blow—his
arm feebly extended toward the street, his face and his
very lips white as ashes—while he uttered, "There—
there—there !"

General Montague started mechanically to his feet,
and, from the window of the drawing-room, saw a figure
corresponding, as well as his hurry would permit him
to discern, with the description of the person, whose
appearance so constantly and dreadfully disturbed the
repose of his friend. The figure was just turning from
the rails of the area upon which it had been leaning,
and, without waiting to see more, the old gentleman
snatched his cane and hat, and rushed down the stairs
and into the street, in the furious hope of securing the
person, and punishing the audacity of the mysterious
stranger. He looked around him, but in vain, for any
trace of the form he had himself distinctly beheld. He
ran breathlessly to the nearest corner, expecting to see
from thence the retreating figure, but no such form was
visible. Back and forward, from crossing to crossing,
he ran, at fault, and it was not until the curious gaze and
laughing countenances of the passers-by reminded him
of the absurdity of his pursuit, that he checked his
hurried pace, lowered his walking-cane from the menacing altitude which he had mechanically given it,
adjusted his hat, and walked composedly back again,

inwardly vexed and flurried. He found Barton pale
and trembling in every joint; they both remained silent,
though under emotions very different. At last Barton
whispered, "You saw it?"

"*It!*—him—some one—you mean—to be sure I did,"
replied Montague, testily. "But where is the good or
the harm of seeing him? The fellow runs like a lamp-
lighter. I wanted to *catch* him, but he had stolen away
before I could reach the hall-door. However, it is no
great matter; next time, I dare say, I'll do better; and,
egad, if I once come within reach of him, I'll introduce
his shoulders to the weight of my cane, in a way to
make him cry *peccavi*."

Notwithstanding General Montague's undertakings
and exhortations, however, Barton continued to suffer
from the self-same unexplained cause. Go how, when,
or where he would, he was still constantly dogged or
confronted by the hateful being who had established
over him so dreadful and mysterious an influence; no-
where and at no time was he secure against the odious
appearance which haunted him with such diabolic per-
severance. His depression, misery, and excitement
became more settled and alarming every day, and the
mental agonies that ceaselessly preyed upon him began
at last so sensibly to affect his general health, that Lady
Rochdale and General Montague succeeded, without,
indeed, much difficulty, in persuading him to try a short
tour on the Continent, in the hope that an entire change
of scene would, at all events, have the effect of breaking
through the influences of local association, which the
more sceptical of his friends assumed to be by no means
inoperative in suggesting and perpetuating what they

conceived to be a mere form of nervous illusion. General
Montague, indeed, was persuaded that the figure which
haunted his intended son-in-law was by no means the
creation of his own imagination, but, on the contrary,
a substantial form of flesh and blood, animated by a
spiteful and obstinate resolution, perhaps with some
murderous object in perspective, to watch and follow
the unfortunate gentleman. Even this hypothesis was
not a very pleasant one; yet it was plain that if Barton
could once be convinced that there was nothing preternatural in the phenomenon which he had hitherto regarded
in that light, the affair would lose all its terrors in his
eyes, and wholly cease to exercise upon his health and
spirits the baleful influence which it had hitherto done.
He therefore reasoned, that if the annoyance were
actually escaped from by mere change of scene, it obviously could not have originated in any supernatural
agency.

Yielding to their persuasions, Barton left Dublin for
England, accompanied by General Montague. They
posted rapidly to London, and thence to Dover, whence
they took the packet with a fair wind for Calais. The
general's confidence in the result of the expedition on
Barton's spirits had risen day by day since their departure from the shores of Ireland; for, to the inex-
pressible relief and delight of the latter, he had not,
since then, so much as even once fancied a repetition of
those impressions which had, when at home, drawn him
gradually down to the very abyss of horror and despair.
This exemption from what he had begun to regard as
the inevitable condition of his existence, and the sense
of security which began to pervade his mind, were inex-

pressibly delightful; and in the exultation of what he
considered his deliverance, he indulged in a thousand
happy anticipations for a future, into which so lately he
had hardly dared to look; and in short, both he and
his companion secretly congratulated themselves upon
the termination of that persecution which had been to
its immediate victim a source of such unspeakable agony.

It was a beautiful day, and a crowd of idlers stood
upon the jetty to receive the packet, and enjoy the bustle
of the new arrivals. Montague walked a few paces in
advance of his friend, and as he made his way through
the crowd, a little man touched his arm, and said to
him, in a broad provincial *patois*—

" Monsieur is walking too fast; he will lose his sick
comrade in the throng, for, by my faith, the poor gentleman seems to be fainting."

Montague turned quickly, and observed that Barton
did indeed look deadly pale. He hastened to his side.

" My dear fellow, are you ill?" he asked anxiously.

The question was unheeded and twice repeated, ere
Barton stammered—

" I saw him—by ——, I saw him!"

" *Him!*—who—where—when did you see him—where
is he?" cried Montague, looking around him.

" I saw him—but he is gone," repeated Barton, faintly.

" But where—where? For God's sake, speak," urged Montague, vehemently.

" It is but this moment—*here*," said he.

" But what did he look like—what had he on—what
did he wear—quick, quick," urged his excited companion, ready to dart among the crowd, and collar the
delinquent on the spot.

"He touched your arm—he spoke to you—he pointed to me. God be merciful to me, there is no escape," said Barton, in the low, subdued tones of intense despair.

Montague had already bustled away in all the flurry of mingled hope and indignation; but though the singular *personnel* of the stranger who had accosted him was vividly and perfectly impressed upon his recollection, he failed to discover among the crowd even the slightest resemblance to him. After a fruitless search, in which he enlisted the services of several of the bystanders, who aided all the more zealously, as they believed he had been robbed, he at length, out of breath and baffled, gave over the attempt.

"Ah, my friend, it won't do," said Barton, with the faint voice and bewildered, ghastly look of one who has been stunned by some mortal shock ; "there is no use in contending with it ; whatever it is, the dreadful association between me and it is now established ; I shall never escape—never, never !"

"Nonsense, nonsense, my dear fellow ; don't talk so," said Montague, with something at once of irritation and dismay ; "you must not ; never mind, I say—never mind, we'll jockey the scoundrel yet."

It was, however, but lost labour to endeavour henceforward to inspire Barton with one ray of hope ; he became utterly desponding. This intangible, and as it seemed, utterly inadequate influence was fast destroying his energies of intellect, character, and health. His first object was now to return to Ireland, there, as he believed, and now almost hoped, speedily to die.

To Ireland, accordingly, he came, and one of the first
faces he saw upon the shore was again that of his implacable and dreaded persecutor. Barton seemed at last
to have lost not only all enjoyment and every hope in
existence, but all independence of will besides. He now
submitted himself passively to the management of the
friends most nearly interested in his welfare. With the
apathy of entire despair, he implicitly assented to whatever measures they suggested and advised ; and as a last
resource, it was determined to remove him to a house
of Lady Rochdale's in the neighbourhood of Clontarf,
where, with the advice of his medical attendant, who
persisted in his opinion that the whole train of impressions resulted merely from some nervous derangement, it
was resolved that he was to confine himself strictly to the
house, and to make use only of those apartments which
commanded a view of an enclosed yard, the gates of
which were to be kept jealously locked.   Those precautions would at least secure him against the casual appearance of any living form, which his excited imagination
might possibly confound with the spectre which, as
it was contended, his fancy recognised in every figure
which bore even a distant or general resemblance to the
traits with which he had at first invested it. A month
or six weeks' absolute seclusion under these conditions,
it was hoped, might, by interrupting the series of these
terrible impressions, gradually dispel the predisposing
apprehension, and effectually break up the associations
which had confirmed the supposed disease, and rendered
recovery hopeless. Cheerful society and that of his
friends was to be constantly supplied, and on the whole,
very sanguine expectations were indulged in, that under

this treatment the obstinate hypochondria of the patient
might at length give way.

Accompanied, therefore, by Lady Rochdale, General
Montague, and his daughter—his own affianced bride—
poor Barton, himself never daring to cherish a hope of
his ultimate emancipation from the strange horrors under which his life was literally wasting away, took possession of the apartments, whose situation protected him
against the dreadful intrusions, from which he shrank
with such unutterable terror.

After a little time, a steady persistence in this system
began to manifest its results, in a very marked though
gradual improvement, alike in the health and spirits of
the invalid. Not, indeed, that anything at all approaching to complete recovery was yet discernible. On the
contrary, to those who had not seen him since the commencement of his strange sufferings, such an alteration
would have been apparent as might well have shocked
them. The improvement, however, such as it was, was
welcomed with gratitude and delight, especially by the
poor young lady, whom her attachment to him, as well
as her now singularly painful position, consequent on
his mysterious and protracted illness, rendered an object
of pity scarcely one degree less to be commiserated than
himself.

A week passed—a fortnight—a month—and yet no
recurrence of the hated visitation had agitated and terrified him as before. The treatment had, so far forth,
been followed by complete success. The chain of association had been broken. The constant pressure upon
the overtasked spirits had been removed, and, under
these comparatively favourable circumstances, the sense

of social community with the world about him, and
something of human interest, if not of enjoyment, began
to reanimate his mind.

It was about this time that Lady Rochdale, who, like
most old ladies of the day, was deep in family receipts,
and a great pretender to medical science, being engaged
in the concoction of certain unpalatable mixtures, of
marvellous virtue, despatched her own maid to the kitchen
garden, with a list of herbs, which were there to be
carefully culled, and brought back to her for the purpose stated. The hand-maiden, however, returned with
her task scarce half completed, and a good deal flurried
and alarmed. Her mode of accounting for her precipitate
retreat and evident agitation was odd, and to the old
lady unpleasantly startling.

It appeared that she had repaired to the kitchen garden, pursuant to her mistress's directions, and had there
begun to make the specified selection among the rank
and neglected herbs which crowded one corner of the
enclosure, and while engaged in this pleasant labour, she
carelessly sang a fragment of an old song, as she said,
" to keep herself company." She was, however, interrupted by a sort of mocking echo of the air she was
singing; and, looking up, she saw through the old
thorn hedge, which surrounded the garden, 'a singularly ill-looking little man, whose countenance wore the
stamp of menace and malignity, standing close to her,
at the other side of the hawthorn screen. She described
herself as utterly unable to move or speak, while he
charged her with a message for Captain Barton; the
substance of which she distinctly remembered to have
been to the effect, that he, Captain Barton, must come

abroad as usual, and shew himself to his friends, out
of doors, or else prepare for a visit in his own chamber.   On concluding this brief message, the stranger
had, with a threatening air, got down into the outer
ditch, and seizing the hawthorn stems in his hands,
seemed on the point of climbing through the fence—a
feat which might have been accomplished without much
difficulty.   Without, of course, awaiting this result, the
girl, throwing down her treasures of thyme and rose-
mary, had turned and run, with the swiftness of terror,
to the house.   Lady Rochdale commanded her, on pain
of instant dismissal, to observe an absolute silence respecting all that portion of the incident which related
to Captain Barton ; and, at the same time, directed instant search to be made by her men in the garden and
fields adjacent.   This measure, however, was attended
with the usual unsuccess, and filled with fearful and
undefinable misgivings, Lady Rochdale communicated
the incident to her brother.   The story, however, until
long afterwards, went no further, and, of course, it was
jealously guarded from Barton, who continued to amend,
though slowly and imperfectly.

Barton now began to walk occasionally in the court-
yard which we have mentioned, and which being surrounded by a high wall, commanded no view beyond its
own extent. Here he, therefore, considered himself perfectly secure ; and, but for a careless violation of orders
by one of the grooms, he might have enjoyed, at least
for some time longer, his much-prized immunity. Opening upon the public road, this yard was entered by a
wooden gate, with a wicket in it, which was further
defended by an iron gate upon the outside. Strict orders

had been given to keep them carefully locked; but, spite
of these, it had happened that one day, as Barton was
slowly pacing this narrow enclosure, in his accustomed
walk, and reaching the further extremity, was turning
to retrace his steps, he saw the boarded wicket ajar, and
the face of his tormentor immoveably looking at him
through the iron bars. For a few seconds he stood
riveted to the earth—breathless and bloodless—in the
fascination of that dreaded gaze, and then fell helplessly
and insensibly upon the pavement.

There was he found a few minutes afterwards, and
conveyed to his room—the apartment which he was never
afterwards to leave alive. Henceforward a marked and
unaccountable change was observable in the tone of his
mind. Captain Barton was now no longer the excited
and despairing man he had been before; a strange alteration had passed upon him—an unearthly tranquillity
reigned in his mind—it was the anticipated stillness of
the grave.

"Montague, my friend, this struggle is nearly ended
now," he said, tranquilly, but with a look of fixed and
fearful awe. "I have, at last, some comfort from that
world of spirits, from which my *punishment* has come.
I know now that my sufferings will be soon over."

Montague pressed him to speak on.

"Yes," said he, in a softened voice, "my punishment is nearly ended. From sorrow, perhaps, I shall
never, in time or eternity, escape; but my *agony* is
almost over. Comfort has been revealed to me, and
what remains of my allotted struggle I will bear with
submission—even with hope."

"I am glad to hear you speak so tranquilly, my dear

fellow," said Montague; "peace and cheerfulness of
mind are all you need to make you what you were."

"No, no—I never can be that," said he, mournfully.
"I am no longer fit for life. I am soon to die: I do
not shrink from death as I did. I am to see *him* but
once again, and then all is ended."

"He said so, then?" suggested Montague.

"*He?*—No, no: good tidings could scarcely come
through him; and these were good and welcome; and
they came so solemnly and sweetly, with unutterable
love and melancholy, such as I could not, without saying more than is needful, or fitting, of other long-past
scenes and persons, fully explain to you." As Barton
said this he shed tears.

"Come, come," said Montague, mistaking the source
of his emotions, "you must not give way. What is it,
after all, but a pack of dreams and nonsense; or, at
worst, the practices of a scheming rascal that enjoys his
power of playing upon your nerves, and loves to exert
it—a sneaking vagabond that owes you a grudge, and
pays it off this way, not daring to try a more manly
one."

"A grudge, indeed, he owes me—you say rightly,"
said Barton, with a sullen shudder; "a grudge as you
call it. Oh God! when the justice of heaven permits
the Evil one to carry out a scheme of vengeance—when
its execution is committed to the lost and frightful victim
of sin, who owes his own ruin to the man, the very man,
whom he is commissioned to pursue—then, indeed, the
torments and terrors of hell are anticipated on earth.
But heaven has dealt mercifully with me—hope has
opened to me at last; and if death could come without

the dreadful sight I am doomed to see, I would gladly close my eyes this moment upon the world. But though death is welcome, I shrink with an agony you cannot understand—a maddening agony, an actual frenzy of terror—from the last encounter with that—that DEMON, who has drawn me thus to the verge of the chasm, and who is himself to plunge me down. I am to see him again—once more—but under circumstances unutterably more terrific than ever."

As Barton thus spoke, he trembled so violently that Montague was really alarmed at the extremity of his sudden agitation, and hastened to lead him back to the topic which had before seemed to exert so tranquillizing an effect upon his mind.

" It was not a dream," he said, after a time ; " I was in a different state—I felt differently and strangely; and yet it was all as real, as clear, and vivid, as what I now see and hear ; it was a reality."

" And what *did* you see and hear ?" urged his companion.

" When I awakened from the swoon I fell into on seeing *him*," said Barton, continuing as if he had not heard the question, " it was slowly, very slowly ; I was reclining by the margin of a broad lake, surrounded by misty hills, and a soft, melancholy, rose-coloured light illuminated it all. It was indescribably sad and lonely, and yet more beautiful than any earthly scene. My head was leaning on the lap of a girl, and she was singing a strange and wondrous song, that told, I know not how, whether by words or harmony, of all my life—all that is past, and all that is still to come; and with the song the old feelings that I thought had perished within

me came back, and tears flowed from my eyes, partly
for the song and its mysterious beauty, and partly for
the unearthly sweetness of her voice; yet I knew the
voice—oh! how well; and I was spell-bound as I listened and looked at the strange and solitary scene, without
stirring, almost without breathing—and, alas! alas!
without turning my eyes toward the face that I knew
was near me, so sweetly powerful was the enchantment
that held me.   And so, slowly and softly, the song and
scene grew fainter, and ever fainter, to my senses, till
all was dark and still again.   And then I wakened to
this world, as you saw, comforted, for I knew that I was
forgiven much."   Barton wept again long and bitterly.

From this time, as we have said, the prevailing tone
of his mind was one of profound and tranquil melancholy. This, however, was not without its interruptions.
He was thoroughly impressed with the conviction that
he was to experience another and a final visitation,
illimitably transcending in horror all he had before experienced.   From this anticipated and unknown agony,
he often shrunk in such paroxysms of abject terror and
distraction, as filled the whole household with dismay
and superstitious panic.   Even those among them who
affected to discredit the supposition of preternatural
agency in the matter, were often in their secret souls
visited, during the darkness and solitude of night, with
qualms and apprehensions, which they would not have
readily confessed; and none of them attempted to dis-
suade Barton from the resolution on which he now syste-
matically acted, of shutting himself up in his own apartment.   The window-blinds of this room were kept
jealously down; and his own man was seldom out of

his presence, day or night, his bed being placed in the same chamber.

This man was an attached and respectable servant; and his duties, in addition to those ordinarily imposed upon *valets*, but which Barton's independent habits generally dispensed with, were to attend carefully to the simple precautions by means of which his master hoped to exclude the dreaded intrusion of the "Watcher," as the strange letter he had at first received had designated his persecutor. And, in addition to attending to these arrangements, which consisted merely in anticipating the possibility of his master's being, through any unscreened window or opened door, exposed to the dreaded influence, the valet was never to suffer him to be for one moment alone: total solitude, even for a minute, had become to him now almost as intolerable as the idea of going abroad into the public ways ; it was an instinctive anticipation of what was coming.

It is needless to say, that, under these mysterious and horrible circumstances, no steps were taken toward the fulfilment of that engagement into which he had entered. There was quite disparity enough in point of years, and indeed of habits, between the young lady and Captain Barton, to have precluded anything like very vehement or romantic attachment on her part. Though grieved and anxious, therefore, she was very far from being heart-broken ; a circumstance which, for the sentimental purposes of our tale, is much to be deplored. But truth must be told, especially in a narrative, whose chief, if not only, pretensions to interest consist in a rigid adherence to facts, or what are so reported to have been.

Miss Montague, however, devoted much of her time to a patient but fruitless attempt to cheer the unhappy invalid. She read for him, and conversed with him ; but it was apparent that whatever exertions he made, the endeavour to escape from the one constant and ever present fear that preyed upon him was utterly and miserably unavailing.

Young ladies, as all the world knows, are much given to the cultivation of pets ; and among those who shared the favour of Miss Montague was a fine old owl, which the gardener, who caught him napping among the ivy of a ruined stable, had dutifully presented to that young lady.

The caprice which regulates such preferences was manifested in the extravagant favour with which this grim and ill-favoured bird was at once distinguished by his mistress; and, trifling as this whimsical circumstance may seem, I am forced to mention it, inasmuch as it is connected, oddly enough, with the concluding scene of the story. Barton, so far from sharing in this liking for the new favourite, regarded it from the first with an antipathy as violent as it was utterly unaccountable. Its very vicinity was insupportable to him. He seemed to hate and dread it with a vehemence absolutely laughable, and which, to those who have never witnessed the exhibition of antipathies of this kind, would seem all but incredible.

With these few words of preliminary explanation, I shall proceed to state the particulars of the last scene in this strange series of incidents. It was almost two o'clock one winter's night, and Barton was, as usual at that hour, in his bed; the servant we have mentioned occupied a smaller bed in the same room, and a candle was burning. The man was on a sudden aroused by his master, who said—

" I can't get it out of my head that that accursed bird has escaped somehow, and is lurking in some corner of the room. I have been dreaming of him. Get up, Smith, and look about ; search for him. Such hateful dreams !"

The servant rose, and examined the chamber, and while engaged in so doing, he heard the well-known sound, more like a long-drawn gasp than a hiss, with which these birds from their secret haunts affright the quiet of the night. This ghostly indication of its proximity, for the sound proceeded from the passage upon which Barton's chamber-door opened, determined the search of the servant, who, opening the door, proceeded a step or two forward for the purpose of driving the bird away. He had, however, hardly entered the lobby, when the door behind him slowly swung to under the impulse, as it seemed, of some gentle current of air; but as immediately over the door there was a kind of window, intended in the day-time to aid in lighting the passage, and through which the rays of the candle were then issuing, the valet could see quite enough for his purpose. As he advanced he heard his master, who, lying in a well-curtained bed, had not, as it seemed, perceived his exit from the room, call him by name, and direct him to place the candle on the table by his bed. The servant, who was now some way in the long passage, and not liking to raise his voice for the purpose of replying, lest he should startle the sleeping inmates of the house, began to walk hurriedly and softly back

again, when, to his amazement, he heard a voice in the
interior of the chamber answering calmly, and actually
saw, through the window which overtopped the door,
that the light was slowly shifting, as if carried across
the chamber in answer to his master's call. Palsied by
a feeling akin to terror, yet not unmingled with a horrible curiosity, he stood breathless and listening at the
threshold, unable to summon resolution to push open
the door and enter.   Then came a rustling of the curtains, and a sound like that of one who in a low voice
hushes a child to rest, in the midst of which he heard
Barton say, in a tone of stifled horror—"Oh, God—oh,
my God!" and repeat the same exclamation several
times.   Then ensued a silence, which again was broken
by the same strange soothing sound; and at last there
burst forth, in one swelling peal, a yell of agony so appalling and hideous, that, under some impulse of ungo-
vernable horror, the man rushed to the door, and with
his whole strength strove to force it open.   Whether it
was that, in his agitation, he had himself but imperfectly turned the handle, or that the door was really
secured upon the inside, he failed to effect an entrance;
and as he tugged and pushed, yell after yell rang louder
and wilder through the chamber, accompanied all the
while by the same hushed sounds. Actually freezing with
terror, and scarce knowing what he did, the man turned
and ran down the passage, wringing his hands in the
extremity of horror and irresolution.   At the stair-head
he was encountered by General Montague, scared and
eager, and just as they met the fearful sounds had
ceased.

"What is it?—who—where is your master?" said

Montague, with the incoherence of extreme agitation.
" Has anything—for God's sake, is anything wrong?"
"Lord have mercy on us, it's all over," said the man,
staring wildly towards his master's chamber. "He's
dead sir ; I'm sure he's dead."

Without waiting for inquiry or explanation, Montague, closely followed by the servant, hurried to the
chamber-door, turned the handle, and pushed it open.
As the door yielded to his pressure, the ill-omened bird
of which the servant had been in search, uttering its
spectral warning, started suddenly from the far side of
the bed, and flying through the door-way close over
their heads, and extinguishing, in his passage, the candle which Montague carried, crashed through the sky-
light that overlooked the lobby, and sailed away into
the darkness of the outer space.

"There it is, God bless us !" whispered the man,
after a breathless pause.

"Curse that bird!" muttered the general, startled by
the suddenness of the apparition, and unable to conceal
his discomposure.

"The candle was moved," said the man, after another
breathless pause ; " see, they put it by the bed!"

" Draw the curtains, fellow, and don't stand gaping
there," whispered Montague, sternly.

The man hesitated.

"Hold this, then," said Montague, impatiently thrusting the candlestick into the servant's hand, and himself advancing to the bedside, he drew the curtains
apart. The light of the candle, which was still burning
at the bedside, fell upon a figure huddled together, and
half upright, at the head of the bed. It seemed as

E

though it had shrunk back as far as the solid panneling
would allow, and the hands were still clutched in the
bed-clothes.

"Barton, Barton, Barton!" cried the general, with a
strange mixture of awe and vehemence.

He took the candle, and held it so that it shone full
upon his face.   The features were fixed, stern, and
white; the jaw was fallen, and the sightless eyes, still
open, gazed vacantly forward toward the front of the
bed.

"God Almighty, he's dead!" muttered the general,
as he looked upon this fearful spectacle.   They both
continued to gaze upon it in silence for a minute or
more.   "And cold, too," whispered Montague, withdrawing his hand from that of the dead man.

"And see, see; may I never have life, sir," added the
man, after another pause, with a shudder, "but there
was something else on the bed with him!   Look there—
look there; see that, sir!"

As the man thus spoke, he pointed to a deep inden-
ture, as if caused by a heavy pressure, near the foot of
the bed.

Montague was silent.

"Come, sir, come away, for God's sake," whispered
the man, drawing close up to him, and holding fast by
his arm, while he glanced fearfully round; "what good
can be done here now?—come away, for God's sake!"

At this moment they heard the steps of more than
one approaching, and Montague, hastily desiring the
servant to arrest their progress, endeavoured to loose
the rigid gripe with which the fingers of the dead man
were clutched in the bed-clothes, and drew, as well as

he was able, the awful figure into a reclining posture; then closing the curtains carefully upon it, he hastened himself to meet those who were approaching.

*   *   *   *   *   *   *

    *   *   *   *   *   *

It is needless to follow the personages so slightly connected with this narrative into the events of their after-lives; it is enough for us to remark, that no clue to the solution of these mysterious occurrences was ever afterwards discovered; and so long an interval having now passed, it is scarcely to be expected that time can throw any new lights upon their inexplicable obscurity. Until the secrets of the earth shall be no longer hidden, therefore, these transactions must remain shrouded in their original mystery.

The only occurrence in Captain Barton's former life to which reference was ever made, as having any possible connexion with the sufferings with which his existence closed, and which he himself seemed to regard as working out a retribution for some grievous sin of his past life, was a circumstance which not for several years after his death was brought to light. The nature of this disclosure was painful to his relatives, and discreditable to his memory.

It appeared, then, that some eight years before Captain Barton's final return to Dublin, he had formed, in the town of Plymouth, a guilty attachment, the object of which was the daughter of one of the ship's crew under his command. The father had visited the frailty of his unhappy child with extreme harshness, and even brutality, and it was said that she had died heart-broken. Presuming upon Barton's implication in her guilt, thiman had conducted himself towards him with marked insolence, and Barton retaliated this, and what he resented with still more exasperated bitterness—his treatment of the unfortunate girl—by a systematic exercise of those terrible and arbitrary severities with which the regulations of the navy arm those who are responsible for its discipline.   The man had at length made his escape, while the vessel was in port at Lisbon, but died, as it was said, in an hospital in that town, of the wounds inflicted in one of his recent and sanguinary punishments.

Whether these circumstances in reality bear, or not, upon the occurrences of Barton's after-life, it is, of course, impossible to say. It seems, however, more than probable that they were, at least in his own mind, closely associated with them.   But however the truth may be, as to the origin and motives of this mysterious persecution, there can be no doubt that, with respect to the agencies by which it was accomplished, absolute and impenetrable mystery is like to prevail until the day of doom.

The Murdered Cousin.

---◆---

" And they lay wait for their own blood : they lurk privily for their own lives.
" So are the ways of every one that is greedy of gain ; which taketh away the life
of the owner thereof."

[THIS story of the Irish peerage is written, as nearly as
possible, in the very words in which it was related by its
" heroine," the late Countess D——, and is therefore
told in the first person.]

MY mother died when I was an infant, and of her I have
no recollection, even the faintest. By her death my
education was left solely to the direction of my surviving
parent. He entered upon his task with a stern appre-
ciation of the responsibility thus cast upon him. My
religious instruction was prosecuted with an almost exaggerated anxiety ; and I had, of course, the best mas-
ters to perfect me in all those accomplishments which my
station and wealth might seem to require. My father
was what is called an oddity, and his treatment of me,
though uniformly kind, was governed less by affection
and tenderness, than by a high and unbending sense of
duty. Indeed I seldom saw or spoke to him except at

meal-times, and then, though gentle, he was usually reserved and gloomy. His leisure hours, which were many, were passed either in his study or in solitary walks ; in short, he seemed to take no further interest in my happiness or improvement, than a conscientious regard to the discharge of his own duty would seem to impose.

Shortly before my birth an event occurred which had contributed much to induce and to confirm my father's unsocial habits ; it was the fact that a suspicion of *murder* had fallen upon his younger brother, though not sufficiently definite to lead to any public proceedings, yet strong enough to ruin him in public opinion. This disgraceful and dreadful doubt cast upon the family name, my father felt deeply and bitterly, and not the less so that he himself was thoroughly convinced of his brother's innocence. The sincerity and strength of this conviction he shortly afterwards proved in a manner which produced the catastrophe of my story.

Before, however, I enter upon my immediate adventures, I ought to relate the circumstances which had awakened that suspicion to which I have referred, inasmuch as they are in themselves somewhat curious, and in their effects most intimately connected with my own after-history.

My uncle, Sir Arthur Tyrrell, was a gay and extravagant man, and, among other vices, was ruinously addicted to gaming. This unfortunate propensity, even after his fortune had suffered so severely as to render retrenchment imperative, nevertheless continued to engross him, nearly to the exclusion of every other pursuit. He was, however, a proud, or rather a vain man, and could not

bear to make the diminution of his income a matter of
triumph to those with whom he had hitherto competed;
and the consequence was, that he frequented no longer
the expensive haunts of his dissipation, and retired from
the gay world, leaving his coterie to discover his reasons
as best they might. He did not, however, forego his favourite vice, for though he could not worship his great
divinity in those costly temples where he was formerly
wont to take his place, yet he found it very possible to
bring about him a sufficient number of the votaries of
chance to answer all his ends. The consequence was,
that Carrickleigh, which was the name of my uncle's
residence, was never without one or more of such visiters
as I have described. It happened that upon one occasion he was visited by one Hugh Tisdall, a gentleman of
loose, and, indeed, low habits, but of considerable wealth,
and who had, in early youth, travelled with my uncle
upon the Continent. The period of this visit was winter, and, consequently, the house was nearly deserted
excepting by its ordinary inmates ; it was, therefore,
highly acceptable, particularly as my uncle was aware
that his visiter's tastes accorded exactly with his own.

Both parties seemed determined to avail themselves of
their mutual suitability during the brief stay which Mr.
Tisdall had promised; the consequence was, that they
shut themselves up in Sir Arthur's private room for nearly
all the day and the greater part of the night, during the
space of almost a week, at the end of which the servant
having one morning, as usual, knocked at Mr. Tisdall's
bed-room door repeatedly, received no answer, and, upon
attempting to enter, found that it was locked. This
appeared suspicious, and the inmates of the house having

been alarmed, the door was forced open, and, on proceeding to the bed, they found the body of its occupant
perfectly lifeless, and hanging halfway out, the head
downwards, and near the floor.   One deep wound had
been inflicted upon the temple, apparently with some
blunt instrument, which had penetrated the brain, and
another blow, less effective—probably the first aimed—
had grazed his head, removing some of the scalp.   The
door had been double locked upon the *inside*, in evidence
of which the key still lay where it had been placed in the
lock.   The window, though not secured on the interior,
was closed ; a circumstance not a little puzzling, as it
afforded the only other mode of escape from the room.
It looked out, too, upon a kind of court-yard, round
which the old buildings stood, formerly accessible by a
narrow doorway and passage lying in the oldest side of
the quadrangle, but which had since been built up, so as
to preclude all ingress or egress; the room was also upon
the second story, and the height of the window considerable ; in addition to all which the stone window-sill
was much too narrow to allow of any one's standing upon
it when the window was closed.   Near the bed were
found a pair of razors belonging to the murdered man,
one of them upon the ground, and both of them open.
The weapon which inflicted the mortal wound was not
to be found in the room, nor were any footsteps or other
traces of the murderer discoverable. At the suggestion of
Sir Arthur himself, the coroner was instantly summoned
to attend, and an inquest was held.   Nothing, however,
in any degree conclusive was elicited.   The walls, ceiling,
and floor of the room were carefully examined, in order
to ascertain whether they contained a trap-door or other

concealed mode of entrance, but no such thing appeared.
Such was the minuteness of investigation employed, that,
although the grate had contained a large fire during the
night, they proceeded to examine even the very chimney,
in order to discover whether escape by it were possible.
But this attempt, too, was fruitless, for the chimney,
built in the old fashion, rose in a perfectly perpendicular
line from the hearth, to a height of nearly fourteen feet
above the roof, affording in its interior scarcely the possibility of ascent, the flue being smoothly plastered, and
sloping towards the top like an inverted funnel ; pro-
mising, too, even if the summit were attained, owing to
its great height, but a precarious descent upon the sharp
and steep-ridged roof ; the ashes, too, which lay in the
grate, and the soot, as far as it could be seen, were
undisturbed, a circumstance almost conclusive upon the
point.

Sir Arthur was of course examined. His evidence was
given with clearness and unreserve, which seemed calculated to silence all suspicion.   He stated that, up to the
day and night immediately preceding the catastrophe, he
had lost to a heavy amount, but that, at their last sitting,
he had not only won back his original loss, but upwards
of £4,000 in addition; in evidence of which he produced
an acknowledgment of debt to that amount in the handwriting of the deceased, bearing date the night of the catastrophe.   He had mentioned the circumstance to Lady
Tyrrell, and in presence of some of his domestics ; which
statement was supported by *their* respective evidence.
One of the jury shrewdly observed, that the circumstance
of Mr. Tisdall's having sustained so heavy a loss might
have suggested to some ill-minded persons, accidentally

hearing it, the plan of robbing him, after having murdered him in such a manner as might make it appear that he had committed suicide; a supposition which was strongly supported by the razors having been found thus displaced and removed from their case. Two persons had probably been engaged in the attempt, one watching by the sleeping man, and ready to strike him in case of his awakening suddenly, while the other was procuring the razors and employed in inflicting the fatal gash, so as to make it appear to have been the act of the murdered man himself. It was said that while the juror was making this suggestion Sir Arthur changed colour. There was nothing, however, like legal evidence to implicate him, and the consequence was that the verdict was found against a person or persons unknown, and for some time the matter was suffered to rest, until, after about five months, my father received a letter from a person signing himself Andrew Collis, and representing himself to be the cousin of the deceased. This letter stated that his brother, Sir Arthur, was likely to incur not merely suspicion but personal risk, unless he could account for certain circumstances connected with the recent murder, and contained a copy of a letter written by the deceased, and dated the very day upon the night of which the murder had been perpetrated. Tisdall's letter contained, among a great deal of other matter, the passages which follow:—

" I have had sharp work with Sir Arthur ; he tried some of his stale tricks, but soon found that *I* was Yorkshire, too ; it would not do—you understand me. We went to the work like good ones, head, heart, and soul ; and in fact, since I came here, I have lost no time. I am

rather fagged, but I am sure to be well paid for my hard-
ship ; I never want sleep so long as I can have the music
of a dice-box, and wherewithal to pay the piper. As I
told you, he tried some of his queer turns, but I foiled
him like a man, and, in return, gave him more than he
could relish of the genuine *dead knowledge*. In short,
I have plucked the old baronet as never baronet was
plucked before; I have scarce left him the stump of a
quill. I have got promissory notes in his hand to the
amount of ——; if you like round numbers, say five-and-
twenty thousand pounds, safely deposited in my portable
strong box, alias, double-clasped pocket-book. I leave
this ruinous old rat-hole early on to-morrow, for two
reasons : first, I do not want to play with Sir Arthur
deeper than I think his security would warrant; and,
secondly, because I am safer a hundred miles away from
Sir Arthur than in the house with him. Look you, my
worthy, I tell you this between ourselves—I may be
wrong—but, by ——, I am as sure as that I am now
living, that Sir A—— attempted to poison me last
night. So much for old friendship on both sides. When
I won the last stake, a heavy one enough, my friend
leant his forehead upon his hands, and you'll laugh when
I tell you that his head literally smoked like a hot
dumpling. I do not know whether his agitation was
produced by the plan which he had against me, or by
his having lost so heavily ; though it must be allowed
that he had reason to be a little funked, whichever way
his thoughts went; but he pulled the bell, and ordered
two bottles of Champagne.   While the fellow was bringing them, he wrote a promissory note to the full amount,
which he signed, and, as the man came in with the bottles and glasses, he desired him to be off. He filled a
glass for me, and, while he thought my eyes were off,
for I was putting up his note at the time, he dropped
something slyly into it, no doubt to sweeten it; but I saw
it all, and, when he handed it to me, I said, with an
emphasis which he might easily understand, 'There is

some sediment in it, I'll not drink it.' 'Is there,' said
he, and at the same time snatched it from my hand
and threw it into the fire. What do you think of
that? Have I not a tender bird in hand? Win or lose,
I will not play beyond five thousand to-night, and to-
morrow sees me safe out of the reach of Sir Arthur's
Champagne."

Of the authenticity of this document, I never heard
my father express a doubt; and I am satisfied that,
owing to his strong conviction in favour of his brother,
he would not have admitted it without sufficient inquiry,
inasmuch as it tended to confirm the suspicions which
already existed to his prejudice. Now, the only point
in this letter which made strongly against my uncle,
was the mention of the "double-clasped pocket-book,"
as the receptacle of the papers likely to involve him,
for this pocket-book was not forthcoming, nor anywhere
to be found, nor had any papers referring to his gaming
transactions been discovered upon the dead man.

But whatever might have been the original intention
of this man, Collis, neither my uncle nor my father ever
heard more of him; he published the letter, however,
in Faulkner's newspaper, which was shortly afterwards
made the vehicle of a much more mysterious attack.
The passage in that journal to which I allude, appeared
about four years' afterwards, and while the fatal occurrence was still fresh in public recollection. It commenced by a rambling preface, stating that "a certain
person whom certain persons thought to be dead, was
not so, but living, and in full possession of his memory,
and moreover, ready and able to make great delinquents
tremble :" it then went on to describe the murder, with-

out, however, mentioning names; and in doing so, it
entered into minute and circumstantial particulars of
which none but an *eye-witness* could have been possessed, and by implications almost too unequivocal to
be regarded in the light of insinuation, to involve the
" *titled gambler*" in the guilt of the transaction.

My father at once urged Sir Arthur to proceed against
the paper in an action of libel, but he would not hear
of it, nor consent to my father's taking any legal steps
whatever in the matter. My father, however, wrote in
a threatening tone to Faulkner, demanding a surrender
of the author of the obnoxious article ; the answer to
this application is still in my possession, and is penned
in an apologetic tone : it states that the manuscript had
been handed in, paid for, and inserted as an advertisement, without sufficient inquiry, or any knowledge as
to whom it referred. No step, however, was taken to
clear my uncle's character in the judgment of the public; and, as he immediately sold a small property, the
application of the proceeds of which were known to
none, he was said to have disposed of it to enable himself to buy off the threatened information ; however the
truth might have been, it is certain that no charges respecting the mysterious murder were afterwards publicly
made against my uncle, and, as far as external distur-
bances were concerned, he enjoyed henceforward perfect
security and quiet.

A deep and lasting impression, however, had been
made upon the public mind, and Sir Arthur Tyrrell was
no longer visited or noticed by the gentry of the county,
whose attentions he had hitherto received. He accordingly affected to despise those courtesies which he no

longer enjoyed, and shunned even that society which he
might have commanded. This is all that I need recapitulate of my uncle's history, and I now recur to my
own.

Although my father had never, within my recollection, visited, or been visited by my uncle, each being
of unsocial, procrastinating, and indolent habits, and
their respective residences being very far apart—the
one lying in the county of Galway, the other in that
of Cork—he was strongly attached to his brother, and
evinced his affection by an active correspondence, and
by deeply and proudly resenting that neglect which had
branded Sir Arthur as unfit to mix in society.

When I was about eighteen years of age, my father,
whose health had been gradually declining, died, leaving
me in heart wretched and desolate, and, owing to his habitual seclusion, with few acquaintances, and almost no
friends. The provisions of his will were curious, and when
I was sufficiently come to myself to listen to, or comprehend them, surprised me not a little: all his vast property
was left to me, and to the heirs of my body, for ever;
and, in default of such heirs, it was to go after my death
to my uncle, Sir Arthur, without any entail. At the same
time, the will appointed him my guardian, desiring that
I might be received within his house, and reside with
his family, and under his care, during the term of my
minority; and in consideration of the increased expense
consequent upon such an arrangement, a handsome al-
lowance was allotted to him during the term of my proposed residence. The object of this last provision I at
once understood; my father desired, by making it the
direct apparent interest of Sir Arthur that I should die

without issue, while at the same time he placed my person wholly in his power, to prove to the world how great and unshaken was his confidence in his brother's innocence and honour. It was a strange, perhaps an idle scheme, but as I had been always brought up in the habit of considering my uncle as a deeply injured man, and had been taught, almost as a part of my religion, to regard him as the very soul of honour, I felt no further uneasiness respecting the arrangement than that likely to affect a shy and timid girl at the immediate prospect of taking up her abode for the first time in her life among strangers. Previous to leaving my home, which I felt I should do with a heavy heart, I received a most tender and affectionate letter from my uncle, calculated, if anything could do so, to remove the bitterness of parting from scenes familiar and dear from my earliest childhood, and in some degree to reconcile me to the measure. It was upon a fine autumn day that I approached the old domain of Carrickleigh. I shall not soon forget the impression of sadness and of gloom which all that I saw produced upon my mind; the sunbeams were falling with a rich and melancholy lustre upon the fine old trees, which stood in lordly groups, casting their long sweeping shadows over rock and sward; there was an air of neglect and decay about the spot, which amounted almost to desolation, and mournfully increased as we approached the building itself, near which the ground had been originally more artificially and carefully cultivated than elsewhere, and where consequently neglect more immediately and strikingly betrayed itself.

As we proceeded, the road wound near the beds of what had been formerly two fish-ponds, which were now

nothing more than stagnant swamps, overgrown with
rank weeds, and here and there encroached upon by
the straggling underwood; the avenue itself was much
broken; and in many places the stones were almost
concealed by grass and nettles; the loose stone walls
which had here and there intersected the broad park,
were, in many places, broken down, so as no longer to
answer their original purpose as fences; piers were now
and then to be seen, but the gates were gone; and to
add to the general air of dilapidation, some huge trunks
were lying scattered through the venerable old trees,
either the work of the winter storms, or perhaps the
victims of some extensive but desultory scheme of de-
nudation, which the projector had not capital or perse-
verance to carry into full effect.

·After the carriage had travelled a full mile of this
avenue, we reached the summit of a rather abrupt emi-
nence, one of the many which added to the picturesque-
ness, if not to the convenience of this rude approach;
from the top of this ridge the grey walls of Carrickleigh
were visible, rising at a small distance in front, and
darkened by the hoary wood which crowded around
them; it was a quadrangular building of considerable
extent, and the front, where the great entrance was
placed, lay towards us, and bore unequivocal marks
of antiquity; the time-worn, solemn aspect of the old
building, the ruinous and deserted appearance of the
whole place, and the associations which connected it
with a dark page in the history of my family, combined
to depress spirits already predisposed for the reception
of sombre and dejecting impressions. When the carriage
drew up in the grass-grown court-yard before the hall-

door, two lazy-looking men, whose appearance well accorded with that of the place which they tenanted,
alarmed by the obstreporous barking of a great chained
dog, ran out from some half-ruinous out-houses, and
took charge of the horses; the hall-door stood open,
and I entered a gloomy and imperfectly-lighted apartment, and found no one within it.   However, I had not
long to wait in this awkward predicament, for before
my luggage had been deposited in the house, indeed
before I had well removed my cloak and other muffles,
so as to enable me to look around, a young girl ran
lightly into the hall, and kissing me heartily and somewhat boisterously exclaimed, " My dear cousin, my dear
Margaret—I am so delighted—so out of breath, we did
not expect you till ten o'clock; my father is somewhere
about the place, he must be close at hand.   James—
Corney—run out and tell your master; my brother is
seldom at home, at least at any reasonable hour; you
must be so tired—so fatigued—let me show you to your
room; see that Lady Margaret's luggage is all brought
up; you must lie down and rest yourself.   Deborah
bring some coffee—up these stairs; we are so delighted
to see you—-you cannot think how lonely I have been;
how steep these stairs are, are not they?   I am so glad
you are come—I could hardly bring myself to believe
that you were really coming; how good of you, dear
Lady Margaret."   There was real good-nature and delight in my cousin's greeting, and a kind of constitu-
tional confidence of manner which placed me at once at
ease, and made me feel immediately upon terms of intimacy with her.   The room into which she ushered
me, although partaking in the general air of decay which

pervaded the mansion and all about it, had, nevertheless, been fitted up with evident attention to comfort,
and even with some dingy attempt at luxury ; but what
pleased me most was that it opened, by a second door,
upon a lobby which communicated with my fair cousin's
apartment ; a circumstance which divested the room, in
my eyes, of the air of solitude and sadness which would
otherwise have characterised it, to a degree almost painful to one so depressed and agitated as I was.

After such arrangements as I found necessary were
completed, we both went down to the parlour, a large
wainscotted room, hung round with grim old portraits,
and, as I was not sorry to see, containing, in its ample
grate, a large and cheerful fire. Here my cousin had
leisure to talk more at her ease ; and from her I learned
something of the manners and the habits of the two
remaining members of her family, whom I had not yet
seen. On my arrival I had known nothing of the family
among whom I was come to reside, except that it consisted of three individuals, my uncle, and his son and
daughter, Lady Tyrrell having been long dead ; in addition to this very scanty stock of information, I shortly
learned from my communicative companion, that my
uncle was, as I had suspected, completely retired in his
habits, and besides that, having been, so far back as she
could well recollect, always rather strict, as reformed
rakes frequently become, he had latterly been growing
more gloomily and sternly religious than heretofore. Her
account of her brother was far less favourable, though
she did not say anything directly to his disadvantage.
From all that I could gather from her, I was led to suppose that he was a specimen of the idle, coarse-man-

nered, profligate "*squirearchy*"—a result which might
naturally have followed from the circumstance of his
being, as it were, outlawed from society, and driven for
companionship to grades below his own—enjoying, too,
the dangerous prerogative of spending a good deal of
money. However, you may easily suppose that I found
nothing in my cousin's communication fully to bear me
out in so very decided a conclusion.

I awaited the arrival of my uncle, which was every
moment to be expected, with feelings half of alarm,
half of curiosity—a sensation which I have often since
experienced, though to a less degree, when upon the
point of standing for the first time in the presence of
one of whom I have long been in the habit of hearing
or thinking with interest. It was, therefore, with some
little perturbation that I heard, first a slight bustle at
the outer door, then a slow step traverse the hall, and
finally witnessed the door open, and my uncle enter the
room. He was a striking looking man; from peculiarities both of person and of dress, the whole effect of his
appearance amounted to extreme singularity. He was
tall, and when young his figure must have been strikingly elegant; as it was, however, its effect was marred
by a very decided stoop; his dress was of a sober
colour, and in fashion anterior to any thing which I
could remember. It was, however, handsome, and by
no means carelessly put on; but what completed the
singularity of his appearance was his uncut, white hair,
which hung in long, but not at all neglected curls, even
so far as his shoulders, and which combined with his
regularly classic features, and fine dark eyes, to bestow
upon him an air of venerable dignity and pride, which

I have seldom seen equalled elsewhere. I rose as he
entered, and met him about the middle of the room; he
kissed my cheek and both my hands, saying—

"You are most welcome, dear child, as welcome as
the command of this poor place and all that it contains
can make you. I am rejoiced to see you—truly rejoiced.
I trust that you are not much fatigued; pray be seated
again." He led me to my chair, and continued, "I
am glad to perceive you have made acquaintance with
Emily already; I see, in your being thus brought together, the foundation of a lasting friendship. You are
both innocent, and both young. God bless you—God
bless you, and make you all that I could wish."

He raised his eyes, and remained for a few moments
silent, as if in secret prayer. I felt that it was impossible
that this man, with feelings manifestly so tender, could
be the wretch that public opinion had represented him
to be. I was more than ever convinced of his innocence.
His manners were, or appeared to me, most fascinating.
I know not how the lights of experience might have
altered this estimate. But I was then very young, and .
I beheld in him a perfect mingling of the courtesy of
polished life with the gentlest and most genial virtues
of the heart. A feeling of affection and respect towards him began to spring up within me, the more
earnest that I remembered how sorely he had suffered
in fortune and how cruelly in fame. My uncle having
given me fully to understand that I was most welcome,
and might command whatever was his own, pressed me
to take some supper; and on my refusing, he observed
that, before bidding me good night, he had one duty
further to perform, one in which he was convinced I

would cheerfully acquiesce. He then proceeded to read
a chapter from the Bible; after which he took his leave
with the same affectionate kindness with which he had
greeted me, having repeated his desire that I should
consider every thing in his house as altogether at my
disposal. It is needless to say how much I was pleased
with my uncle—it was impossible to avoid being so;
and I could not help saying to myself, if such a man
as this is not safe from the assaults of slander, who is?
I felt much happier than I had done since my father's
death, and enjoyed that night the first refreshing sleep
which had visited me since that calamity. My curiosity
respecting my male cousin did not long remain unsatisfied; he appeared upon the next day at dinner. His
manners, though not so coarse as I had expected, were
exceedingly disagreeable; there was an assurance and a
forwardness for which I was not prepared; there was
less of the vulgarity of manner, and almost more of that
of the mind, than I had anticipated. I felt quite uncomfortable in his presence; there was just that confidence
in his look and tone, which would read encouragement
even in mere toleration; and I felt more disgusted and
annoyed at the coarse and extravagant compliments
which he was pleased from time to time to pay me, than
perhaps the extent of the atrocity might fully have warranted. It was, however, one consolation that he did
not often appear, being much engrossed by pursuits
about which I neither knew nor cared anything; but
when he did, his attentions, either with a view to his
amusement, or to some more serious object, were so obviously and perseveringly directed to me, that young
and inexperienced as I was, even *I* could not be ig-

norant of their significance. I felt more provoked by
this odious persecution than I can express, and dis-
couraged him with so much vigour, that I did not stop
even at rudeness to convince him that his assiduities
were unwelcome ; but all in vain.

This had gone on for nearly a twelvemonth, to my
infinite annoyance, when one day, as I was sitting at
some needlework with my companion, Emily, as was my
habit, in the parlour, the door opened, and my cousin
Edward entered the room. There was something, I
thought, odd in his manner, a kind of struggle between
shame and impudence, a kind of flurry and ambiguity,
which made him appear, if possible, more than ordinarily disagreeable.

"Your servant, ladies," he said, seating himself
at the same time; "sorry to spoil your *tête-à-tête;*
but never mind, I'll only take Emily's place for a
minute or two, and then we part for a while, fair
cousin. Emily, my father wants you in the corner turret ; no shilly, shally, he's in a hurry." She hesitated.
"Be off—tramp, march, I say," he exclaimed, in a tone
which the poor girl dared not disobey.

She left the room, and Edward followed her to the
door. He stood there for a minute or two, as if reflecting what he should say, perhaps satisfying himself
that no one was within hearing in the hall. At length
he turned about, having closed the door, as if carelessly, with his foot, and advancing slowly, in deep
thought, he took his seat at the side of the table opposite to mine. There was a brief interval of silence,
after which he said :—

"I imagine that you have a shrewd suspicion of the

object of my early visit; but I suppose I must go into particulars. Must I ?"

"I have no conception," I replied, "what your object may be."

"Well, well," said he becoming more at his ease as he proceeded, "it may be told in a few words. You know that it is totally impossible, quite out of the question, that an off-hand young fellow like me, and a good-looking girl like yourself, could meet continually as you and I have done, without an attachment—a liking growing up on one side or other; in short, I think I have let you know as plainly as if I spoke it, that I have been in love with you, almost from the first time I saw you." He paused, but I was too much horrified to speak. He interpreted my silence favourably. "I can tell you," he continued, "I'm reckoned rather hard to please, and very hard to *hit*. I can't say when I was taken with a girl before, so you see fortune reserved me ——."

Here the odious wretch actually put his arm round my waist: the action at once restored me to utterance, and with the most indignant vehemence I released myself from his hold, and at the same time said :—

"I *have*, sir, of course, perceived your most disagreeable attentions ; they have long been a source of great annoyance to me ; and you must be aware that I have marked my disapprobation, my disgust, as unequivocally as I possibly could, without actual indelicacy."

I paused, almost out of breath from the rapidity with which I had spoken ; and without giving him time to renew the conversation, I hastily quitted the room, leaving him in a paroxysm of rage and mortification. As

I ascended the stairs, I heard him open the parlour-
door with violence, and take two or three rapid strides
in the direction in which I was moving. I was now
much frightened, and ran the whole way until I reached
my room, and having locked the door, I listened breathlessly, but heard no sound. This relieved me for the
present ; but so much had I been overcome by the agitation and annoyance attendant upon the scene which I had
just passed through, that when my cousin Emily knocked at the door, I was weeping in great agitation. You
will readily conceive my distress, when you reflect upon
my strong dislike to my cousin Edward, combined with
my youth and extreme inexperience. Any proposal of
such a nature must have agitated me ; but that it should
come from the man whom, of all others, I instinctively
most loathed - and abhorred, and to whom I had, as
clearly as manner could do it, expressed the state of my
feelings, was almost too annoying to be borne ; it was
a calamity, too, in which I could not claim the sympathy
of my cousin Emily, which had always been extended
to me in my minor grievances. Still I hoped that it
might not be unattended with good ; for I thought that
one inevitable and most welcome consequence would result from this painful *eclaircissement,* in the discontinu-
ance of my cousin's odious persecution.

When I arose next morning, it was with the fervent
hope that I might never again behold his face, or even
hear his name ; but such a consummation, though de-
voutedly to be wished, was hardly likely to occur. The
painful impressions of yesterday were too vivid to be at
once erased ; and I could not help feeling some dim
foreboding of coming annoyance and evil. To expect on

my cousin's part anything like delicacy or consideration
for me, was out of the question.   I saw that he had set
his heart upon my property, and that he was not likely
easily to forego such a prize, possessing what might
have been considered opportunities and facilities almost
to compel my compliance.   I now keenly felt the unreasonableness of my father's conduct in placing me to
reside with a family, with all the members of which,
with one exception, he was wholly unacquainted, and I
bitterly felt the helplessness of my situation.   I determined, however, in the event of my cousin's persevering
in his addresses, to lay all the particulars before my
uncle, although he had never, in kindness or intimacy,
gone a step beyond our first interview, and to throw myself upon his hospitality and his sense of honour for
protection against a repetition of such annoyances.

My cousin's conduct may appear to have been an inadequate cause for such serious uneasiness ; but my
alarm was awakened neither by his acts nor by words,
but entirely by his manner, which was strange and
even intimidating.   At the beginning of our yesterday's interview, there was a sort of bullying swagger in
his air, which, towards the end, gave place to something
bordering upon the brutal vehemence of an undisguised
ruffian, a transition which had tempted me into a belief
that he might seek, even forcibly, to extort from me a
consent to his wishes, or by means still more horrible,
of which I scarcely dared to trust myself to think, to
possess himself of my property.

I was early next day summoned to attend my uncle
in his private room, which lay in a corner turret of the
old building; and thither I accordingly went, wondering

all the way what this unusual measure might prelude.
When I entered the room, he did not rise in his usual
courteous way to greet me, but simply pointed to a chair
opposite to his own ; this boded nothing agreeable.   I
sat down, however, silently waiting until he should open
the conversation.

"Lady Margaret," at length he said, in a tone of
greater sternness than I thought him capable of using,
"I have hitherto spoken to you as a friend, but I have
not forgotten that I am also your guardian, and that
my authority as such gives me a right to controul your
conduct.   I shall put a question to you, and I expect
and will demand a plain, direct answer. Have I rightly
been informed that you have contemptuously rejected
the suit and hand of my son Edward ?"

I stammered forth with a good deal of trepidation :—

"I believe, that is, I have, sir, rejected my cousin's
proposals ; and my coldness and discouragement might
have convinced him that I had determined to do so."

"Madame," replied he, with suppressed, but, as it
appeared to me, intense anger, "I have lived long
enough to know that *coldness* and discouragement, and
such terms, form the common cant of a worthless co-
quette. You know to the full, as well as I, that *coldness
and discouragement* may be so exhibited as to convince
their object that he is neither distasteful nor indifferent
to the person who wears that manner.   You know, too,
none better, that an affected neglect, when skilfully
managed, is amongst the most formidable of the allure-
ments which artful beauty can employ.   I tell you, madame, that having, without one word spoken in discouragement, permitted my son's most marked attentions

for a twelvemonth or more, you have no *right* to dismiss him with no further explanation than demurely
telling him that you had always looked coldly upon him,
and neither your wealth nor *your ladyship* (there was
an emphasis of scorn on the word which would have
become Sir Giles Overreach himself) can warrant you
in treating with contempt the affectionate regard of an
honest heart."

I was too much shocked at this undisguised attempt
to bully me into an acquiescence in the interested and
unprincipled plan for their own aggrandisement, which
I now perceived my uncle and his son had deliberately
formed, at once to find strength or collectedness to
frame an answer to what he had said.   At length I replied, with a firmness that surprised myself :—

"In all that you have just now said, sir, you have
grossly misstated my conduct and motives.   Your information must have been most incorrect, as far as it regards my conduct towards my cousin ; my manner
towards him could have conveyed nothing but dislike ;
and if anything could have added to the strong aversion
which I have long felt towards him, it would be his attempting thus to frighten me into a marriage which he
knows to be revolting to me, and which is sought by
him only as a means for securing to himself whatever
property is mine."

As I said this, I fixed my eyes upon those of my
uncle, but he was too old in the world's ways to falter
beneath the gaze of more searching eyes than mine ; he
simply said—

"Are you acquainted with the provisions of your
father's will?"

I answered in the affirmative; and he continued:—
"Then you must be aware that if my son Edward
were, which God forbid, the unprincipled, reckless
man, the ruffian you pretend to think him"—(here he
spoke very slowly, as if he intended that every word
which escaped him should be registered in my memory,
while at the same time the expression of his countenance
underwent a gradual but horrible change, and the eyes
which he fixed upon me became so darkly vivid, that I
almost lost sight of every thing else)—"if he were
what you have described him, do you think, child, he
would have found no shorter way than marriage to gain
his ends. A single blow, an outrage not a degree
worse than you insinuate, would transfer your property
to us!!"

I stood staring at him for many minutes after he had
ceased to speak, fascinated by the terrible, serpent-like
gaze, until he continued with a welcome change of
countenance :—

"I will not speak again to you, upon this topic, until
one month has passed. You shall have time to consider the relative advantages of the two courses which
are open to you. I should be sorry to hurry you to a
decision. I am satisfied with having stated my feelings
upon the subject, and pointed out to you the path of
duty. Remember this day month ; not one word
sooner."

He then rose, and I left the room, much agitated and
exhausted.

This interview, all the circumstances attending it, but
most particularly the formidable expression of my uncle's
countenance while he talked, though hypothetically, of

murder, combined to arouse all my worst suspicions of
him.   I dreaded to look upon the face that had so recently worn the appalling livery of guilt and malignity.
I regarded it with the mingled fear and loathing with
which one looks upon an object which has tortured them
in a night-mare.

In a few days after the interview, the particulars of
which I have just detailed, I found a note upon my
toilet-table, and on opening it I read as follows :—

" MY DEAR LADY MARGARET,—You will be, perhaps,
surprised to see a strange face in your room to-day.   I
have dismissed your Irish maid, and secured a French
one to wait upon you ; a step rendered necessary by my
proposing shortly to visit the Continent with all my
family.   Your faithful guardian,

                          "ARTHUR TYRRELL."

On inquiry, I found that my faithful attendant was
actually gone, and far on her way to the town of Galway ; and in her stead there appeared a tall, raw-boned,
ill-looking, elderly Frenchwoman, whose sullen and presuming manners seemed to imply that her vocation had
never before been that of a lady's-maid.   I could not
help regarding her as a creature of my uncle's, and
therefore to be dreaded, even had she been in no other
way suspicious.

Days and weeks passed away without any, even a momentary doubt upon my part, as to the course to be
pursued by me.   The allotted period had at length
elapsed ; the day arrived upon which I was to communicate my decision to my uncle.   Although my resolution had never for a moment wavered, I could not

shake off the dread of the approaching colloquy; and
my heart sank within me as I heard the expected sum-
mons. I had not seen my cousin Edward since the
occurrence of the grand *eclaircissement;* he must have
studiously avoided me; I suppose from policy, it could
not have been from delicacy. I was prepared for a terrific burst of fury from my uncle, as soon as I should
make known my determination; and I not unreasonably
feared that some act of violence or of intimidation would
next be resorted to.   Filled with these dreary forebod-
ings, I fearfully opened the study door, and the next
minute I stood in my uncle's presence. He received me
with a courtesy which I dreaded, as arguing a favourable anticipation respecting the answer which I was to
give; and after some slight delay he began by saying—
    "It will be a relief to both of us, I believe, to bring
this conversation as soon as possible to an issue. You
will excuse me, then, my dear niece, for speaking with
a bluntness which, under other circumstances, would be
unpardonable. You have, I am certain, given the subject of our last interview fair and serious consideration;
and I trust that you are now prepared with candour to
lay your answer before me. A few words will suffice;
we perfectly understand one another."
    He paused; and I, though feeling that I stood upon
a mine which might in an instant explode, nevertheless
answered with perfect composure: "I must now, sir,
make the same reply which I did upon the last occasion,
and I reiterate the declaration which I then made, that
I never can nor will, while life and reason remain, consent to a union with my cousin Edward."
    This announcement wrought no apparent change in

Sir Arthur, except that he became deadly, almost lividly pale. He seemed lost in dark thought for a minute, and then, with a slight effort, said, "You have answered me honestly and directly; and you say your resolution is unchangeable; well, would it had been otherwise—would it had been otherwise—but be it as it is; I am satisfied."

He gave me his hand—it was cold and damp as death; under an assumed calmness, it was evident that he was fearfully agitated. He continued to hold my hand with an almost painful pressure, while, as if unconsciously, seeming to forget my presence, he muttered, "Strange, strange, strange, indeed! fatuity, helpless fatuity!" there was here a long pause. "Madness *indeed* to strain a cable that is rotten to the very heart; it must break—and then—all goes." There was again a pause of some minutes, after which, suddenly changing his voice and manner to one of wakeful alacrity, he exclaimed,

"Margaret, my son Edward shall plague you no more. He leaves this country to-morrow for France; he shall speak no more upon this subject—never, never more; whatever events depended upon your answer must now take their own course; but as for this fruitless proposal, it has been tried enough; it can be repeated no more."

At these words he coldly suffered my hand to drop, as if to express his total abandonment of all his projected schemes of alliance; and certainly the action, with the accompanying words, produced upon my mind a more solem and depressing effect than I believed possible to have been caused by the course which I had determined to pursue; it struck upon my heart with an awe and heaviness which *will* accompany the accomplishment of an important and irrevocable act, even though no doubt

or scruple remains to make it possible that the agent
should wish it undone.

"Well," said my uncle, after a little time, "we now
cease to speak upon this topic, never to resume it again.
Remember you shall have no farther uneasiness from
Edward; he leaves Ireland for France to-morrow; this
will be a relief to you; may I depend upon your *honour*
that no word touching the subject of this interview shall
ever escape you?" I gave him the desired assurance;
he said, "It is well; I am satisfied; we have nothing
more, I believe, to say upon either side, and my presence must be a restraint upon you, I shall therefore bid
you farewell." I then left the apartment, scarcely knowing what to think of the strange interview which had
just taken place.

On the next day my uncle took occasion to tell me
that Edward had actually sailed, if his intention had
not been prevented by adverse winds or weather; and
two days after he actually produced a letter from his
son, written, as it said, *on board*, and despatched while
the ship was getting under weigh. This was a great
satisfaction to me, and as being likely to prove so, it
was no doubt communicated to me by Sir Arthur.

During all this trying period I had found infinite consolation in the society and sympathy of my dear cousin
Emily. I never, in after-life, formed a friendship so
close, so fervent, and upon which, in all its progress, I
could look back with feelings of such unalloyed pleasure,
upon whose termination I must ever dwell with so deep,
so yet unembittered a sorrow. In cheerful converse with
her I soon recovered my spirits considerably, and passed
my time agreeably enough, although still in the utmost

seclusion. Matters went on smoothly enough, although I could not help sometimes feeling a momentary, but horrible uncertainty respecting my uncle's character ; which was not altogether unwarranted by the circumstances of the two trying interviews, the particulars of which I have just detailed. The unpleasant impression which these conferences were calculated to leave upon my mind was fast wearing away, when there occurred a circumstance, slight indeed in itself, but calculated irrepressibly to awaken all my worst suspicions, and to overwhelm me again with anxiety and terror.

I had one day left the house with my cousin Emily, in order to take a ramble of considerable length, for the purpose of sketching some favourite views, and we had walked about half a mile when I perceived that we had forgotten our drawing materials, the absence of which would have defeated the object of our walk. Laughing at our own thoughtlessness, we returned to the house, and leaving Emily outside, I ran up stairs to procure the drawing-books and pencils which lay in my bed-room. As I ran up the stairs, I was met by the tall, ill-looking Frenchwoman, evidently a good deal flurried ; "Que veut, Madame ?" said she, with a more decided effort to be polite, than I had ever known her make before. " No, no—no matter," said I, hastily running by her in the direction of my room. "Madame," cried she, in a high key, "restez ici si vous plait, votre chambre n'est pas faite." I continued to move on without heeding her. She was some way behind me, and feeling that she could not otherwise prevent my entrance, for I was now upon the very lobby, she made a desperate attempt to seize hold of my person ; she succeeded in grasping the

G

end of my shawl, which she drew from my shoulders, but slipping at the same time upon the polished oak floor, she fell at full length upon the boards. A little frightened as well as angry at the rudeness of this strange woman, I hastily pushed open the door of my room, at which I now stood, in order to escape from her; but great was my amazement on entering to find the apartment pre-occupied. The window was open, and beside it stood two male figures; they appeared to be examining the fastenings of the casement, and their backs were turned towards the door. One of them was my uncle; they both had turned on my entrance, as if startled; the stranger was booted and cloaked, and wore a heavy, broad-leafed hat over his brows; he turned but for a moment, and averted his face; but I had seen enough to convince me that he was no other than my cousin Edward. My uncle had some iron instrument in his hand, which he hastily concealed behind his back ; and coming towards me, said something as if in an explanatory tone ; but I was too much shocked and confounded to understand what it might be. He said something about "*repairs*—window-frames—cold, and safety." I did not wait, however, to ask or to receive explanations, but hastily left the room. As I went down stairs I thought I heard the voice of the Frenchwoman in all the shrill volubility of excuse, and others uttering suppressed but vehement imprecations, or what seemed to me to be such.

I joined my cousin Emily quite out of breath. I need not say that my head was too full of other things to think much of drawing for that day. I imparted to her frankly the cause of my alarms, but, at the same time,

as gently as I could; and with tears she promised vigilance, devotion, and love. I never had reason for a
moment to repent the unreserved confidence which I then
reposed in her. She was no less surprised than I at the
unexpected appearance of Edward, whose departure for
France neither of us had for a moment doubted, but
which was now proved by his actual presence to be
nothing more than an imposture practised, I feared, for
no good end. The situation in which I had found my
uncle had very nearly removed all my doubts as to his
designs; I magnified suspicions into certainties, and
dreaded night after night that I should be murdered in
my bed. The nervousness produced by sleepless nights
and days of anxious fears increased the horrors of my
situation to such a degree, that I at length wrote a letter
to a Mr. Jefferies, an old and faithful friend of my
father's, and perfectly acquainted with all his affairs,
praying him, for God's sake, to relieve me from my present terrible situation, and communicating without reserve the nature and grounds of my suspicions. This
letter I kept sealed and directed for two or three days
always about my person, for discovery would have been
ruinous, in expectation of an opportunity, which might
be safely trusted, of having it placed in the post-office;
as neither Emily nor I were permitted to pass beyond
the precincts of the demesne itself, which was surrounded by high walls formed of dry stone, the difficulty of
procuring such an opportunity was greatly enhanced.

At this time Emily had a short conversation with her
father, which she reported to me instantly. After some
indifferent matter, he had asked her whether she and I
were upon good terms, and whether I was unreserved in

my disposition.   She answered in the affirmative ; and
he then inquired whether I had been much surprised to
find him in my chamber on the other day. She answered
that I had been both surprised and amused.   " And
what did she think of George Wilson's appearance ?"
" Who ?" inquired she.   " Oh ! the architect," he
answered, " who is to contract for the repairs of the
house ; he is accounted a handsome fellow."   " She
could not see his face," said Emily, " and she was in
such a hurry to escape that she scarcely observed him."
Sir Arthur appeared satisfied, and the conversation
ended.

This slight conversation, repeated accurately to me by
Emily, had the effect of confirming, if indeed any thing
was required to do so, all that I had before believed as
to Edward's actual presence ; and I naturally became,
if possible, more anxious than ever to despatch the letter
to Mr. Jefferies. An opportunity at length occurred.
As Emily and I were walking one day near the gate of
the demesne, a lad from the village happened to be passing down the avenue from the house ; the spot was secluded, and as this person was not connected by service
with those whose observation I dreaded, I committed
the letter to his keeping, with strict injunctions that he
should put it, without delay, into the receiver of the
town post-office ; at the same time I added a suitable
gratuity, and the man having made many protestations
of punctuality, was soon out of sight.   He was hardly
gone when I began to doubt my discretion in having
trusted him ; but I had no better or safer means of
despatching the letter, and I was not warranted in
suspecting him of such wanton dishonesty as a disposi-

tion to tamper with it ; but I could not be quite satisfied of its safety until I had received an answer, which
could not arrive for a few days. Before I did, however,
an event occurred which a little surprised me. I was
sitting in my bed-room early in the day, reading by
myself, when I heard a knock at the door. "Come in,"
said I, and my uncle entered the room. "Will you excuse me," said he, "I sought you in the parlour, and
thence I have come here. I desired to say a word to
you. I trust that you have hitherto found my conduct
to you such as that of a guardian towards his ward
should be." I dared not withhold my assent. "And,"
he continued, "I trust that you have not found me
harsh or unjust, and that you have perceived, my dear
niece, that I have sought to make this poor place as
agreeable to you as may be ?" I assented again ; and
he put his hand in his pocket, whence he drew a folded
paper, and dashing it upon the table with startling emphasis he said, "Did you write that letter ?" The sudden and fearful alteration of his voice, manner, and face,
but more than all, the unexpected production of my
letter to Mr. Jefferies, which I at once recognised, so
confounded and terrified me, that I felt almost choking.
I could not utter a word. "Did you write that letter ?"
he repeated, with slow and intense emphasis. "You did,
liar and hypocrite. You dared to write that foul and
infamous libel; but it shall be your last. Men will
universally believe you mad, if I choose to call for an
inquiry. I can make you appear so. The suspicions
expressed in this letter are the hallucinations and alarms
of a moping lunatic. I have defeated your first attempt,
madam ; and by the holy God, if ever you make another,

chains, darkness, and the keeper's whip shall be your portion." With these astounding words he left the room, leaving me almost fainting.

I was now almost reduced to despair; my last cast had failed; I had no course left but that of escaping secretly from the castle, and placing myself under the protection of the nearest magistrate. I felt if this were not done, and speedily, that I should be *murdered*. No one, from mere description, can have an idea of the unmitigated horror of my situation; a helpless, weak, inexperienced girl, placed under the power, and wholly at the mercy of evil men, and feeling that I had it not in my power to escape for one moment from the malignant influences under which I was probably doomed to fall; with a consciousness, too, that if violence, if murder were designed, no human being would be near to aid me; my dying shriek would be lost in void space.

I had seen Edward but once during his visit, and as I did not meet him again, I began to think that he must have taken his departure; a conviction which was to a certain degree satisfactory, as I regarded his absence as indicating the removal of immediate danger. Emily also arrived circuitously at the same conclusion, and not without good grounds, for she managed indirectly to learn that Edward's black horse had actually been for a day and part of a night in the castle stables, just at the time of her brother's supposed visit. The horse had gone, and as she argued, the rider must have departed with it.

This point being so far settled, I felt a little less uncomfortable; when being one day alone in my bed-room, I happened to look out from the window, and to my unutterable horror, I beheld peering through an opposite casement, my cousin Edward's face. Had I seen the evil one himself in bodily shape, I could not have experienced a more sickening revulsion. I was too much appalled to move at once from the window, but I did so soon enough to avoid his eye. He was looking fixedly down into the narrow quadrangle upon which the window opened. I shrunk back unperceived, to pass the rest of the day in terror and despair. I went to my room early that night, but I was too miserable to sleep.

At about twelve o'clock, feeling very nervous, I determined to call my cousin Emily, who slept, you will remember, in the next room, which communicated with mine by a second door. By this private entrance I found my way into her chamber, and without difficulty persuaded her to return to my room and sleep with me. We accordingly lay down together, she undressed, and I with my clothes on, for I was every moment walking up and down the room, and felt too nervous and miserable to think of rest or comfort. Emily was soon fast asleep, and I lay awake, fervently longing for the first pale gleam of morning, and reckoning every stroke of the old clock with an impatience which made every hour appear like six.

It must have been about one o'clock when I thought I heard a slight noise at the partition door between Emily's room and mine, as if caused by somebody's turning the key in the lock. I held my breath, and the same sound was repeated at the second door of my room, that which opened upon the lobby ; the sound was here distinctly caused by the revolution of the bolt in the lock, and it was followed by a slight pressure

upon the door itself, as if to ascertain the security of
the lock. The person, whoever it might be, was probably satisfied, for I heard the old boards of the lobby
creak and strain, as if under the weight of somebody moving cautiously over them. My sense of hearing became unnaturally, almost painfully acute. I suppose the imagination added distinctness to sounds vague
in themselves. I thought that I could actually hear
the breathing of the person who was slowly returning
along the lobby.

At the head of the stair-case there appeared to occur a pause; and I could distinctly hear two or three
sentences hastily whispered; the steps then descended
the stairs with apparently less caution. I ventured
to walk quickly and lightly to the lobby door, and attempted to open it; it was indeed fast locked upon the
outside, as was also the other. I now felt that the
dreadful hour was come; but one desperate expedient
remained—it was to awaken Emily, and by our united
strength, to attempt to force the partition door, which
was slighter than the other, and through this to pass to
the lower part of the house, whence it might be possible
to escape to the grounds, and so to the village. I returned
to the bed-side, and shook Emily, but in vain; nothing
that I could do availed to produce from her more than
a few incoherent words; it was a death-like sleep. She
had certainly drunk of some narcotic, as, probably, had I
also, in spite of all the caution with which I had examined
every thing presented to us to eat or drink. I now attempted, with as little noise as possible, to force first
one door, then the other; but all in vain. I believe no
strength could have effected my object, for both doors

opened inwards. I therefore collected whatever move-
ables I could carry thither, and piled them against the
doors, so as to assist me in whatever attempts I should
make to resist the entrance of those without. I then returned to the bed and endeavoured again, but fruitlessly,
to awaken my cousin. It was not sleep, it was torpor, le-
thargy, death. I knelt down and prayed with an agony
of earnestness ; and then seating myself upon the bed, I
awaited my fate with a kind of terrible tranquillity.

I heard a faint clanking sound from the narrow court
which I have already mentioned, as if caused by the
scraping of some iron instrument against stones or
rubbish. I at first determined not to disturb the calmness
which I now experienced, by uselessly watching the proceedings of those who sought my life ; but as the sounds
continued, the horrible curiosity which I felt overcame
every other emotion, and I determined, at all hazards,
to gratify it. I, therefore, crawled upon my knees to
the window, so as to let the smallest possible portion of
my head appear above the sill.

The moon was shining with an uncertain radiance
upon the antique grey buildings, and obliquely upon
the narrow court beneath ; one side of it was therefore clearly illuminated, while the other was lost in obscurity, the sharp outlines of the old gables, with their
nodding clusters of ivy, being at first alone visible.
Whoever or whatever occasioned the noise which had
excited my curiosity, was concealed under the shadow
of the dark side of the quadrangle. I placed my hand
over my eyes to shade them from the moonlight, which
was so bright as to be almost dazzling, and, peering into
the darkness, I first dimly, but afterwards gradually,

almost with full distinctness, beheld the form of a man
engaged in digging what appeared to be a rude hole
close under the wall. Some implements, probably a
shovel and pickaxe, lay beside him, and to these he
every now and then applied himself as the nature of the
ground required. He pursued his task rapidly, and
with as little noise as possible. "So," thought I, as
shovelful after shovelful, the dislodged rubbish mounted
into a heap, "they are digging the grave in which,
before two hours pass, I must lie, a cold, mangled
corpse. I am *their's*—I cannot escape." I felt as if
my reason was leaving me. I started to my feet, and
in mere despair I applied myself again to each of the
two doors alternately. I strained every nerve and sinew,
but I might as well have attempted, with my single
strength, to force the building itself from its foundations.
I threw myself madly upon the ground, and clasped my
hands over my eyes as if to shut out the horrible images
which crowded upon me.

The paroxysm passed away. I prayed once more
with the bitter, agonised fervour of one who feels that
the hour of death is present and inevitable. When I
arose, I went once more to the window and looked out,
just in time to see a shadowy figure glide stealthily along
the wall. The task was finished. The catastrophe of
the tragedy must soon be accomplished. I determined
now to defend my life to the last; and that I might be
able to do so with some effect, I searched the room for
something which might serve as a weapon; but either
through accident, or else in anticipation of such a possibility, every thing which might have been made available for such a purpose had been removed.

The Shadow of Death.

I must then die tamely and without an effort to defend myself. A thought suddenly struck me ; might it not be possible to escape through the door, which the assassin must open in order to enter the room? I resolved to make the attempt. I felt assured that the door through which ingress to the room would be effected was that which opened upon the lobby. It was the more direct way, besides being, for obvious reasons, less liable to interruption than the other. I resolved, then, to place myself behind a projection of the wall, the shadow would serve fully to conceal me, and when the door should be opened, and before they should have discovered the identity of the occupant of the bed, to creep noise-lessly from the room, and then to trust to Providence for escape. In order to facilitate this scheme, I removed all the lumber which I had heaped against the door ; and I had nearly completed my arrangements, when I perceived the room suddenly darkened, by the close approach of some shadowy object to the window. On turning my eyes in that direction, I observed at the top of the casement, as if suspended from above, first the feet, then the legs, then the body, and at length the whole figure of a man present itself. It was Edward Tyrrel. He appeared to be guiding his descent so as to bring his feet upon the centre of the stone block which occupied the lower part of the window ; and having secured his footing upon this, he kneeled down and began to gaze into the room. As the moon was gleaming into the chamber, and the bed-curtains were drawn, he was able to distinguish the bed itself and its contents. He appeared satisfied with his scrutiny, for he looked up and made a sign with his hand. He then applied his hand-to the window-frame, which must have been ingeniously contrived for the purpose, for with apparently no resistance the whole frame, containing casement and all, slipped from its position in the wall, and was by him lowered into the room.   The cold night wind waved the bed-curtains, and he paused for a moment; all was still again, and he stepped in upon the floor of the room.   He held in his hand what appeared to be a steel instrument, shaped something like a long hammer.   This he held rather behind him, while, with three long, *tip-toe* strides, he brought himself to the bedside. I felt that the discovery must now be made, and held my breath in momentary expectation of the execration in which he would vent his surprise and disappointment. I closed my eyes; there was a pause, but it was a short one.   I heard two dull blows, given in rapid succession; a quivering sigh, and the long-drawn, heavy breathing of the sleeper was for ever suspended.   I unclosed my eyes, and saw the murderer fling the quilt across the head of his victim; he then, with the instrument of death still in his hand, proceeded to the lobby-door, upon which he tapped sharply twice or thrice.   A quick step was then heard approaching, and a voice whispered something from without.   Edward answered, with a kind of shuddering chuckle, "her ladyship is past complaining; unlock the door, in the devil's name, unless you're afraid to come in, and help me to lift her out of the window."   The key was turned in the lock, the door opened, and my uncle entered the room.   I have told you already that I had placed myself under the shade of a projection of the wall, close to the door.   I had instinctively shrunk down cowering towards the ground on the entrance of Edward through the window. When my uncle entered the room, he and his son both stood so very close to me that his hand was every moment upon the point of touching my face. I held my breath, and remained motionless as death.

"You had no interruption from the next room?" said my uncle.

"No," was the brief reply.

"Secure the jewels, Ned; the French harpy must not lay her claws upon them. You're a steady hand, by G—d; not much blood—eh?"

"Not twenty drops," replied his son, "and those on the quilt."

"I'm glad it's over," whispered my uncle again; "we must lift the—the *thing* through the window, and lay the rubbish over it."

They then turned to the bedside, and, winding the bed-clothes round the body, carried it between them slowly to the window, and exchanging a few brief words with some one below, they shoved it over the window-sill, and I heard it fall heavily on the ground underneath.

"I'll take the jewels," said my uncle; "there are two caskets in the lower drawer."

He proceeded, with an accuracy which, had I been more at ease, would have furnished me with matter of astonishment, to lay his hand upon the very spot where my jewels lay; and having possessed himself of them, he called to his son:—

"Is the rope made fast above?"

"I'm no fool; to be sure it is," replied he.

They then lowered themselves from the window; and I rose lightly and cautiously, scarcely daring to

breathe, from my place of concealment, and was creep-
ing towards the door, when I heard my uncle's voice,
in a sharp whisper, exclaim, "Get up again; G—d
d——n you, you've forgot to lock the room door;"
and I perceived, by the straining of the rope which hung
from above, that the mandate was instantly obeyed.
Not a second was to be lost.   I passed through the
door, which was only closed, and moved as rapidly as
I could, consistently with stillness, along the lobby.
Before I had gone many yards, I heard the door through
which I had just passed roughly locked on the inside. I
glided down the stairs in terror, lest, at every corner, I
should meet the murderer or one of his accomplices. I
reached the hall, and listened, for a moment, to ascertain whether all was silent around.   No sound was audible; the parlour windows opened on the park, and
through one of them I might, I thought, easily effect
my escape.   Accordingly, I hastily entered; but, to my
consternation, a candle was burning in the room, and
by its light I saw a figure seated at the dinner-table,
upon which lay glasses, bottles, and the other accom-
paniments of a drinking party.   Two or three chairs
were placed about the table, irregularly, as if hastily
abandoned by their occupants.   A single glance satisfied me that the figure was that of my French attendant.   She was fast asleep, having, probably, drank
deeply.   There was something malignant and ghastly
in the calmness of this bad woman's features, dimly illuminated as they were by the flickering blaze of the
candle.   A knife lay upon the table, and the terrible
thought struck me—"Should I kill this sleeping accomplice in the guilt of the murderer, and thus secure

my retreat?" Nothing could be easier; it was but to draw the blade across her throat, the work of a second.

,An instant's pause, however, corrected me. " No," thought I, "the God who has conducted me thus far through the valley of the shadow of death, will not abandon me now. I will fall into their hands, or I will escape hence, but it shall be free from the stain of blood; His will be done." I felt a confidence arising from this reflection, an assurance of protection which I cannot describe. There were no other means of escape, so I advanced, with a firm step and collected mind, to the window. I noiselessly withdrew the bars, and unclosed the shutters; I pushed open the casement, and, without waiting to look behind me, I ran with my utmost speed, scarcely feeling the ground beneath me, down the avenue, taking care to keep upon the grass which bordered it. I did not for a moment slacken my speed, and I had now gained the central point between the park-gate and the mansion-house. Here the avenue made a wider circuit, and in order to avoid delay, I directed my way across the smooth sward round which the carriageway wound, intending, at the opposite side of the level, at a point which I distinguished by a group of old birch trees, to enter again upon the beaten track, which was from thence tolerably direct to the gate. I had, with my utmost speed, got about half way across this broad flat, when the rapid tramp of a horse's hoofs struck upon my ear. My heart swelled in my bosom, as though I would smother. The clattering of golloping hoofs approached; I was pursued; they were now upon the sward on which I was running; there was not a bush or a bramble to shelter me; and,

as if to render escape altogether desperate, the moon,
which had hitherto been obscured, at this moment shone
forth with a broad, clear light, which made every object
distinctly visible. The sounds were now close behind me.
I felt my knees bending under me, with the sensation
which unnerves one in a dream. I reeled, I stumbled,
I fell; and at the same instant the cause of my alarm
wheeled past me at full gallop. It was one of the young
fillies which pastured loose about the park, whose frolics
had thus all but maddened me with terror. I scrambled
to my feet, and rushed on with weak but rapid steps,
my sportive companion still galloping round and round
me with many a frisk and fling, until, at length, more
dead than alive, I reached the avenue-gate, and crossed
the stile, I scarce knew how. I ran through the village,
in which all was silent as the grave, until my progress
was arrested by the hoarse voice of a sentinel, who cried
"Who goes there?" I felt that I was now safe. I
turned in the direction of the voice, and fell fainting
at the soldier's feet. When I came to myself, I was sitting in a miserable hovel, surrounded by strange faces,
all bespeaking curiosity and compassion. Many sol-
diers were in it also; indeed, as I afterwards found, it
was employed as a guard-room by a detachment of
troops quartered for that night in the town. In a few
words I informed their officer of the circumstances
which had occurred, describing also the appearance of
the persons engaged in the murder; and he, without
further loss of time than was necessary to procure the
attendance of a magistrate, proceeded to the mansion-
house of Carrickleigh, taking with him a party of his
men. But the villains had discovered their mistake,

and had effected their escape before the arrival of the military.

The Frenchwoman was, however, arrested in the neighbourhood upon the next day. She was tried and condemned at the ensuing assizes; and previous to her execution confessed that " *she had a hand in making Hugh Tisdal's bed*." She had been a housekeeper in the castle at the time, and a *chere amie* of my uncle's. She was, in reality, able to speak English like a native, but had exclusively used the French language, I suppose to facilitate her designs. She died the same hardened wretch she had lived, confessing her crimes only, as she alleged, that her doing so might involve Sir Arthur Tyrrel, the great author of her guilt and misery, and whom she now regarded with unmitigated detestation.

With the particulars of Sir Arthur's and his son's escape, as far as they are known, you are acquainted. You are also in possession of their after fate; the terrible, the tremendous retribution which, after long delays of many years, finally overtook and crushed them. Wonderful and inscrutable are the dealings of God with his creatures!

Deep and fervent as must always be my gratitude to heaven for my deliverance, effected by a chain of providential occurrences, the failing of a single link of which must have ensured my destruction, it was long before I could look back upon it with other feelings than those of bitterness, almost of agony. The only being that had ever really loved me, my nearest and dearest friend, ever ready to sympathise, to counsel, and to assist; the gayest, the gentlest, the warmest heart; the only

H

creature on earth that cared for me; *her* life had been the price of my deliverance; and I then uttered the wish, which no event of my long and sorrowful life has taught me to recall, that she had been spared, and that, in her stead, *I* were mouldering in the grave, forgotten, and at rest.

Schalken the Painter.

THERE exists, at this moment, in good preservation, a
remarkable work of Schalken's.   The curious management of its lights constitutes, as usual in his pieces, the
chief apparent merit of the picture.   I say *apparent*,
for in its subject and not in its handling, however ex-
quisite, consists its real value.   The picture represents
the interior of what might be a chamber in some antique
religious building; and its foreground is occupied by a
female figure, in a species of white robe, part of which is
arranged so as to form a veil.   The dress, however, is
not that of any religious order.   In her hand she bears
a lamp, by which alone her figure and face are illuminated; and her features wear such an arch smile as
well becomes a pretty woman when practising some
prankish roguery; in the back ground, and, excepting
where the dim red light of an expiring fire serves to define the form, in total shadow, stands the figure of a

man dressed in the old Flemish fashion, in an attitude of
alarm, his hand being placed on the hilt of his sword,
which he appears to be in the act of drawing.

There are some pictures which impress one, I know
not how, with a conviction that they represent not the
mere ideal shapes and combinations which have floated
through the imagination of the artist, but scenes, faces,
and situations which have actually existed. There is in
that strange picture something that stamps it as the
representation of reality.

And such in truth it is, for it faithfully records a remarkable and mysterious occurrence, and perpetuates,
in the face of the female figure, which occupies the
most prominent place in the design, an accurate portrait
of Rose Velderkaust, the niece of Gerard Douw, the
first, and, I believe, the only love of Godfrey Schalken.
My great grandfather knew the painter well; from
Schalken himself he learned the fearful story of the
painting, and from him too he ultimately received the
picture itself as a bequest. The story and the picture
have become heir-looms in my family, and having de-
cribed the latter, I shall, if you please, attempt to relate
the tradition which has descended with the canvass.

There are few forms on which the mantle of romance
hangs more ungracefully than upon that of the uncouth
Schalken—the boorish but most cunning worker in oils,
whose pieces delight the critics of our day almost as
much as his manners disgusted the refined of his own;
and yet this man, so rude, so dogged, so slovenly in
the midst of his celebrity, had, in his obscure, but
happier days, played the hero in a wild romance of
mystery and passion.

When Schalken studied under the renowned Gerard
Douw, he was a very young man; and in spite of his phlegmatic temperament, he at once fell over head and ears in
love with the beautiful niece of his wealthy master.
Rose Velderkaust was still younger than he, having not
yet attained her seventeenth year, and if tradition speaks
truth, she possessed all the soft and dimpling charms of
the fair, light-haired, Flemish maidens. The young
painter loved honestly and fervently. His frank adoration
was rewarded. He declared his love, and extracted a
faltering confession in return. He was the happiest and
proudest painter in all Christendom. But there was
somewhat to dash his elation ; he was poor and undis-
tinguished. He dared not ask old Gerard for the hand
of his sweet ward. He must first win a reputation and
a competence.

There were, therefore, many dread uncertainties and
cold delays before him ; he had to fight his way against
sore odds. But he had won the heart of dear Rose
Velderkaust, and that was half the battle. It is needless
to say his exertions were redoubled, and his lasting
celebrity proves that his industry was not unrewarded.
by success.

These ardent labours, and worse still, the hopes that
elevated and beguiled them, were, however, destined
to experience a sudden interruption—of a character so
mysterious as to baffle all inquiry, and to throw over
the events themselves a shadow of preternatural horror.

Schalken had one evening outstayed all his fellow-pu-
pils, and still pursued his work in the deserted room.
As the daylight was fast failing, he laid aside his co-
lours, and applied himself to the completion of a sketch

on which he had expended extraordinary pains. It was
a religious composition, and represented the temptations
of a pot-bellied Saint Anthony. The young artist, however destitute of elevation, had, nevertheless, discern-
ment enough to be dissatisfied with his own work,
and many were the patient erasures and improve-
ments which saint and devil underwent, yet all in
vain. The large, old-fashioned room was silent, and,
with the exception of himself, quite emptied of its usual
inmates. An hour had thus passed away, nearly
two, without any improved result. Daylight had already declined, and twilight was deepening into the
darkness of night. The patience of the young painter
was exhausted, and he stood before his unfinished production, angry and mortified, one hand buried in the
folds of his long hair, and the other holding the
piece of charcoal which had so ill-performed its office,
and which he now rubbed, without much regard to the
sable streaks it produced, with irritable pressure upon
his ample Flemish inexpressibles.

"Curse the subject!" said the young man, aloud ;
."curse the picture, the devils, the saint ——"

At this moment a short, sudden sniff, uttered close
beside him, made the artist turn sharply round, and he
now, for the first time, became aware that his labours
had been overlooked by a stranger.

Within about a yard and half, and rather behind him,
there stood the figure of an elderly man, in a cloak
and a broad-brimmed, conical hat; in his hand, which
was protected with a heavy gauntlet-shaped glove, he carried a long ebony walking-stick, surmounted with what
appeared, as it glittered dimly in the twilight, to be a

massive head of gold, and upon his breast, through the
folds of the cloak, there shone the links of a rich chain
of the same metal.   The room was so obscure that nothing further of the appearance of the figure could be
ascertained, and the heavy flap of his hat threw his
features into profound shadow.   It would not have been
easy to conjecture the age of the intruder; but a quantity of dark hair escaping from beneath this sombre hat,
as well as his firm and upright carriage, seemed to indicate that his years could not yet exceed threescore, or
thereabouts.   There was an air of gravity and importance about the garb of this person, and something indescribably odd, I might say awful, in the perfect, stone-
like stillness of the figure, that effectually checked the
testy comment which had at once risen to the lips of
the irritated artist.   He therefore, as soon as he had
sufficiently recovered his surprise, asked the stranger,
civilly, to be seated, and desired to know if he had any
message to leave for his master.

"Tell Gerard Douw," said the unknown, without
altering his attitude in the smallest degree, "that
Minheer Vanderhausen, of Rotterdam, desires to speak.
with him on to-morrow evening at this hour, and if
he please, in this room, upon matters of weight; that
is all."

The stranger, having finished this message, turned
abruptly, and, with a quick, but silent step, quitted the
room, before Schalken had time to say a word in reply.
The young man felt a curiosity to see in what direction
the burgher of Rotterdam would turn, on quitting the
studio, and for that purpose. he went directly to the
window which commanded the door.   A lobby of con-

siderable extent intervened between the inner door of
the painter's room and the street entrance, so that
Schalken occupied the post of observation, as he conjectured, before the old man could possibly have reached
the street. He watched in vain, however. There was no
other mode of exit. Had the queer old man vanished, or
was he lurking about the recesses of the lobby for some
sinister purpose? This last suggestion filled the mind of
Schalken with a vague uneasiness, which was so unac-
countably intense as to make him alike afraid to remain
in the room alone, and reluctant to pass through the
lobby. However, with an effort apparently very dispro-
portioned to the occasion, he summoned resolution to
leave the room, and having locked the door, and thrust
the key into his pocket, without looking to the right or
left, he traversed the passage which had so recently,
perhaps still, contained the person of his mysterious
visitant, scarcely venturing to breathe till he had arrived
in the open street.

"Minheer Vanderhausen !" said Gerard Douw within
himself, as the appointed hour approached, "Minheer
Vanderhausen, of Rotterdam! I never heard of the
man till yesterday. What can he want of me? A portrait, perhaps, to be painted; or a poor relation to
be apprenticed; or a collection to be valued; or—pshaw!
there's no one in Rotterdam to leave me a legacy.
Well, whatever the business may be, we shall soon know
it all."

It was now the close of day, and again every easel, except that of Schalken, was deserted. Gerard Douw was
pacing the apartment with the restless step of impatient
expectation, sometimes pausing to glance over the work

of one of his absent pupils, but more frequently placing himself at the window, from whence he might observe the passengers who threaded the obscure by-street in which his studio was placed.

" Said you not, Godfrey," exclaimed Douw, after a long and fruitless gaze from his post of observation, and turning to Schalken, "that the hour he appointed was about seven by the clock of the Stadhouse ?"

" It had just told seven when I first saw him, sir," answered the student.

" The hour is close at hand, then," said the master, consulting a horologe as large and as round as an orange. " Minheer Vanderhausen, from Rotterdam—is it not so ?"

" Such was the name."

" And an elderly man, richly clad?" pursued Douw, musingly.

" As well as I might see," replied his pupil; "he could not be young, nor yet very old, neither ; and his dress was rich and grave, as might become a citizen of wealth and consideration."

At this moment the sonorous boom of the Stadhouse clock told, stroke after stroke, the hour of seven ; the eyes of both master and student were directed to the door ; and it was not until the last peal of the old bell had ceased to vibrate, that Douw exclaimed—

" So, so ; we shall have his worship presently, that is, if he means to keep his hour ; if not, you may wait for him, Godfrey, if you court his acquaintance. But what, after all, if it should prove but a mummery, got up by Vankarp, or some such wag. I wish you had run all risks, and cudgelled the old burgomaster soundly.   I'd wager a dozen of Rhenish his worship would have unmasked, and pleaded old acquaintance in a trice."

"Here he comes, sir," said Schalken, in a low, monitory tone; and instantly, upon turning towards the door, Gerard Douw observed the same figure which had, on the day before, so unexpectedly greeted his pupil Schalken.

There was something in the air of the figure which at once satisfied the painter that there was no masquerading in the case, and that he really stood in the presence of a man of worship; and so, without hesitation, he doffed his cap, and, courteously saluting the stranger, requested him to be seated.   The visiter waved his hand slightly, as if in acknowledgment of the courtesy, but remained standing.

"I have the honour to see Minheer Vanderhausen of Rotterdam?" said Gerard Douw.

"The same," was the laconic reply of his visiter.

"I understand your worship desires to speak with me," continued Douw, "and I am here by appointment to wait your commands."

"Is that a man of trust?" said Vanderhausen, turning towards Schalken, who stood at a little distance behind his master.

"Certainly," replied Gerard.

"Then let him take this box, and get the nearest jeweller or goldsmith to value its contents, and let him return hither with a certificate of the valuation."

At the same time, he placed a small case about nine inches square in the hands of Gerard Douw, who was as much amazed at its weight as at the strange abruptness

with which it was handed to him.   In accordance with
the wishes of the stranger, he delivered it into the hands
of Schalken, and repeating his directions, despatched
him upon the mission.

Schalken disposed his precious charge securely beneath the folds of his cloak, and rapidly traversing two
or three narrow streets, he stopped at a corner house,
the lower part of which was then occupied by the shop
of a Jewish goldsmith.   He entered the shop, and
calling the little Hebrew into the obscurity of its back
recesses, he proceeded to lay before him Vanderhausen's
casket.   On being examined by the light of a lamp, it
appeared entirely cased with lead, the outer surface of
which was much scraped and soiled, and nearly white
with age.   This having been partially removed, there
appeared beneath a box of some hard wood, which
also they forced open, and after the removal of two
or three folds of linen, they discovered its contents
to be a mass of golden ingots, closely packed, and,
as the Jew declared, of the most perfect quality.
Every ingot underwent the scrutiny of the little Jew,
who seemed to feel an epicurean delight in touching
and testing these morsels of the glorious metal; and
each one of them was replaced in its berth with the
exclamation: "*Meinn Gott,* how very perfect! not one
grain of alloy—beautiful, beautiful!"   The task was at
length finished, and the Jew certified under his hand
the value of the ingots submitted to his examination, to amount to many thousand rix-dollars.   With
the desired document in his pocket, and the rich box of
gold carefully pressed under his arm, and concealed by
his cloak, he retraced his way, and entering the studio,

found his master and the stranger in close conference. Schalken had no sooner left the room, in order to execute the commission he had taken in charge, than Vanderhausen addressed Gerard Douw in the following terms :—

" I cannot tarry with you to-night more than a few minutes, and so I shall shortly tell you the matter upon which I come. You visited the town of Rotterdam some four months ago, and then I saw in the Church of St. Lawrence your niece, Rose Velderkaust. I desire to marry her ; and if I satisfy you that I am wealthier than any other husband you can dream of for her, I expect that you will forward my suit with your authority. If you approve my proposal, you must close with it here and now, for I cannot wait for calculations and delays."

Gerard Douw was hugely astonished at the nature of Minheer Vanderhausen's communication, but he did not venture to express his surprise ; for besides the motives supplied by prudence and politeness, the painter experienced a sort of chill and oppression, like that which is said to supervene when one is placed in unconscious proximity with the object of a natural antipathy— an undefined but overpowering sensation, while standing in the presence of the eccentric stranger, which made him very unwilling to say anything which might reasonably offend him.

" I have no doubt," said Gerard, after two or three prefatory hems, "that the alliance which you propose would prove alike advantageous and honourable to my niece ; but you must be aware that she has a will of her own, and may not acquiesce in what *we* may design for her advantage."

" Do not seek to deceive me, sir painter," said Vanderhausen ; "you are her guardian—she is your ward ; she is mine if *you* like to make her so."

The man of Rotterdam moved forward a little as he spoke, and Gerard Douw, he scarce knew why, inwardly prayed for the speedy return of Schalken.

" I desire," said the mysterious gentleman, " to place in your hands at once an evidence of my wealth, and a security for my liberal dealing with your niece. The lad will return in a minute or two with a sum in value five times the fortune which she has a right to expect from her husband. This shall lie in your hands, together with her dowry, and you may apply the united sum as suits her interest best ; it shall be all exclusively hers while she lives : is that liberal ?"

Douw assented, and inwardly acknowledged that fortune had been extraordinarily kind to his niece; the stranger, he thought, must be both wealthy and generous, and such an offer was not to be despised, though made by a humourist, and one of no very prepossessing presence. Rose had no very high pretensions, for she had but a modest dowry, which she owed entirely to the generosity of her uncle; neither had she any right to raise exceptions on the score of birth, for her own origin was far from splendid ; and as to other objections, Gerard resolved, and, indeed, by the usages of the time, was warranted in resolving, not to listen to them for a moment.

" Sir," said he, addressing the stranger, " your offer is liberal, and whatever hesitation I may feel in closing with it immediately, arises solely from my not having the honour of knowing anything of your family or station. Upon these points you can, of course, satisfy me without difficulty ?"

" As to my respectability," said the stranger, drily, " you must take that for granted at present ; pester me with no inquiries ; you can discover nothing more about me than I choose to make known. You shall have sufficient security for my respectability—my word, if you are honourable ; if you are sordid, my gold."

" A testy old gentleman," thought Douw, " he will have his own way ; but, all things considered, I am not justified in declining his offer. I will not pledge myself unnecessarily, however."

" You will not pledge yourself unnecessarily," said Vanderhausen, strangely uttering the very words which had just floated through the mind of ·his companion ; " but you will do so if it *is* necessary, I presume ; and I will show you that I consider it indispensable. If the gold I mean to leave in your hands satisfy you, and if you don't wish my proposal to be at once withdrawn, you must, before I leave this room, write your name to this engagement."

Having thus spoken, he placed a paper in the hands of the master, the contents of which expressed an engagement entered into by Gerard Douw, to give to Wilken Vanderhausen of Rotterdam, in marriage, Rose Velderkaust, and soforth, within one week of the date thereof. While the painter was employed in reading this covenant, by the light of a twinkling oil lamp in the far wall of the room, Schalken, as we have stated, entered the studio, and having delivered the box and the valuation of the Jew, into the hands of the stranger, he was about to retire, when Vanderhausen called to him to wait ;

and, presenting the case and the certificate to Gerard Douw, he paused in silence until he had satisfied himself, by an inspection of both, respecting the value of the pledge left in his hands.   At length he said—

" Are you content ?"

The painter said he would fain have another day to consider.

" Not an hour," said the suitor, apathetically.

" Well then," said Douw, with a sore effort, " I *am* content, it is a bargain."

" Then sign," said Vanderhausen, " for I am weary."

At the same time he produced a small case of writing materials, and Gerard signed the important document.

" Let this youth witness the covenant," said the old man ; and Godfrey Schalken unconsciously attested the instrument which for ever bereft him of his dear Rose Velderkaust.

The compact being thus completed, the strange visiter folded the paper, and stowed it safely in an inner pocket.

" I will visit you to-morrow night at nine o'clock, at your own house, Gerard Douw, and will see the object of our contract ;" and so saying, Wilken Vanderhausen moved stiffly, but rapidly, out of the room.

Schalken, eager to resolve his doubts, had placed himself by the window, in order to watch the street entrance ; but the experiment served only to support his suspicions, for the old man did not issue from the door. This was *very* strange—odd, nay fearful.   He and his master returned together, and talked but little on the way, for each had his own subjects of reflection, of anxiety, and of hope.   Schalken, however, did not know the ruin which menaced his dearest projects.

Gerard Douw knew nothing of the attachment which had sprung up between his pupil and his niece; and even if he had, it is doubtful whether he would have regarded its existence as any serious obstruction to the wishes of Minheer Vanderhausen. Marriages were then and there matters of traffic and calculation; and it would have appeared as absurd in the eyes of the guardian to make a mutual attachment an essential element in a contract of the sort, as it would have been to draw up his bonds and receipts in the language of romance.

The painter, however, did not communicate to his niece the important step which he had taken in her behalf, a forbearance caused not by any anticipated opposition on her part, but solely by a ludicrous consciousness that if she were to ask him for a description of her destined bridegroom, he would be forced to confess that he had not once seen his face, and if called upon, would find it absolutely impossible to identify him. Upon the next day, Gerard Douw, after dinner, called his niece to him, and having scanned her person with an air of satisfaction, he took her hand, and looking upon her pretty innocent face with a smile of kindness, he said :—

"Rose, my girl, that face of yours will make your fortune." Rose blushed and smiled. "Such faces and such tempers seldom go together, and when they do, the combination is a love-charm such as few heads or hearts can resist; trust me, you will soon be a bride, girl. But this is trifling, and I am pressed for time; so make ready the large room by eight o'clock to-night, and give directions for supper at nine. I expect a friend; and observe me, child, do you trick yourself out hand-

somely. I will not have him think us poor or slut-
tish."

With these words he left her, and took his way to the
room in which his pupils worked.

When the evening closed in, Gerard called Schalken,
who was about to take his departure to his own obscure and
comfortless lodgings, and asked him to come home and
sup with Rose and Vanderhausen. The invitation was,
of course, accepted, and Gerard Douw and his pupil soon
found themselves in the handsome and, even then, antique chamber, which had been prepared for the reception of the stranger. A cheerful wood fire blazed in the
hearth, a little at one side of which an old-fashioned
table, which shone in the fire-light like burnished gold,
was awaiting the supper, for which preparations were
going forward; and ranged with exact regularity, stood
the tall-backed chairs, whose ungracefulness was more
than compensated by their comfort. The little party,
consisting of Rose, her uncle, and the artist, awaited the
arrival of the expected visiter with considerable impatience. Nine o'clock at length came, and with it a sum-
mons at the street door, which being speedily answered,
was followed by a slow and emphatic tread upon the
staircase; the steps moved heavily across the lobby,
the door of the room in which the party we have
described were assembled slowly opened, and there
entered a figure which startled, almost appalled, the
phlegmatic Dutchmen, and nearly made Rose scream
with terror. It was the form, and arrayed in the garb of
Minheer Vanderhausen; the air, the gait, the height
were the same, but the features had never been seen by
any of the party before. The stranger stopped at the
door of the room, and displayed his form and face com-

I

pletely. He wore a dark-coloured cloth cloak, which
was short and full, not falling quite to his knees; his
legs were cased in dark purple silk stockings, and his
shoes were adorned with roses of the same colour. The
opening of the cloak in front showed the under-suit to
consist of some very dark, perhaps sable material, and
his hands were enclosed in a pair of heavy leather gloves,
which ran up considerably above the wrist, in the manner of a gauntlet. In one hand he carried his walking-
stick and his hat, which he had removed, and the other
hung heavily by his side. A quantity of grizzled hair descended in long folds from his head, and rested upon the
plaits of a stiff ruff, which effectually concealed his neck.
So far all was well; but the face!—all the flesh of the
face was coloured with the bluish leaden hue which is
sometimes induced by metallic medicines, administered
in excessive quantities; the eyes showed an undue proportion of muddy white, and had a certain indefinable
character of insanity; the hue of the lips bearing the
usual relation to that of the face, was, consequently, nearly
black; and the entire character of the countenance was
sensual, malignant, and even satanic. It was remarkable that the worshipful stranger suffered as little
as possible of his flesh to appear, and that during his
visit he did not once remove his gloves. Having stood
for some moments at the door, Gerard Douw at length
found breath and collectedness to bid him welcome, and
with a mute inclination of the head, the stranger stepped forward into the room. There was something indescribably odd, even horrible, about all his motions,
something undefinable, that was unnatural, unhuman;
it was as if the limbs were guided and directed by a
spirit unused to the management of bodily machinery.

The stranger spoke hardly at all during his visit, which did not exceed half an hour ; and the host himself could scarcely muster courage enough to utter the few necessary salutations and courtesies ; and, indeed, such was the nervous terror which the presence of Vanderhausen inspired, that very little would have made all his entertainers fly in downright panic from the room. They had not so far lost all self-possession, however, as to fail to observe two strange peculiarities of their visiter. During his stay his eyelids did not once close, or, indeed, move in the slightest degree ; and farther, there was a death-like stillness in his whole person, owing to the absence of the heaving motion of the chest, caused by the process of respiration. These two peculiarities, though when told they may appear trifling, produced a very striking and unpleasant effect when seen and observed. Vanderhausen at length relieved the painter of Leyden of his inauspicious presence; and with no trifling sense of relief the little party heard the street door close after him.

" Dear uncle," said Rose, " what a frightful man ! I would not see him again for the wealth of the States."

" Tush, foolish girl," said Douw, whose sensations were anything but comfortable. " A man may be as ugly as the devil, and yet, if his heart and actions are good, he is worth all the pretty-faced perfumed puppies that walk the Mall. Rose, my girl, it is very true he has not thy pretty face, but I know him to be wealthy and liberal ; and were he ten times more ugly, these two virtues would be enough to counterbalance all his deformity, and if not sufficient actually to alter the shape and hue of his features, at least enough to prevent one's thinking them so much amiss.''

" Do you know uncle," said Rose, " when I saw him
standing at the door, I could not get it out of my head
that I saw the old painted wooden figure that used to
frighten me so much in the Church of St. Laurence at
Rotterdam."

Gerard laughed, though he could not help inwardly
acknowledging the justness of the comparison.   He was
resolved, however, as far as he could, to check his
niece's disposition to dilate upon the ugliness of her intended bridegroom, although he was not a little pleased,
as well as puzzled, to observe that she appeared totally
exempt from that mysterious dread of the stranger which,
he could not disguise it from himself, most painfully
affected him, as also his pupil Godfrey Schalken.

Early on the next day there arrived, from various
quarters of the town, presents of silks, velvets, jewellery,
and soforth, for Rose ; and also a packet directed to
Gerard Douw, which, on being opened, was found to
contain a contract of marriage, formally drawn up between Wilken Vanderhausen of the *Boom-quay*, in Rotterdam, and Rose Velderkaust of Leyden, niece to Gerard Douw, master in ·the art of painting, also of the
same city ; and containing engagements on the part of
Vanderhausen to make settlements upon his bride, far
more splendid than he had before led her guardian to
believe likely, and which were to be secured to her use in
the most unexceptionable manner possible—the money
being placed in the hand of Gerard Douw himself.

I have no sentimental scenes to describe, no cruelty of
guardians, no magnanimity of wards, no agonies, or
transports of lovers.   The record I have to make is one
of sordidness, levity, and heartlessness.   In less than a

week after the first interview which we have just described, the contract of marriage was fulfilled, and
Schalken saw the prize which he would have risked existence to secure, carried off in solemn pomp by his repulsive rival.   For two or three days he absented himself from the school; he then returned and worked, if
with less cheerfulness, with far more dogged resolution
than before : the stimulus of love had given place to that
of ambition.   Months passed away, and, contrary to his
expectation, and, indeed, to the direct promise of the
parties, Gerard Douw heard nothing of his niece or her
worshipful spouse.   The interest of the money, which
was to have been demanded in quarterly sums, lay un-
claimed in his hands.

He began to grow extremely uneasy.   Minheer Vanderhausen's direction in Rotterdam he was fully possessed
of; after some irresolution he finally determined to journey thither—a trifling undertaking, and easily accomplished—and thus to satisfy himself of the safety and
comfort of his ward, for whom he entertained an honest
and strong affection.   His search was in vain, however;
no one in Rotterdam had ever heard of Minheer Vanderhausen.   Gerard Douw left not a house in the Boom-
quay untried, but all in vain.   No one could give him
any information whatever touching the object of his inquiry, and he was obliged to return to Leyden, nothing
wiser, and far more anxious, than when he left it.

On his arrival he hastened to the establishment from
which Vanderhausen had hired the lumbering, though,
considering the times, most luxurious vehicle, which the
bridal party had employed to convey them to Rotterdam.
From the driver of this machine he learned, that having

proceeded by slow stages, they had late in the evening
approached Rotterdam ; but that before they entered the
city, and while yet nearly a mile from it, a small party
of men, soberly clad, and after the old fashion, with
peaked beards and moustaches, standing in the centre of
the road, obstructed the further progress of the carriage.
The driver reined in his horses, much fearing, from the
obscurity of the hour, and the loneliness of the road, that
some mischief was intended.   His fears were, however,
somewhat allayed by his observing that these strange
men carried a large litter, of an antique shape, and which
they immediately set down upon the pavement, where-
upon the bridegroom, having opened the coach door
from within, descended, and having assisted his bride
to do likewise, led her, weeping bitterly and wringing
her hands, to the litter, which they both entered. It
was then raised by the men who surrounded it, and
speedily carried towards the city, and before it had proceeded very far, the darkness concealed it from the view
of the Dutch coachman.   In the inside of the vehicle he
found a purse, whose contents more than thrice paid the
hire of the carriage and man.   He saw and could tell
nothing more of Minheer Vanderhausen and his beautiful lady.

   This mystery was a source of profound anxiety, and
even of grief, to Gerard Douw.   There was evidently
fraud in the dealing of Vanderhausen with him, though
for what purpose committed he could not imagine.   He
greatly doubted how far it was possible for a man possessing such a countenance to be in reality anything but a
villain, and every day that passed without his hearing
from or of his niece, instead of inducing him to forget

his fears, on the contrary tended more and more to aggravate them.   The loss of her cheerful society tended
also to depress his spirits; and in order to dispel the
gloom which often stole upon his mind after his daily
occupations were over, he was wont frequently to ask
Schalken to accompany him home, and share his otherwise solitary supper.

One evening, the painter and his pupil were sitting by
the fire, having accomplished a comfortable meal, and
had yielded to the silent and delicious melancholy of
digestion, when their ruminations were disturbed by a
loud sound at the street door, as if occasioned by some person rushing and scrambling vehemently against it.   A domestic had run without delay to ascertain the cause of
the disturbance, and they heard him twice or thrice in-
terrogate the applicant for admission, but without eliciting any other answer but a sustained reiteration of the
sounds.   They heard him then open the hall-door, and
immediately there followed a light and rapid tread upon
the staircase.   Schalken advanced towards the door.   It
opened before he reached it, and Rose rushed into the
room.   She looked wild, fierce, and haggard with terror
and exhaustion, but her dress surprised them as much
even as her unexpected appearance.   It consisted of a
kind of white woollen wrapper, made close about the neck,
and descending to the very ground.   It was much de-
ranged and travel-soiled.   The poor creature had hardly
entered the chamber when she fell senseless on the
floor.   With some difficulty they succeeded in reviving
her, and on recovering her senses she instantly exclaimed,
in a tone of terror rather than mere impatience—

" Wine! wine!—quickly, or I'm lost!"

Astonished and almost scared at the strange agitation in which the call was made, they at once administered to her wishes, and she drank some wine with a haste and eagerness which surprised them.   She had hardly swallowed it, when she exclaimed, with the same urgency—

"Food, for God's sake, food, at once, or I perish!"

A large fragment of a roast joint was upon the table, and Schalken immediately began to cut some, but he was anticipated ; for no sooner did she see it than she caught it, a more than mortal image of famine, and with her hands, and even with her teeth, she tore off the flesh, and swallowed it.   When the paroxysm of hunger had been a little appeased, she appeared on a sudden overcome with shame, or it may have been that other more agitating thoughts overpowered and scared her, for she began to weep bitterly, and to wring her hands.

"Oh, send for a minister of God," said she ; "I am not safe till he comes : send for him speedily !"

Gerard Douw despatched a messenger instantly, and prevailed on his niece to allow him to surrender his bedchamber to her use.   He also persuaded her to retire there at once to rest : her consent was extorted upon the condition that they would not leave her for a moment.

"Oh, that the holy man were here !" she said : "he can deliver me : the dead and the living can never be one : God has forbidden it !"

With these mysterious words, she surrendered herself to their guidance, and they proceeded to the chamber which Gerard Douw had assigned to her use.

" Do not, do not leave me for a moment !" she said ; " I am lost for ever if you do."

Gerard Douw's chamber was approached through a spacious apartment, which they were now about to enter. He and Schalken each carried a candle, so that a sufficiency of light was cast upon all surrounding objects. They were now entering the large chamber, which, as I have said, communicated with Douw's apartment, when Rose suddenly stopped, and, in a whisper which thrilled them both with horror, she said—

"Oh, God! he is here! he is here! See, see!—there he goes!"

She pointed towards the door of the inner room, and Schalken thought he saw a shadowy and ill-defined form gliding into that apartment. He drew his sword, and, raising the candle so as to throw its light with increased distinctness upon the objects in the room, he entered the chamber into which the shadow had glided. No figure was there—nothing but the furniture which belonged to the room; and yet he could not be deceived as to the fact that something had moved before them into the chamber. A sickening dread came upon him, and the cold perspiration broke out in heavy drops upon his forehead: nor was he more composed when he heard the increased urgency and agony of entreaty with which Rose implored them not to leave her for a moment.

"I saw him," said she; "he's here. I cannot be deceived; I know him; he's by me; he is with me; he's in the room. Then, for God's sake, as you would save me, do not stir from beside me."

They at length prevailed upon her to lie down upon the bed, where she continued to urge them to stay by her. She frequently uttered incoherent sentences, repeating again and again, "The dead and the living cannot be one:

God has forbidden it!" And then again, " Rest to the
wakeful—sleep to the sleep-walkers !" These and such
mysterious and broken sentences she continued to utter
until the clergyman arrived. Gerard Douw began to fear,
naturally enough, that terror or ill-treatment had unsettled the poor girl's intellect; and he half suspected,
from the suddenness of her appearance, the unseason-
ableness of the hour, and, above all, from the wildness
and terror of her manner, that she had made her escape
from some place of confinement for lunatics, and was in
imminent fear of pursuit. He resolved to summon medical advice as soon as the mind of his niece had been
in some measure set at rest by the offices of the clergyman whose attendance she had so earnestly desired; and
until this object had been attained, he did not venture
to put any questions to her which might possibly, by reviving painful or horrible recollections, increase her agitation. The clergyman soon arrived—a man of ascetic
countenance and venerable age—one whom Gerard Douw
respected much, forasmuch as he was a veteran polemic,
though one perhaps more dreaded as a combatant than
beloved as a Christian—of pure morality, subtle brain,
and frozen heart. He entered the chamber which communicated with that in which Rose reclined, and immediately on his arrival she requested him to pray for her,
as for one who lay in the hands of Satan, and who could
hope for deliverance only from heaven.

That you may distinctly understand all the circumstances of the event which I am going to describe, it is
necessary to state the relative position of the parties who
were engaged in it. The old clergyman and Schalken
were in the ante-room of which I have already spoken;

Rose lay in the inner chamber, the door of which was open; and by the side of the bed, at her urgent desire, stood her guardian; a candle burned in the bedchamber, and three were lighted in the outer apartment. The old man now cleared his voice, as if about to commence, but before he had time to begin, a sudden gust of air blew out the candle which served to illuminate the room in which the poor girl lay, and she, with hurried alarm, exclaimed—

"Godfrey, bring in another candle; the darkness is unsafe."

Gerard Douw, forgetting for the moment her repeated injunctions, in the immediate impulse, stepped from the bedchamber into the other, in order to supply what she desired.

"Oh God! do not go, dear uncle," shrieked the unhappy girl—and at the same time she sprung from the bed, and darted after him, in order, by her grasp, to detain him. But the warning came too late, for scarcely had he passed the threshold, and hardly had his niece had time to utter the startling exclamation, when the door which divided the two rooms closed violently after him, as if swung to by a strong blast of wind. Schalken and he both rushed to the door, but their united and desperate efforts could not avail so much as to shake it. Shriek after shriek burst from the inner chamber, with all the piercing loudness of despairing terror. Schalken and Douw strained every nerve to force open the door; but all in vain. There was no sound of struggling from within, but the screams seemed to increase in loudness, and at the same time they heard the bolts of the latticed window withdrawn, and the window itself grated

upon the sill as if thrown open. One *last* shriek, so
long, and piercing, and agonised, as to be scarcely human, swelled from the room, and suddenly there followed a death-like silence.   A light step was heard
crossing the floor, as if from the bed to the window ;
and almost at the same instant the door gave way,
and, yielding to the pressure of the external applicants,
they were nearly precipitated into the room.   It was
empty.   The window was open, and Schalken sprung
to a chair, and gazed out upon the street and canal
below.   There was no one there; but he saw, or thought
he saw, the waters of the broad canal beneath settling
ring after ring in heavy circles, as if a moment before disturbed by the submersion of some ponderous
body.

No trace of Rose was ever after found, nor was anything certain respecting her mysterious wooer discovered
or even suspected—no clue whereby to trace the intricacies of the labyrinth, and to arrive at its solution, presented itself.   But an incident occurred, which, though
it will not be received by our rational readers in lieu of
evidence, produced, nevertheless, a strong and a lasting
impression upon the mind of Schalken.   Many years
after the events which we have detailed, Schalken, then
residing far away, received an intimation of his father's
death, and of his intended burial upon a fixed day in the
church of Rotterdam.   It was necessary that a very
considerable journey should be performed by the funeral
procession, which, as it will readily be believed, was
not very numerously attended.   Schalken with difficulty
arrived in Rotterdam late in the day upon which the
funeral was appointed to take place.   It had not then

arrived.   Evening closed in, and still it did not appear.

Schalken strolled down to the church; he found it
open; notice of the approach of the funeral had been
given, and the vault in which the body was to be laid
had been opened.   The sexton, on seeing a well-dressed
gentleman, whose object was to attend the expected
obsequies, pacing the aisle of the church, hospitably invited him to share with him the comforts of a blazing
fire, which, as was his custom in winter time upon such
occasions, he had kindled in the hearth of a chamber
in which he was accustomed to await the arrival of such
grisly guests, and which communicated, by a flight of
steps, with the vault below.   In this chamber, Schalken
and his entertainer seated themselves; and the sexton,
after some fruitless attempts to engage his guest in conversation, was obliged to apply himself to his tobacco-
pipe and can, to solace his solitude.   In spite of his
grief and cares, the fatigues of a rapid journey of nearly
forty hours gradually overcame the mind and body of
Godfrey Schalken, and he sank into a deep sleep, from
which he was awakened by some one's shaking him
gently by the shoulder.   He first thought that the old
sexton had called him, but *he* was no longer in the room.
He roused himself, and as soon as he could clearly see
what was around him, he perceived a female form,
clothed in a kind of light robe of white, part of which was
so disposed as to form a veil, and in her hand she carried
a lamp.   She was moving rather away from him, in the
direction of the flight of steps which conducted towards
the vaults.   Schalken felt a vague alarm at the sight of
this figure, and at the same time an irresistible impulse

to follow its guidance. He followed it towards the vaults, but when it reached the head of the stairs, he paused ; the figure paused also, and, turning gently round, displayed, by the light of the lamp it carried, the face and features of his first love, Rose Velderkaust. There was nothing horrible, or even sad, in the countenance. On the contrary, it wore the same arch smile which used to enchant the artist long before in his happy days. A feeling of awe and of interest, too intense to be resisted, prompted him to follow the spectre, if spectre it were. She descended the stairs—he followed—and, turning to the left, through a narrow passage, she led him, to his infinite surprise, into what appeared to be an old-fashioned Dutch apartment, such as the pictures of Gerard Douw have served to immortalise. Abundance of costly antique furniture was disposed about the room, and in one corner stood a four-post bed, with heavy black cloth curtains around it; the figure frequently turned towards him with the same arch smile ; and when she came to the side of the bed, she drew the curtains, and, by the light of the lamp, which she held towards its contents, she disclosed to the horror-stricken painter, sitting bolt upright in the bed, the livid and demoniac form of Vanderhausen. Schalken had hardly seen him, when he fell senseless upon the floor, where he lay until discovered, on the next morning, by persons employed in closing the passages into the vaults. He was lying in a cell of considerable size, which had not been disturbed for a long time, and he had fallen beside a large coffin, which was supported upon small stone pillars, a security against the attacks of vermin.

To his dying day Schalken was satisfied of the reality

of the vision which he had witnessed, and he has left
behind him a curious evidence of the impression which
it wrought upon his fancy, in a painting executed shortly
after the event I have narrated, and which is valuable
not only as exhibiting the peculiarities which have
made Schalken's pictures sought after, but even more
so as presenting a portrait of his early love, Rose Velderkaust, whose mysterious fate must always remain
matter of speculation.

The Evil Guest.

———•———

" When Lust hath conceived, it bringeth forth Sin : and Sin, when it is finished, bringeth forth Death."

ABOUT sixty years ago, and somewhat more than twenty miles from the ancient town of Chester, in a southward direction, there stood a large, and, even then, an old-fashioned mansion-house. It lay in the midst of a demesne of considerable extent, and richly wooded with venerable timber; but, apart from the sombre majesty of these giant groups, and the varieties of the undulating ground on which they stood, there was little that could be deemed attractive in the place. A certain air of neglect and decay, and an indescribable gloom and melancholy, hung over it. In darkness, it seemed darker than any other tract; when the moonlight fell upon its glades and hollows, they looked spectral and awful, with a sort of churchyard loneliness ; and even when the blush of the morning kissed its broad woodlands, there was a melancholy in the salute which saddened rather than cheered the heart of the beholder.

This antique, melancholy, and neglected place, we shall call, for distinctness sake, Gray Forest. It was then the property of the younger son of a nobleman, once celebrated for his ability and his daring, but who had long since passed to that land where human wisdom and courage avail nought. The representative of this noble house resided at the family mansion in Sussex, and the cadet, whose fortunes we mean to sketch in these pages, lived upon the narrow margin of an encumbered income, in a reserved and unsocial discontent, deep among the solemn shadows of the old woods of Gray Forest.

The Hon. Richard Marston was now somewhere between forty and fifty years of age—perhaps nearer the latter; he still, however, retained, in an eminent degree, the traits of manly beauty, not the less remarkable for its unquestionably haughty and passionate character. He had married a beautiful girl, of good family, but without much money, somewhere about eighteeen years before; and two children, a son and a daughter, had been the fruit of this union. The boy, Harry Marston, was at this time at Cambridge; and his sister, scarcely fifteen, was at home with her parents, and under the training of an accomplished governess, who had been recommended to them by a noble relative of Mrs. Marston. She was a native of France, but thoroughly mistress of the English language, and, except for a foreign accent, which gave a certain prettiness to all she said, she spoke it as perfectly as any native Englishwoman. This young Frenchwoman was eminently handsome and attractive. Expressive, dark eyes, a clear olive complexion, small even teeth, and a beautifully-dimpling smile, more perhaps than a strictly classic regularity of features, were the secrets of her unquestionable in-

K

fluence, at first sight, upon the fancy of every man of
taste who beheld her.

Mr. Marston's fortune, never very large, had been
shattered by early dissipation. Naturally of a proud and
somewhat exacting temper, he acutely felt the mortifying
consequences of his poverty. The want of what he felt
ought to have been his position and influence in the
county in which he resided, fretted and galled him; and
he cherished a resentful and bitter sense of every slight,
imaginary or real, to which the same fruitful source of
annoyance and humiliation had exposed him. He held,
therefore, but little intercourse with the surrounding
gentry, and that little not of the pleasantest possible
kind; for, not being himself in a condition to entertain,
in that style which accorded with his own ideas of his
station, he declined, as far as was compatible with good
breeding, all the proffered hospitalities of the neighbourhood; and, from his wild and neglected park, looked
out upon the surrounding world in a spirit of moroseness
and defiance, very unlike, indeed, to that of neighbourly
good-will.

In the midst, however, of many of the annoyances
attendant upon crippled means, he enjoyed a few of
those shadowy indications of hereditary importance,
which are all the more dearly prized, as the substantial
accessories of wealth have disappeared. The mansion
in which he dwelt was, though old-fashioned, imposing
in its aspect, and upon a scale unequivocally aristocratic;
its walls were hung with ancestral portraits, and he
managed to maintain about him a large and tolerably
respectable staff of servants. In addition to these, he
had his extensive demesne, his deer-park, and his un-

rivalled timber, wherewith to console himself; and, in
the consciousness of these possessions, he found some
imperfect assuagement of those bitter feelings of suppressed scorn and resentment, which a sense of lost
station and slighted importance engendered. Mr. Marston's early habits had, unhappily, been of a kind to
aggravate, rather than alleviate, the annoyances inci-
dental to reduced means. He had been a gay man, a
voluptuary, and a gambler. His vicious tastes had sur-
vived the means of their gratification. His love for his
wife had been nothing more than one of those vehement
and headstrong fancies, which, in self-indulgent men,
sometimes result in marriage, and which seldom outlive
the first few months of that life-long connexion. Mrs.
Marston was a gentle, noble-minded woman. After
agonies of disappointment, which none ever suspected,
she had at length learned to submit, in sad and gentle
acquiescence, to her fate. Those feelings, which had
been the charm of her young days, were gone,, and, as
she bitterly felt, for ever. For them there was no recall
—they could not return; and, without complaint or reproach, she yielded to what she felt was inevitable. It was
impossible to look at Mrs. Marston, and not to discern, at
a glance, the ruin of a surpassingly beautiful woman ; a
good deal wasted, pale, and chastened with a deep, untold sorrow, but still possessing the outlines, both in
face and form, of that noble beauty and matchless grace,
which had made her, in happier days, the admired of all
observers. But equally impossible was it to converse
with her, for even a minute, without hearing, in the
gentle and melancholy music of her voice, the sad echoes
of those griefs to which her early beauty had been sa-

crificed, an undying sense of lost love, and happiness departed, never to come again.

One morning, Mr. Marston had walked, as was his custom when he expected the messenger who brought from the neighbouring post-office his letters, some way down the broad, straight avenue, with its double rows of lofty trees at each side, when he encountered the nimble emissary on his return. He took the letter-bag in silence. It contained but two letters—one addressed to "Mademoiselle de Barras, chez M. Marston," and the other to himself. He took them both, dismissed the messenger, and opening that addressed to himself, read as follows, while he slowly retraced his steps towards the house :—

"DEAR RICHARD,—I am a whimsical fellow, as you doubtless remember, and have lately grown, they tell me, rather hippish besides. I do not know to which infirmity I am to attribute a sudden fancy which urges me to pay you a visit, if you will admit me. To say truth, my dear Dick, I wish to see a little of your part of the world, and, I will confess it, *en passant*, to see a little of *you* too. I really wish to make acquaintance with your family; and though they tell me my health is very much shaken, I must say, in self-defence, I am not a troublesome inmate. I can perfectly take care of myself, and need no nursing or caudling whatever. Will you present this, my petition, to Mrs. Marston, and report her decision thereon to me. Seriously, I know that your house may be full, or some other *contre-temps* may make it impracticable for me just now to invade you. If it be so, tell me, my dear Richard, frankly, as my movements are perfectly free, and my time all my own, so that I can arrange my visit to suit your convenience.—Yours, &c.,

"WYNSTON E. BERKLEY.

"P.S.—Direct to me at —— Hotel, in Chester, as I shall probably be there by the time this reaches you."

"Ill-bred and pushing as ever," quoth Mr. Marston, angrily, as he thrust the unwelcome letter into his pocket. "This fellow, wallowing in wealth, without one nearer relative on earth than I, and associated more nearly still with me by the—psha! not affection—the *recollections* of early and intimate companionship, leaves me unaided, for years of desertion and suffering, to the buffetings of the world, and the troubles of all but overwhelming pecuniary difficulties, and now, with the cool confidence of one entitled to respect and welcome, invites himself to my house. Coming here," he continued, after a gloomy pause, and still pacing slowly towards the house, "to collect amusing materials for next season's gossip—stories about the married Benedick—the bankrupt beau—the outcast tenant of a Cheshire wilderness;" and, as he said this, he looked at the neglected prospect before him with an eye almost of hatred. "Ay, to see the nakedness of the land is he coming, but he shall be disappointed. His money may buy him a cordial welcome at an inn, but curse me if it shall purchase him a reception here."

He again opened and glanced through the letter.

"Ay, purposely put in such a way that I can't decline it without affronting him," he continued doggedly. "Well, then, he has no one to blame but himself—affronted he shall be; I shall effectually put an end to this humorous excursion. Egad, it is rather hard if a man cannot keep his poverty to himself."

Sir Wynston Berkley was a baronet of large fortune—a selfish, fashionable man, and an inveterate bachelor. He and Marston had been schoolfellows, and the violent and implacable temper of the latter had as little im-

pressed his companion with feelings of regard, as the
frivolity and selfishness of the baronet had won the
esteem of his relative.   As boys, they had little in
common upon which to rest the basis of a friendship,
or even a mutual liking.   Berkley was gay, cold, and
satirical; his cousin—for cousins they were—was jealous,
haughty, and relentless.   Their negative disinclination
to one another's society, not unnaturally engendered by
uncongenial and unamiable dispositions, had for a time
given place to actual hostility, while the two young men
were at Oxford.   In some intrigue, Marston discovered
in his cousin a too-successful rival; the consequence
was, a bitter and furious quarrel, which, but for the
prompt and peremptory interference of friends, Marston
would undoubtedly have pushed to a bloody issue.
Time had, however, healed this rupture, and the young
men came to regard one another with the same feelings,
and eventually to re-establish the same sort of cold and
indifferent intimacy which had subsisted between them
before their angry collision.

Under these circumstances, whatever suspicion Marston might have felt on the receipt of the unexpected,
and indeed unaccountable proposal, which had just reached
him, he certainly had little reason to complain of any
violation of early friendship in the neglect with which
Sir Wynston had hitherto treated him.   In deciding to
decline his proposed visit, however, Marston had not
consulted the impulses of spite or anger.   He knew the
baronet well; he knew that he cherished no good-will
towards him, and that in the project which he had thus
unexpectedly broached, whatever indirect or selfish
schemes might possibly be at the bottom of it, no

friendly feeling had ever mingled. He was therefore
resolved to avoid the trouble and the expense of a visit
in all respects distasteful to him, and in a gentlemanlike
way, but, at the same time, as the reader may suppose,
with very little anxiety as to whether or not his gay
correspondent should take offence at his reply, to decline,
once for all, the proposed distinction.

With this resolution, he entered the spacious and
somewhat dilapidated mansion which called him master; and entering a sitting-room, appropriated to his
daughter's use, he found her there, in company with
her beautiful French governess. He kissed his child,
and saluted her young preceptress with formal courtesy.

"Mademoiselle," said he, "I have got a letter for
you; and, Rhoda," he continued, addressing his pretty
daughter, "bring this to your mother, and say, I
request her to read it."

He gave her the letter he himself had just received,
and the girl tripped lightly away upon her mission.

Had he narrowly scrutinised the countenance of the
fair Frenchwoman, as she glanced at the direction of
that which he had just placed in *her* hand, he might
have seen certain transient, but very unmistakeable
evidences of excitement and agitation. She quickly concealed the letter, however, and with a sigh, the momentary flush which it had called to her cheek subsided,
and she was tranquil as usual.

Mr. Marston remained for some minutes—five, eight,
or ten, we cannot say precisely—pretty much where he
had stood on first entering the chamber, doubtless
awaiting the return of his messenger, or the appearance
of his wife. At length, however, he left the room

himself to seek her ; but, during his brief stay, his
previous resolution had been removed. By what influence we cannot say ; but removed completely it
unquestionably was, and a final determination that Sir
Wynston Berkley should become his guest had fixedly
taken its place.

As Marston walked along the passages which led
from this room, he encountered Mrs. Marston and his
daughter.

"Well," said he, "you have read Wynston's letter ?"

"Yes," she replied, returning it to him ; "and what
answer, Richard, do you purpose giving him ?"

She was about to hazard a conjecture, but checked
herself, remembering that even so faint an evidence of a
disposition to advise might possibly be resented by her
cold and imperious lord.

"I have considered it, and decided to receive him,"
he replied.

"Ah! I am afraid—that is, I hope—he may find our
housekeeping such as he can enjoy," she said, with an
involuntary expression of surprise ; for she had scarcely
had a doubt that her husband would have preferred
evading the visit of his fine friend, under his gloomy
circumstances.

"If our modest fare does not suit him," said Marston, with sullen bitterness, "he can depart as easily as
he came. We, poor gentlemen, can but do our best.
I have thought it over, and made up my mind."

"And how soon, my dear Richard, do you intend
fixing his arrival ?" she inquired, with the natural uneasiness of one upon whom, in an establishment whose

pretensions considerably exceeded its resources, the perplexing cares of housekeeping devolved.

"Why, as soon as he pleases," replied he. "I suppose you can easily have his room prepared by to-morrow or next day. I shall write by this mail, and tell him to come down at once."

Having said this in a cold, decisive way, he turned and left her, as it seemed, not caring to be teased with further questions. He took his solitary way to a distant part of his wild park, where, far from the likelihood of disturbance or intrusion, he was often wont to amuse himself for the live-long day, in the sedentary sport of shooting rabbits. And there we leave him for the present, signifying to the distant inmates of his house the industrious pursuit of his unsocial occupation, by the dropping fire which sullenly, from hour to hour, echoed from the remote woods.

Mrs. Marston issued her orders; and having set on foot all the necessary preparations for so unwonted an event as a stranger's visit of some duration, she betook herself to her little boudoir—the scene of many an hour of patient but bitter suffering, unseen by human eye, and unknown, except to the just Searcher of hearts, to whom belongs mercy and VENGEANCE.

Mrs. Marston had but two friends to whom she had ever spoken upon the subject nearest her heart—the estrangement of her husband, a sorrow to which even time had failed to reconcile her. From her children this grief was carefully concealed. To them she never uttered the semblance of a complaint. Anything that could by possibility have reflected blame or dishonour upon their father, she would have perished rather than have allowed them so much as to suspect. The two friends who did understand her feelings, though in different degrees, were, one, a good and venerable clergyman, the Rev. Doctor Danvers, a frequent visiter and occasional guest at Gray Forest where his simple manners and unaffected benignity and tenderness of heart had won the love of all, with the exception of its master, and commanded even his respect. The second was no other than the young French governess, Mademoiselle de Barras, in whose ready sympathy and consolatory counsels she found no small happiness. The society of this young lady had indeed become, next to that of her daughter, her greatest comfort and pleasure.

Mademoiselle de Barras was of a noble though ruined French family, and a certain nameless elegance and dignity attested, spite of her fallen condition, the purity of her descent. She was accomplished—possessed of that fine perception and sensitiveness, and that ready power of self-adaptation to the peculiarities and moods of others, which we term tact—and was, moreover, gifted with a certain natural grace, and manners the most winning imaginable. In short, she was a fascinating companion; and when the melancholy circumstances of her own situation, and the sad history of her once rich and noble family, were taken into account, with her striking attractions of person and air, the combination of all these associations and impressions rendered her one of the most interesting persons that could well be imagined. The circumstances of Mademoiselle de Barras's history and descent seemed to warrant, on Mrs. Marston's part, a closer intimacy and confidence than usually subsists between parties mutually occupying such a relation.

Mrs. Marston had hardly established herself in this little apartment, when a light foot approached, a gentle tap was given at the door, and Mademoiselle de Barras entered.

"Ah, mademoiselle, so kind—such pretty flowers. Pray sit down," said the lady, with a sweet and grateful smile, as she took from the taper fingers of the foreigner the little bouquet which she had been at the pains to gather.

Mademoiselle sat down, and gently took the lady's hand and kissed it. A small matter will overflow a heart charged with sorrow—a chance word, a look, some little office of kindness—and so it was with mademoiselle's bouquet and gentle kiss. Mrs. Marston's heart was touched; her eyes filled with bright tears; she smiled gratefully upon her fair and humble companion, and as she smiled, her tears overflowed, and she wept in silence for some minutes.

"My poor mademoiselle," she said, at last, "you are so very, very kind."

Mademoiselle said nothing; she lowered her eyes, and pressed the poor lady's hand.

Apparently to interrupt an embarrassing silence, and to give a more cheerful tone to their little interview, the governess, in a gay tone, on a sudden said—

"And so, madame, we are to have a visiter, Miss Rhoda tells me—a baronet, is he not?"

"Yes, indeed, mademoiselle—Sir Wynston Berkley, a gay London gentleman, and a cousin of Mr. Marston's," she replied.

"Ha—a cousin!" exclaimed the young lady, with a little more surprise in her tone than seemed altogether called for—"a cousin? oh, then, that is the reason of

his visit. Do, pray, madame, tell me all about him ; I
am so much afraid of strangers, and what you call men
of the world. Oh, dear Mrs. Marston, I am not worthy
to be here, and he will see all that in a moment ; indeed,
indeed, I am afraid. Pray tell me all about him."

She said this with a simplicity which made the elder
lady smile, and while mademoiselle re-adjusted the tiny
flowers which formed the bouquet she had just presented to her, Mrs. Marston good-naturedly recounted
to her all she knew of Sir Wynston Berkley, which, in
substance, amounted to no more than we have already
stated. When she concluded, the young Frenchwoman
continued for some time silent, still busy with her
flowers. But, suddenly, she heaved a deep sigh, and
shook her head.

"You seem disquieted, mademoiselle," said Mrs.
Marston, in a tone of kindness.

"I am thinking, madame," she said, still looking
upon the flowers which she was adjusting, and again
sighing profoundly, "I am thinking of what you said
to me a week ago ; alas !"

"I do not remember what it was, my good mademoiselle—nothing, I am sure, that ought to grieve you—
at least nothing that was intended to have that effect,"
replied the lady, in a tone of gentle encouragement.

"No, not intended, madame," said the young Frenchwoman, sorrowfully.

"Well, what was it ? Perhaps you misunderstood;
perhaps I can explain what I said," replied Mrs. Marston, affectionately.

"Ah, madame, you think—you think I am *unlucky*,"
answered the young lady, slowly and faintly.

" Unlucky! Dear mademoiselle, you surprise me," rejoined her companion.

"I mean—what I mean is this, madame; you date unhappiness—if not its beginning, at least its great aggravation and increase," she answered, dejectedly, "from the time of my coming here, madame; and though I know you are too good to dislike me on that account, yet I must, in your eyes, be ever connected with calamity, and look like an ominous thing."

" Dear mademoiselle, allow no such thought to enter your mind. You do me great wrong, indeed you do," said Mrs. Marston, laying her hand upon the young lady's, kindly.

There was a silence for a little time, and the elder lady resumed :—

" I remember now what you allude to, dear mademoiselle—the increased estrangement, the widening separation which severs me from one unutterably dear to me—the first and bitter disappointment of my life, which seems to grow more hopelessly incurable day by day."

Mrs. Marston paused, and, after a brief silence, the governess said :—

" I am very superstitious myself, dear madame, and I thought I must have seemed to you an inauspicious inmate—in short, *unlucky*—as I have said; and the thought made me very unhappy—so unhappy, that I was going to leave you, madame—I may now tell you frankly —going away; but you have set my doubts at rest, and I am quite happy again."

" Dear mademoiselle !" cried the lady, tenderly, and rising, as she spake, to kiss the cheek of her humble friend; "never—never speak of this again. God knows

I have too few friends on earth, to spare the kindest and tenderest among them all. No, no. You little think what comfort I have found in your warm-hearted and ready sympathy, and how dearly I prize your affection, my poor mademoiselle."

The young Frenchwoman rose, with downcast eyes, and a dimpling, happy smile; and, as Mrs. Marston drew her affectionately toward her, and kissed her, she timidly returned the embrace of her kind patroness. For a moment her graceful arms encircled her, and she whispered her, "Dear madame, how happy—how very happy you make me."

Had Ithuriel touched with his spear the beautiful young woman, thus for a moment, as it seemed, lost in a trance of gratitude and love, would that angelic form have stood the test unscathed? A spectator, marking the scene, might have observed a strange gleam in her eyes—a strange expression in her face—an influence for a moment *not* angelic, like a shadow of some passing spirit, cross her visibly, as she leaned over the gentle lady's neck, and murmured, "Dear madame, how happy —how very happy you make me." Such a spectator, as he looked at that gentle lady, might have seen, for one dreamy moment, a lithe and painted serpent, coiled round and round, and hissing in her ear.

A few minutes more, and mademoiselle was in the solitude of her own apartment. She shut and bolted the door, and taking from her desk the letter which she had that morning received, threw herself into an arm-chair, and studied the document profoundly. Her actual revision and scrutiny of the letter itself was interrupted by long intervals of profound abstraction; and, after a

full hour thus spent, she locked it carefully up again,
and with a clear brow, and a gay smile, rejoined her
pretty pupil for a walk.

We must now pass over an interval of a few days, and
come at once to the arrival of Sir Wynston Berkley,
which duly occurred upon the evening of the day
appointed. The baronet descended from his chaise but
a short time before the hour at which the little party,
which formed the family at Gray Forest were wont to
assemble for the social meal of supper. A few minutes
devoted to the mysteries of the toilet, with the aid of
an accomplished valet, enabled him to appear, as he conceived, without disadvantage at this domestic re-union.

Sir Wynston Berkley was a particularly gentlemanlike
person. He was rather tall, and elegantly made, with
gay, easy manners, and something indefinably aristocratic in his face, which, however, was a little more worn
than his years would have strictly accounted for. But
Sir Wynston had been a *roué*, and, spite of the clever-
est possible making up, the ravages of excess were very
traceable in the lively beau of fifty. Perfectly well
dressed, and with a manner that was ease and gaiety
itself, he was at home from the moment he entered the
room. Of course, anything like genuine cordiality was
out of the question; but Mr. Marston embraced his
relative with perfect good breeding, and the baronet
appeared determined to like everybody, and be pleased
with everything.

He had not been five minutes in the parlour, chatting
gaily with Mr. and Mrs. Marston and their pretty
daughter, when Mademoiselle de Barras entered the
room. As she moved towards Mrs. Marston, Sir Wyn-

ston rose, and, observing her with evident admiration,
said in an under-tone, inquiringly, to Marston, who was
beside him—

" And *this ?*"

" That is Mademoiselle de Barras, my daughter's
governess, and Mrs. Marston's companion," said Marston, drily.

" Ha !" said Sir Wynston ; " I *thought* you were but
three at home just now, and I was right. Your son is
at Cambridge ; I heard so from our old friend, Jack
Manbury. Jack has his boy there too. Egad, Dick,
it seems but last week that you and I were there together."

" Yes," said Marston, looking gloomily into the fire,
as if he saw, in its smoke and flicker, the phantoms of
murdered time and opportunity ; " but I hate looking
back, Wynston. The past is to me but a medley of ill-
luck and worse management."

" Why what an ungrateful dog you are !" returned Sir
Wynston, gaily, turning his back upon the fire, and
glancing round the spacious and handsome, though
somewhat faded apartment. "I was on the point of
congratulating you on the possession of the finest park
and noblest demesne in Cheshire, when you begin to
grumble. Egad, Dick, all I can say to your complaint
is, that *I* don't pity you, and there are dozens who may
honestly *envy* you—that is all."

In spite of this cheering assurance, Marston remained
sullenly silent. Supper, however, had now been served,
and the little party assumed their places at the table.

"I am sorry, Wynston, I have no sport of any kind
to offer you here," said Marston, " except, indeed, some

good trout-fishing, if you like it. I have three miles of excellent fishing at your command."

" My dear fellow, I am a mere cockney," rejoined Sir Wynston; " I am not a sportsman; I never tried it, and should not like to begin now. No, Dick, what I much prefer is, abundance of your fresh air, and the enjoyment of your scenery. When I was at Rouen three years ago ——."

" Ha !—Rouen? Mademoiselle will feel an interest in that; it is her birth-place," interrupted Marston, glancing at the Frenchwoman.

" Yes—Rouen—ah—yes !" said mademoiselle, with very evident embarrassment.

Sir Wynston appeared for a moment a little disconcerted too, but rallied speedily, and pursued his detail of his doings at that fair town of Normandy.

Marston knew Sir Wynston well ; and he rightly calculated that whatever effect his experience of the world might have had in intensifying his selfishness or hardening his heart, it certainly could have had none in improving a character originally worthless and unfeeling. He knew, moreover, that his wealthy cousin was gifted with a great deal of that small cunning which is available for masking the little scheming of frivolous and worldly men ; and that Sir Wynston never took trouble of any kind without a sufficient purpose, having its centre in his own personal gratification.

This visit greatly puzzled Marston ; it gave him even a vague sense of uneasiness. Could there exist any flaw in his own title to the estate of Gray Forest ? He had an unpleasant, doubtful sort of remembrance of some apprehensions of this kind, when he was but a child, hav-

L

ing been whispered in the family. Could this really be
so, and could the baronet have been led to make this
unexpected visit merely for the purpose of personally
examining into the condition of a property of which he
was about to become the legal invader? The nature of
this suspicion affords, at all events, a fair gauge of Marston's estimate of his cousin's character. And as he
revolved these doubts from time to time, and as he
thought of Mademoiselle de Barras's transient, but unaccountable embarrassment at the mention of Rouen
by Sir Wynston—an embarrassment which the baronet
himself appeared for a moment to reciprocate—undefined, glimmering suspicions of another kind flickered
through the darkness of his mind. He was effectually
puzzled; his surmises and conjectures baffled; and he
more than half repented that he had acceded to his
cousin's proposal, and admitted him as an inmate of his
house.

Although Sir Wynston comported himself as if he were
conscious of being the very most welcome visiter who
could possibly have established himself at Gray Forest,
he was, doubtless, fully aware of the real feelings with
which he was regarded by his host. If he had in reality
an object in prolonging his stay, and wished to make
the postponement of his departure the direct interest of
his entertainer, he unquestionably took effectual measures for that purpose.

The little party broke up every evening at about ten
o'clock, and Sir Wynston retired to his chamber at the
same hour. He found little difficulty in inducing Marston to amuse him there with a quiet game of picquet.
In his own room, therefore, in the luxurious ease of

dressing-gown and slippers he sate at cards with his host, often until an hour or two past midnight. Sir Wynston was exorbitantly wealthy, and very reckless in expenditure. The stakes for which they played, although they gradually became in reality pretty heavy, were in his eyes a very unimportant consideration. Marston, on the other hand, was poor, and played with the eye of a lynx and the appetite of a shark. The ease and perfect good-humour with which Sir Wynston lost were not unimproved by his entertainer, who, as may readily be supposed, was not sorry to reap this golden harvest, provided without the slightest sacrifice, on his part, of pride or independence. If, indeed, he sometimes suspected that his guest was a little more anxious to lose than to win, he was also quite resolved not to perceive it, but calmly persisted in, night after night, giving Sir Wynston, as he termed it, his revenge; or, in other words, treating him to a repetition of his losses. All this was very agreeable to Marston, who began to treat his visiter with, at all events, more external cordiality and distinction than at first.

An incident, however, occurred, which disturbed these amicable relations in an unexpected way. It becomes necessary here to mention that Mademoiselle de Barras's sleeping apartment opened from a long corridor. It was *en suite* with two dressing-rooms, each opening also upon the corridor, but wholly unused and unfurnished. Some five or six other apartments also opened at either side, upon the same passage. These little local details being premised, it so happened that one day Marston, who had gone out with the intention of angling in the trout-stream which flowed through his park, though at a con-

siderable distance from the house, having unexpectedly
returned to procure some tackle which he had forgotten,
was walking briskly through the corridor in question to
his own apartment, when, to his surprise, the door of
one of the deserted dressing-rooms, of which we have
spoken, was cautiously pushed open, and Sir Wynston
Berkley issued from it. Marston was almost beside him
as he did so, and Sir Wynston made a motion as if about
instinctively to draw back again, 'and at the same time
the keen ear of his host distinctly caught the sound of
rustling silks and a tip-toe tread hastily withdrawing
from the deserted chamber. Sir Wynston looked nearly
as much confused as a man of the world can look. Marston stopped short, and scanned his visiter for a moment with a very peculiar expression.

"You have caught me peeping, Dick. I am an inveterate explorer," said the baronet, with an effectual
effort to shake off his embarrassment. "An open door
in a fine old house is a temptation which ——"

"That door is usually closed, and ought to be kept
so," interrupted Marston, drily; "there is nothing
whatever to be seen in the room but dust and cobwebs."

"Pardon me," said Sir Wynston, more easily, "you
forget the view from the window."

"Ay, the view, to be sure; there *is* a good view from
it," said Marston, with as much of his usual manner as
he could resume so soon; and, at the same time, carelessly opening the door again, he walked in, accompanied
by Sir Wynston, and both stood at the window together,
looking out in silence upon a prospect which neither of
them saw.

"Yes, I do think it is a good view," said Marston;

and as he turned carelessly away, he darted a swift glance round the chamber. The door opening toward the French lady's apartment was closed, but not actually shut. This was enough; and as they left the room, Marston repeated his invitation to his guest to accompany him; but in a tone which showed that he scarcely followed the meaning of what he himself was saying.

He walked undecidedly toward his own room, then turned and went down stairs. In the hall he met his pretty child.

" Ha! Rhoda," said he, " you have not been out to-day ?"

" No, papa; but it is so very fine, I think I shall go now."

" Yes ; go, and mademoiselle can accompany you. Do you hear, Rhoda, mademoiselle goes with you, and you had better go at once."

A few minutes more, and Marston, from the parlour-window, beheld Rhoda and the elegant French girl walking together towards the woodlands. He watched them gloomily, himself unseen, until the crowding underwood concealed their receding figures. Then, with a sigh, he turned, and reascended the great stair case.

" I shall sift this mystery to the bottom," thought he. " I shall foil the conspirators, if so they be, with their own weapons ; art with art ; chicane with chicane; duplicity with duplicity."

He was now in the long passage which we have just spoken of, and glancing back and before him, to ascertain that no chance eye discerned him, he boldly entered mademoiselle's chamber. Her writing-desk lay upon

the table. It was locked ; and coolly taking it in his
hands, Marston carried it into his own room, bolted his
chamber-door, and taking two or three bunches of keys,
he carefully tried nearly a dozen in succession, and when
almost despairing of success, at last found one which
fitted the lock, turned, and opened the desk.

Sustained throughout his dishonourable task by some
strong and angry passion, the sight of the open escri-
toire checked and startled him for a moment.   Violated
privilege, invaded secrecy, base, perfidious espionage
upbraided and stigmatised him, as the intricacies of the
outraged sanctuary opened upon his intrusive gaze.   He
felt for a moment shocked and humbled.   He was im-
pelled to lock and replace the desk where he had originally found it, without having effected his meditated
treason ; but this hesitation was transient ; the fiery and
reckless impulse which had urged him to the act returned to enforce its consummation.   With a guilty eye
and eager hands, he searched the contents of this tiny
repository of the fair Norman's written secrets.

"Ha! the very thing," he muttered, as he detected
the identical letter which he himself had handed to Mademoiselle de Barras but a few days before.   "The
handwriting struck me, ill-disguised; I thought I knew
it; we shall see."

He had opened the letter; it contained but a few
lines : he held his breath while he read it.   First he
grew pale, then a shadow came over his face, and then
another, and another, darker and darker, shade upon
shade, as if an exhalation from the pit was momentarily blackening the air about him.   He said nothing;
there was but one long, gentle sigh, and in his face a

mortal sternness, as he folded the letter again, replaced it, and locked the desk.

Of course, when Mademoiselle de Barras returned from her accustomed walk, she found everything in her room, to all appearance, undisturbed, and just as when she left it. While this young lady was making her toilet for the evening, and while Sir Wynston Berkley was worrying himself with conjectures as to whether Marston's evil looks, when he encountered him that morning in the passage, existed only in his own fancy, or were, in good' truth, very grim and significant realities, Marston himself was striding alone through the wildest and darkest solitudes of his park, haunted by his own unholy thoughts, and, it may be, by those other evil and unearthly influences which wander, as we know, "in desert places." Darkness overtook him, and the chill of night, in these lonely tracts. In his *solitary* walk, what fearful *company* had he been keeping! As the shades of night deepened round him, the sense of the neighbourhood of ill, the consciousness of the foul fancies of which, where he was now treading, he had been for hours the sport, oppressed him with a vague and unknown terror ; a certain horror of the thoughts which had been his comrades through the day, which he could not now shake off, and which haunted him with a ghastly and defiant pertinacity, scared, while they half-enraged him. He stalked swiftly homewards, like a guilty man pursued.

Marston was not perfectly satisfied, though very nearly, with the evidence now in his possession. The letter, the stolen perusal of which had so agitated him that day, bore no signature ; but, independently of the

handwriting, which seemed, spite of the constraint of
an attempted disguise, to be familiar to his eye, there
existed, in the matter of the letter, short as it was, certain internal evidences, which, although not actually
conclusive, raised, in conjunction with all the other circumstances, a powerful presumption in aid of his suspicions. He resolved, however, to sift the matter further,
and to bide his time.   Meanwhile, his manner must indicate no trace of his dark surmises and bitter thoughts.
Deception, in its two great branches, simulation and
*dis*simulation, was easy to him.   His habitual reserve
and gloom would divest any accidental and momentary
disclosure of his inward trouble of everything suspicious
or unaccountable, which would have characterized such
displays and eccentricities in another man.

His rapid and reckless ramble, a kind of physical
vent for the paroxysm which had so agitated him
throughout the greater part of the day, had soiled and
disordered his dress, and thus had helped to give to his
whole appearance a certain air of haggard wildness,
which, in the privacy of his chamber, he hastened carefully and entirely to remove.

At supper, Marston was apparently in unusually good
spirits.   Sir Wynston and he chatted gaily and fluently
upon many subjects, grave and gay.   Among them the
inexhaustible topic of popular superstition happened to
turn up, and especially the subject of strange prophe-
cies of the fates and fortunes of individuals, singularly
fulfilled in the events of their after-life.

" By-the-by, Dick, this is rather a nervous topic for
me to discuss," said Sir Wynston.

" How so?" asked his host.

"Why, don't you remember?" urged the baronet.

"No, I don't recollect what you allude to," replied Marston, in all sincerity.

"Why, don't you remember Eton?" pursued Sir Wynston.

"Yes, to be sure," said Marston.

"*Well?*" continued his visiter.

"Well, I really don't recollect the prophecy," replied Marston.

"What! do you forget the gipsy who predicted that you were to murder *me*, Dick—eh?"

"Ah—ha, ha!" laughed Marston, with a start.

"Don't you remember it now?" urged his companion.

"Ah, why yes, I believe I do," said Marston; "but another prophecy was running in my mind; a gipsy prediction, too. At Ascot, do you recollect the girl told me I was to be lord chancellor of England, and a duke besides."

"Well, Dick," rejoined Sir Wynston, merrily, "if both are to be fulfilled, or neither, I trust you may never sit upon the woolsack of England."

The party soon after broke up: Sir Wynston and his host, as usual, to pass some hours at picquet; and Mrs. Marston, as was her wont, to spend some time in her own boudoir, over notes and accounts, and the worrying details of housekeeping.

While thus engaged, she was disturbed by a respectful tap at her door, and an elderly servant, who had been for many years in the employment of Mr. Marston, presented himself.

"Well, Merton, do you want anything?" asked the lady.

"Yes, ma'am, please, I want to give warning; I wish to leave the service, ma'am;" replied he, respectfully, but doggedly.

"To leave us, Merton!" echoed his mistress, both surprised and sorry, for the man had been long her servant, and had been much liked and trusted.

"Yes, ma'am," he repeated.

"And why do you wish to do so, Merton? has anything occurred to make the place unpleasant to you?" urged the lady.

"No, ma'am—no, indeed," said he, earnestly, "I have nothing to complain of—nothing, indeed, ma'am."

"Perhaps, you think you can do better, if you leave us?" suggested his mistress.

"No, indeed, ma'am, I have no such thought," he said, and seemed on the point of bursting into tears; "but—but, somehow—ma'am, there is something come over me, lately, and I can't help, but think, if I stay here, ma'am—some—some—*misfortune* will happen us all—and that is the truth, ma'am."

"This is very foolish, Merton—a mere childish fancy," replied Mrs. Marston; "you like your place, and have no better prospect before you; and now, for a mere superstitious fancy, you propose giving it up, and leaving us. No, no, Merton, you had better think the matter over—and if you still, upon reflection, prefer going away, you can then speak to your master."

"Thank you ma'am—God bless you," said the man, withdrawing.

Mrs. Marston rang the bell for her maid, and retired to her room.

"Has anything occurred lately," she asked, "to annoy Merton?"

"No, ma'am, I don't know of anything; but he is very changed, indeed, of late," replied the maid.

"He has not been quarrelling?" inquired she.

"Oh, no, ma'am, he never quarrels; he is very quiet, and keeps to himself always; he thinks a wonderful deal of himself," replied the servant.

"But, you said that he is much changed—did you not?" continued the lady; for there was something strangely excited and unpleasant in the man's manner, in this little interview, which struck Mrs. Marston, and alarmed her curiosity. He had seemed like one charged with some horrible secret—intolerable, and which he yet dared not reveal.

"What," proceeded Mrs. Marston, "is the nature of the change of which you speak?"

"Why, ma'am, he is like one frightened, and in sorrow," she replied; "he will sit silent, and now and then shaking his head, as if he wanted to get rid of something that is teasing him, for an hour together."

"Poor man!" said she.

"And, then, when we are at meals, he will, all on a sudden, get up, and leave the table; and Jem Boulter, that sleeps in the next room to him, says, that, almost as often as he looks through the little window between the two rooms, no matter what hour in the night, he sees Mr. Merton on his knees by the bedside, praying or crying, he don't know which; but, any way, he is not happy—poor man!—and that is plain enough."

" It is very strange," said the lady, after a pause ;
" but, I think, and hope, after all, it will prove to have
been no more than a little nervousness."

" Well, ma'am, I do hope it is not his conscience that
is coming against him, now," said the maid.

" We have no reason to suspect anything of the kind,"
said Mrs. Mraston, gravely ; " quite the reverse ; he has
been always a particularly proper man."

" Oh, indeed," responded the attendant, " goodness
forbid I should say or think anything against him ; but
I could not help telling you my mind, ma'am, meaning
no harm."

" And, how long is it since you observed this sad
change in poor Merton ?" persisted the lady.

" Not, indeed, to say very long, ma'am," replied the
girl; "somewhere about a week, or very little more—
at least, as we remarked, ma'am."

Mrs. Marston pursued her inquiries no further that
night. But, although she affected to treat the matter
thus lightly, it had, somehow, taken a painful hold upon
her imagination, and left in her mind those undefinable
and ominous sensations, which, in certain mental tem-
peraments, seem to foreshadow the approach of unknown misfortune.

For two or three days, everything went on smoothly,
and pretty much as usual. At the end of this brief interval, however, the attention of Mrs. Marston was recalled to the subject of her servant's mysterious anxiety
to leave, and give up his situation. Merton again stood
before her, and repeated the intimation he had already
given.

" Really, Merton, this is very odd," said the lady.

" You like your situation, and yet you persist in desiring
to leave it. What am I to think ?"

" Oh, ma'am," said he, " I am unhappy ; I am tormented, ma'am. I can't tell you, ma'am ; I can't indeed, ma'am!"'

"If anything weighs upon your mind, Merton, I would
advise you to consult our good clergyman, Dr. Danvers,"
urged the lady.

The servant hung his head, and mused for a time
gloomily; and then said decisively—

" No, ma'am ; no use."

" And pray, Merton, how long is it since you first entertained this desire ?" asked Mrs. Marston.

"Since Sir Wynston Berkley came, ma'am," answered he.

" Has Sir Wynston annoyed you in any way ?" continued she.

" Far from it, ma'am," he replied ; "he is a very
kind gentleman."

" Well, his *man*, then ; is *he* a respectable, inoffensive
person ?" she inquired.

" I never met one more so," said the man, promptly,
and raising his head.

" What I wish to know is, whether your desire to go
is connected with Sir Wynston and his servant ?" said
Mrs. Marston.

The man hesitated, and shifted his position unea-
sily. ·

" You need not answer, Merton, if you don't wish it,"
she said kindly.

" Why, ma'am, yes, it *has* something to say to them
both," he replied, with some agitation.

" I really cannot understand this," said she.

Merton hesitated for some time, and appeared much troubled.

" It was something, ma'am—something that Sir Wynston's man said to me; and there it is out," he said at last, with an effort.

" Well, Merton," said she, " I won't press you further; but I must say, that as this communication, whatever it may be, has caused *you*, unquestionably, very great uneasiness, it seems to me but probable that it affects the safety or the interests of some person—I cannot say of whom ; and, if so, there can be no doubt that it is your duty to acquaint those who are so involved in the disclosure, with its purport."

" No, ma'am, there is nothing in what I heard that could touch anybody but myself. It was nothing but what others heard, without remarking it, or thinking about it. I can't tell you any more, ma'am ; but I am very unhappy, and uneasy in my mind."

As the man said this, he began to weep bitterly.

The idea that his mind was affected now seriously occurred to Mrs. Marston, and she resolved to convey her suspicions to her husband, and to leave him to deal with the case as to him should seem good.

" Dont agitate yourself so, Merton ; I shall speak to your master upon what you have said ; and you may rely upon it, that no surmise to the prejudice of your character has entered my mind," said Mrs. Marston, very kindly.

" Oh, ma'am, you are too good," sobbed the poor man, vehemently. " You don't know me, ma'am ; I never knew myself till lately. I am a miserable man.

nuch

Su
" he

fur-
tion,
ibly,
that
—I
)ubt
red

hat
but
ing
am

slr
ey
)al

to
ıy
ır
l,

r
[

.

Treason

I am frightened at myself, ma'am—frightened terribly.
Christ knows, it would be well for me I was dead this
minute."

"I am very sorry for your unhappiness, Merton,"
said Mrs. Marston; "and, especially, that I can do
nothing to alleviate it; I can but speak, as I have said,
to your master, and he will give you your discharge, and
arrange whatever else remains to be done."

"God bless you, ma'am," said the servant, still much
agitated, and left her.

Mr. Marston usually passed the early part of the day
in active exercise, and she, supposing that he was, in all
probability, at that moment far from home, went to
"mademoiselle's" chamber, which was at the other end
of the spacious house, to confer with her in the interval
upon the strange application thus urged by poor Merton.

Just as she reached the door of Mademoiselle de Barras's chamber, she heard voices within exerted in evident
excitement. She stopped in amazement. They were
those of her husband and mademoiselle. Startled, confounded, and amazed, she pushed open the door, and
entered. Her husband was sitting, one hand clutched
upon the arm of the chair he occupied, and the other extended, and clenched, as it seemed, with the emphasis
of rage, upon the desk which stood upon the table. His
face was darkened with the stormiest passions, and his
gaze was fixed upon the Frenchwoman, who was standing
with a look half-guilty, half-imploring, at a little distance.

There was something, to Mrs. Marston, so utterly
unexpected, and even so shocking, in this *tableau*, that
she stood for some seconds pale and breathless, and
gazing with a vacant stare of fear and horror from her

husband to the French girl, and from her to her husband
again. The three figures in this strange group remained
fixed, silent, and aghast, for several seconds. Mrs. Marston endeavoured to speak ; but, though her lips moved,
no sound escaped her ; and, from very weakness, she
sank, half-fainting, into a chair.

Marston rose, throwing, as he did so, a guilty and
furious glance at the young Frenchwoman, and walked a
step or two toward the door; he hesitated, however, and
turned, just as mademoiselle, bursting into tears, threw
her arms round Mrs. Marston's neck, and passionately
exclaimed—

"Protect me, madame, I implore, from the insults
and suspicions of your husband."

Marston stood a little behind his wife, and he and the
governess exchanged a glance of keen significance, as the
latter sank, sobbing, like an injured child into its mother's embrace, upon the poor lady's tortured bosom.

"Madame, madame! he says—Mr. Marston says—
I have presumed to give you advice, and to meddle, and
to interfere ; that I am endeavouring to make you despise
his authority. Madame, speak for me. Say, madame,
have I ever done so ?—say, madame, am I the cause of
bitterness and contumacy? Ah, *mon Dieu! c'est trop*—
it is too much, madame. I shall go—I must go, madame. Why, ah! why, did I stay for this ?"

As she thus spoke, mademoiselle again burst into a
paroxysm of weeping, and again the same significant
glance was interchanged.

"Go ; yes, you shall go," said Marston, striding toward the window. "I will have no whispering or con-
spiring in my house : I have heard of your confidences

and consultations. Mrs. Marston, I meant to have done this quietly," he continued, addressing his wife ; " I meant to have given Mademoiselle de Barras my opinion and her dismissal without your assistance ; but it seems you wish to interpose. You are sworn friends, and never fail one another, of course, at a pinch. I take it for granted that I owe your presence at our interview which I am resolved shall be, as respects mademoiselle, a final one, to a message from that intriguing young lady—eh?"

"I have had no message, Richard," said Mrs. Marston ; "I don't know—do tell me, for God's sake, what is all this about ?" And as the poor lady thus spoke, her overwrought feelings found vent in a violent flood of tears.

"Yes, madame, that is the question. I have asked him frequently what is all this anger, all these reproaches about ; what have I done ?" interposed mademoiselle, with indignant vehemence, standing erect, and viewing Marston with a flashing eye and a flushed cheek. " Yes, I am called conspirator, meddler, *intriguante*. Ah, madame, it is intolerable."

"But what have I done, Richard ?" urged the poor lady, stunned and bewildered ; " how have I offended you ?"

"Yes, yes," continued the Frenchwoman, with angry volubility, " what has she done that you call contumacy and disrespect ? Yes, dear madame, *there* is the question ; and if he cannot answer, is it not most cruel to call me conspirator, and spy, and *intriguante*, because I talk to my dear madame, who is my only friend in this place ?"

"Mademoiselle de Barras, I need no declamation from

M

you ; and, pardon me, Mrs. Marston, nor from you
either," retorted he ; " I have my information from one
on whom I can rely ; let that suffice. Of course you are
both agreed in a story. I dare say you are ready to
swear you never so much as canvassed my conduct, and
my *coldness* and *estrangement*—eh ? These are the
words, are not they ?"

" I have done you no wrong, sir ; madame can tell
you. I am no mischief-maker ; no, I never was such
a thing. Was I, madame ?" persisted the governess—
" bear witness for me ?"

" I have told you my mind, Mademoiselle de Barras,"
interrupted Marston ; " I will have no altercation, if you
please. I think, Mrs. Marston, we have had enough of
this ; may I accompany you hence ?"

So saying, he took the poor lady's passive hand, and
led her from the room. Mademoiselle stood in the
centre of the apartment, alone, erect, with heaving breast
and burning cheek—beautiful, thoughtful, guilty—the
very type of the fallen angelic. There for a time, her
heart all confusion, her mind darkened, we must leave
her ; various courses before her, and as yet without resolution to choose among them ; a lost spirit, borne on the
eddies of the storm ; fearless and self-reliant, but with
no star to guide her on her dark, malign, and forlorn
way.

Mrs. Marston, in her own room, reviewed the agitating scene through which she had just been so unexpectedly carried. The tremendous suspicion which, at
the first disclosure of the *tableau* we have described,
smote the heart and brain of the poor lady with the stun
of a thunderbolt, had been, indeed, subsequently dis-

turbed, and afterwards contradicted ; but the shock of
her first impression remained still upon her mind and
heart. She felt still through every nerve the vibrations
of that maddening terror and despair which had overcome
her senses for a moment. The surprise, the shock, the
horror, outlived the obliterating influence of what followed. She was in this agitation when Mademoiselle de
Barras entered her chamber, resolved with all her art to
second and support the success of her prompt measures
in the recent critical emergency. She had come, she
said, to bid her dear madame farewell, for she was resolved to go. Her own room had been invaded, that
insult and reproach might be heaped upon her ; how
utterly unmerited Mrs. Marston knew. She had been
called by every foul name which applied to the spy and
the maligner; she could not bear it. Some one had
evidently been endeavouring to procure her removal, and
had but too effectually succeeded. Mademoiselle was
determined to go early the next morning; nothing should
prevent or retard her departure ; her resolution was
taken. In this strain did mademoiselle run on, but in a
subdued and melancholy tone, and weeping profusely.

The wild and ghastly suspicions which had for a moment flashed terribly upon the mind of Mrs. Marston,
had faded away under the influences of reason and reflection, · although, indeed, much painful excitement still
remained, before Mademoiselle de Barras had visited
her room. Marston's temper she knew but too well ; it
was violent, bitter, and impetuous ; and though he cared
little, if at all, for her, she had ever perceived that he was
angrily jealous of the slightest intimacy or confidence by
which any other than himself might establish an influ-

ence over her mind. That he had learned the subject
of some of her most interesting conversations with mademoiselle she could not doubt, for he had violently upbraided that young lady in her presence with having
discussed it, and here now was mademoiselle herself
taking refuge with her from galling affront and unjust
reproach, incensed, wounded, and weeping. The whole
thing was consistent; all the circumstances bore plainly
in the same direction; the evidence was conclusive; and
Mrs. Marston's thoughts and feelings respecting her fair
young confidante quickly found their old level, and
flowed on tranquilly and sadly in their accustomed
channel.

While Mademoiselle de Barras was thus, with the
persevering industry of the spider, repairing the meshes
which a chance breath had shattered, she would,
perhaps, have been in her turn shocked and startled,
could she have glanced into Marston's mind, and
seen, in what was passing there, the real extent of her
danger.

Marston was walking, as usual, alone, and in the most
solitary region of his lonely park. One hand grasped
his walking-stick, not to lean upon it, but as if it were
the handle of a battle-axe; the other was buried in his
bosom; his dark face looked upon the ground, and he
strode onward with a slow but energetic step, which had
the air of deep resolution. He found himself at last in
a little churchyard, lying far among the wild forest of his
demesne, and in the midst of which, covered with ivy
and tufted plants, now ruddy with autumnal tints, stood
the ruined walls of a little chapel. In the dilapidated
vault close by lay buried many of his ancestors, and un-

der the little wavy hillocks of fern and nettles, slept many an humble villager. He sat down upon a worn tombstone in this lowly ruin, and with his eyes fixed upon the ground, he surrendered his spirit to the stormy and evil thoughts which he had invited. Long and motionless he sat there, while his foul fancies and schemes began to assume shape and order. The wind rushing through the ivy roused him for a moment, and as he raised his gloomy eye it alighted accidentally upon a skull, which some wanton hand had fixed in a crevice of the wall. He averted his glance quickly, but almost as quickly refixed his gaze upon the impassive symbol of death, with an expression lowering and contemptuous, and with an angry gesture struck it down among the weeds with his stick. He left the place, and wandered on through the woods.

"Men can't control the thoughts that flit across their minds," he muttered, as he went along, "any more than they can direct the shadows of the clouds that sail above them. They come and pass, and leave no stain behind. What, then, of omens, and that wretched effigy of death? Stuff—psha! *Murder*, indeed! I'm incapable of murder. I have drawn my sword upon a man in fair duel; but *murder!* Out upon the thought, out upon it."

He stamped upon the ground with a pang at once of fury and horror. He walked on a little, stopped again, and folding his arms, leaned against an ancient tree.

"Mademoiselle de Barras, vous etes une traitresse, and you shall go. Yes, go you shall; you have deceived me, and we must part."

He said this with melancholy bitterness; and, after a pause, continued :—

" I will have no other revenge. No ; though, I dare say, she will care but little for this; very little, if at all."

" And then, as to the other person," he resumed, after a pause, " it is not the first time he has acted like a trickster. He has crossed me before, and I will choose an opportunity to tell him my mind. I won't mince matters with him either, and will not spare him one insulting syllable that he deserves. He wears a sword, and so do I ; if he pleases, he may draw it ; he shall have the opportunity; but, at all events, I will make it impossible for him to prolong his disgraceful visit at my house."

On reaching home and his own study, the servant, Merton, presented himself, and his master, too deeply excited to hear him then, appointed the next day for the purpose. There was no contending against Marston's peremptory will, and the man reluctantly withdrew. Here was, apparently, a matter of no imaginable moment ; whether this menial should be discharged on that day, or on the morrow; and yet mighty things were involved in the alternative.

There was a deeper gloom than usual over the house. The servants seemed to know that something had gone wrong, and looked grave and mysterious. Marston was more than ever dark and moody. Mrs. Marston's dimmed and swollen eyes showed that she had been weeping. Mademoiselle absented herself from supper, on the plea of a bad headach. Rhoda saw that something, she knew not what, had occurred to agitate her elders, and was depressed and anxious. The old clergy-man, whom we have already mentioned, had called, and stayed to supper. Dr. Danvers was a man of consider-able learning, strong sense, and remarkable simplicity of character. His thoughtful blue eye, and well-marked countenance, were full of gentleness and benevolence, and elevated by a certain natural dignity, of which pu-rity and goodness, without one debasing shade of self-esteem and arrogance, were the animating spirit. Mrs. Marston loved and respected this good minister of God; and many a time had sought and found, in his gentle and earnest counsels, and in the overflowing tenderness of his sympathy, much comfort and support in the pro-gress of her sore and protracted earthly trial. Most especially at one critical period in her history had he endeared himself to her, by interposing, and success-fully, to prevent a formal separation which (as ending for ever the one hope that cheered her on, even in the front of despair) she would probably not long have sur-vived.

With Mr. Marston, however, he was far from being a favourite. There was that in his lofty and simple purity which abashed and silently reproached the sensual, bit-ter, disappointed man of the world. The angry pride of the scornful man felt its own meanness in the grand presence of a simple and humble Christian minister. And the very fact that all his habits had led him to hold such a character in contempt, made him but the more unreasonably resent the involuntary homage which its exhibition in Dr. Danvers's person invariably ex-torted from him. He felt in this good man's presence

under a kind of irritating restraint; that he was in the
presence of one with whom he had, and could have, no
sympathy whatever, and yet one whom he could not
help both admiring and respecting; and in these conflicting feelings were involved certain gloomy and
humbling inferences about himself, which he hated, and
almost feared to contemplate.

It was well, however, for the indulgence of Sir Wynston's conversational propensities, that Dr. Danvers had
happened to drop in; for Marston was doggedly silent
and sullen, and Mrs. Marston was herself scarcely more
disposed than he to maintain her part in a conversation;
so that, had it not been for the opportune arrival of the
good clergyman, the supper must have been despatched
with a very awkward and unsocial taciturnity.

Marston thought, and, perhaps, not erroneously, that
Sir Wynston suspected something of the real state of
affairs, and he was, therefore, incensed to perceive, as
he thought, in his manner, very evident indications of
his being in unusually good spirits. Thus disposed, the
party sat down to supper.

"One of our number is missing," said Sir Wynston,
affecting a slight surprise, which, perhaps, he did not
feel.

"Mademoiselle de Barras—I trust she is well?" said
Doctor Danvers, looking towards Marston.

"I suppose she is; I don't know," said Marston,
drily.

"Why, how should _he_ know," said the baronet,
gaily, but with something almost imperceptibly sarcas-
tic in his tone. "Our friend, Marston, is privileged
to be as ungallant as he pleases, except where he has

the happy privilege to owe allegiance ; but I, a gay
young bachelor of fifty, am naturally curious. I really
do trust that our charming French friend is not unwell."

He addressed his inquiry to Mrs. Marston, who, with
some slight confusion, replied :—

"No; nothing, at least, serious ; merely a slight
headach. I am sure she will be quite well enough to
come down to breakfast."

"She is, indeed, a very charming and interesting
young person," said Doctor Danvers. "There is a certain simplicity about her which argues a good and kind
heart, and an open nature."

"Very true, indeed, doctor," observed Berkley, with
the same faint, but, to Marston, exquisitely provoking
approximation to sarcasm. "There is, as you say, a
very charming simplicity. Don't you think so, Marston ?"

Marston looked at him for a moment, but continued
silent.

"Poor mademoiselle!—she is, indeed, a most affectionate creature," said Mrs. Marston, who felt called
upon to say something.

"Come, Marston, will you contribute nothing to the
general fund of approbation ?" said Sir Wynston, who
was gifted by nature with an amiable talent for teasing,
which he was fond of exercising in a quiet way. "We
have all, but you, said something handsome of our absent young friend."

"I never praise anybody, Wynston ; not even *you*,"
said Marston, with an obvious sneer.

"Well, well, I must comfort myself with the belief
that your silence covers a great deal of good-will, and,

perhaps, a little admiration, too," answered his cousin,
significantly.

"Comfort yourself in any *honest* way you will, my
dear Sir Wynston," retorted Marston, with a degree of
asperity, which, to all but the baronet himself, was unaccountable. "You may be right, you may be wrong;
on a subject so unimportant it matters very little which;
you are at perfect liberty to practise delusions, if you
will, upon *yourself.*"

"By-the-bye, Mr. Marston, is not your son about
to come down here?" asked Doctor Danvers, who
perceived that the altercation was becoming, on Marston's part, somewhat testy, if not positively rude.

"Yes; I expect him in a few days," replied he, with
a sudden gloom.

"You have not seen him, Sir Wynston?" asked the
clergyman.

"I have that pleasure yet to come," said the baronet.

"A pleasure it is, I do assure you, said Doctor
Danvers, heartily. "He is a handsome lad, with the
heart of a hero—a fine, frank, generous lad, and as merry
as a lark."

"Yes, yes," interrupted Marston; "he is well enough,
and has done pretty well at Cambridge. Doctor Danvers, take some wine."

It was strange, but yet mournfully true, that the
praises which the good Doctor Danvers thus bestowed
upon his son were bitter to the soul of the unhappy
Marston. They jarred upon his ear, and stung his
heart; for his conscience converted them into so many
latent insults and humiliations to himself.

"Your wine is very good, Marston. I think your

clarets are many degrees better than any I can get,"
said Sir Wynston, sipping a glass of his favourite wine.
"You country gentlemen are sad selfish dogs; and, with
all your grumbling, manage to collect the best of whatever is worth having about you."

"We sometimes succeed in collecting a pleasant party,"
retorted Marston, with ironical courtesy, "though we do
not always command the means of entertaining them
quite as we would wish."

It was the habit of Doctor Danvers, without respect
of persons or places, to propose, before taking his departure from whatever domestic party he chanced to be
thrown among for the evening, to read some verses from
that holy Book, on which his own hopes and peace were
founded, and to offer up a prayer for all to the throne of
grace. Marston, although he usually absented himself
from such exercises, did not otherwise discourage them;
but upon the present occasion, starting from his gloomy
reverie, he himself was the first to remind the clergyman
of his customary observance. Evil thoughts loomed
upon the mind of Marston, like measureless black mists
upon a cold, smooth sea. They rested, grew, and darkened there; and no heaven-sent breath came silently to
steal them away. Under this dread shadow his mind
lay waiting, like the DEEP, before the Spirit of God
moved upon its waters, passive and awful. Why for the
first time now did religion interest him? The unseen,
intangible, was even now at work within him. A dreadful power shook his very heart and soul. There was
some strange, ghastly wrestling going on in his own immortal spirit, a struggle which made him faint, which he
had no power to determine. He looked upon the holy

influence of the good man's prayer—a prayer in which
he could not join—with a dull, superstitious hope that
the words, inviting better influence, though uttered by
another, and with other objects, would, like a spell,
chase away the foul fiend that was busy with his soul.
Marston sate, looking into the fire, with a countenance
of stern gloom, upon which the wayward lights of the
flickering hearth sported fitfully; while at a distant table
Doctor Danvers sate down, and, taking his well-worn
Bible from his pocket, turned over its leaves, and began,
in gentle but impressive tones, to read.

Sir Wynston was much too well-bred to evince the
slightest disposition to aught but the most proper and
profound attention. The faintest imaginable gleam of
ridicule might, perhaps, have been discerned in his features, as he leaned back in his chair, and, closing his
eyes, composed himself to at least an attitude of attention. No man could submit with more cheerfulness to
an inevitable bore.

In these things, then, thou hast no concern; the
judgment troubles thee not; thou hast no fear of *death*,
Sir Wynston Berkley; yet there is a heart beating near
thee, the mysteries of which, could they glide out and
stand before thy face, would perchance appal thee, cold,
easy man of the world. Ay, couldst thou but see with
those cunning eyes of thine, but twelve brief hours into
futurity, each syllable that falls from that good man's
lips unheeded would peal through thy heart and brain
like maddening thunder. Hearken, hearken, Sir Wynston Berkley, perchance these are the farewell words of
thy better angel—the last pleadings of despised mercy!

*   *   *   *   *   *   *

The party broke up. Doctor Danvers took his leave, and rode homeward, down the broad avenue, between the gigantic ranks of elm that closed it in. The full moon was rising above the distant hills; the mists lay like sleeping lakes in the laps of the hollows; and the broad demesne looked tranquil and sad under this chastened and silvery glory. The good old clergyman thought, as he pursued his way, that here at least, in a spot so beautiful and sequestered, the stormy passions and fell contentions of the outer world could scarcely penetrate. Yet, in that calm secluded spot, and under the cold, pure light which fell so holily, what a hell was weltering and glaring!—what a spectacle was that moon to go down upon!

As Sir Wynston was leaving the parlour for his own room, Marston accompanied him to the hall, and said—

"I shan't play to-night, Sir Wynston."

"Ah, ha! very particularly engaged?" suggested the baronet, with a faint, mocking smile. "Well, my dear fellow, we must endeavour to make up for it to-morrow —eh?"

"I don't know *that*," said Marston, "and—— In a word, there is no use, sir, in our masquerading with one another. Each knows the other; each *understands* the other. I wish to have a word or two with you in your room to-night, when we shan't be interrupted."

Marston spoke in a fierce and grating whisper, and his countenance, more even than his accents, betrayed the intensity of his bridled fury. Sir Wynston, however, smiled upon his cousin as if his voice had been melody, and his looks all sunshine.

" Very good, Marston, just as you please," he said ;
" only don't be later than one, as I shall be getting into
bed about that hour.

" Perhaps, upon second thoughts, it is as well to defer
what I have to say," said Marston, musingly. " To-
morrow will do as well; so, *perhaps*, Sir Wynston, I
may not trouble you to-night."

" Just as suits you best, my dear Marston," replied
the baronet, with a tranquil smile; " only don't come
after the hour I have stipulated."

So saying, the baronet mounted the stairs, and made
his way to his chamber. He was in excellent spirits,
and in high good-humour with himself: the object of his
visit to Gray Forest had been, as he now flattered himself, attained. He had conducted an affair requiring the
profoundest mystery in its prosecution, and the nicest
tactique in its management, almost to a triumphant
issue. He had perfectly masked his design, and completely outwitted Marston ; and to a person who piqued
himself upon his clever diplomacy, and vaunted that he
had never yet sustained a defeat in any object which he
had seriously proposed to himself, such a combination of
successes was for the moment quite intoxicating.

Sir Wynston not only enjoyed his own superiority with
all the vanity of a selfish nature, but he no less enjoyed,
with a keen and malicious relish, the intense mortification which, he was well assured, Marston must experience; and all the more acutely, because of the utter im-
possibility, circumstanced as he was, of his taking any
steps to manifest his vexation, without compromising
himself in a most unpleasant way.

· Animated by these amiable feelings, Sir Wynston Berkley sate down, and wrote the following short letter, addressed to Mrs. Gray, Wynston Hall :—

"Mrs. Gray—On receipt of this have the sitting-rooms and several bed-rooms put in order, and thoroughly aired. Prepare for my use the suite of three rooms over the library and drawing-room ; and have the two great wardrobes, and the cabinet in the *state* bed-room, removed into the large dressing-room which opens upon the bed-room I have named. Make everything as comfortable as possible. If anything is wanted in the way of furniture, drapery, ornament, &c., you need only write to John Skelton, Esq., Spring-garden, London, stating what is required, and he will order and send them down. You must be expeditious, as I shall probably go down to Wynston, with two or three friends, at the beginning of next month.
                                 "Wynston Berkley.

"P.S.—I have written to direct Arkins and two or three of the other servants to go down at once. Set them all to work immediately."

He then applied himself to another letter of considerably greater length, and from which, therefore, we shall only offer a few extracts. It was addressed to John Skelton, Esq., and began as follows :—

"My dear Skelton,—You are, doubtless, surprised . at my long silence, but I have had nothing very particular to say. My visit to this dull and uncomfortable place was (as you rightly surmise) not without its object —a little bit of wicked romance ; the pretty demoiselle of Rouen, whom I mentioned to you more than once— la belle de Barras—was, in truth, the attraction that drew me hither ; and, I *think* (for, as yet, she affects

hesitation), I shall have no further trouble with her. She
is a fine creature, and you will admit, when you have
seen her, well worth taking some trouble about. She is,
however, a very knowing little minx, and evidently suspects me of being a sad, fickle dog—and, as I surmise,
has some plans, moreover, respecting my morose cousin,
Marston, a kind of wicked Penruddock, who has carried all his London tastes into his savage retreat, a para-
dise of bogs and bushes. There is, I am very confident,
a *liaison* in that quarter. The young lady is evidently
a dood deal afraid of him, and insists upon such precautions in our interviews, that they have been very few,
and far between, indeed. To-day, there has been a *fracas* of some kind. I have no doubt that Marston, poor
devil, is jealous. His situation is really pitiably comic—
with an intriguing mistress, a saintly wife, and a devil of a
jealous temper of his own. I shall meet Mary on reaching town. Has Clavering (shabby dog!) paid his I. O.
U. yet? Tell the little opera woman she had better be
quiet. She ought to know me by this time; I shall do
what is right, but won't submit to be bullied. If she
is troublesome, snap your fingers at her, on my behalf,
and leave her to her remedy. I have written to Gray,
to get things at Wynston in order. She will draw upon
you for what money she requires. Send down two or
three of the servants, if they have not already gone. The
place is very dusty and dingy, and needs a great deal of
brushing and scouring. I shall see you in town very
soon. By the way, has the claret I ordered from the
Dublin house arrived yet? it is consigned to you, and
goes by the 'Lizard;' pay the freightage, and get Ed-
wards to pack it; ten dozen or so may as well go down
to Wynston, and send other wines in proportion. I leave
details to you." . . . .

Some further directions upon other subjects followed;
and having subscribed the despatch, and addressed it to

the gentlemanlike scoundrel who filled the onerous office
of factotum to this profligate and exacting man of the
world, Sir Wynston Berkley rang his bell, and gave the
two letters into the hand of his man, with special directions to carry them *himself*, in person, to the post-office
in the neighbouring village, early next morning. These
little matters completed, Sir Wynston stirred his fire,
leaned back in his easy chair, and smiled blandly over
the sunny prospect of his imaginary triumphs.

It here becomes necessary to describe, in a few words,
some of the local relations of Sir Wynston's apartments.
The bedchamber which he occupied opened from the
long passage of which we have already spoken—and
there were two other smaller apartments opening from
it in train. In the further of these, which was entered
from a lobby, communicating by a back stair with the
kitchen and servants' apartments, lay Sir Wynston's
valet, and the intermediate chamber was fitted up as a
dressing-room for the baronet himself. These circumstances it is necessary to mention, that what follows may
be clearly intelligible.

While the baronet was penning these records of vicious
schemes—dire waste of wealth and time—irrevocable
time !—Marston paced his study in a very different frame
of mind. There were a gloom and disorder in the room
accordant with those of his own mind. Shelves of ancient tomes, darkened by time, and upon which the dust
of years lay sleeping—dark oaken cabinets, filled with
piles of deeds and papers, among which the nimble spi-
ders were crawling—and, from the dusky walls, several
stark, pale ancestors, looking down coldly from their
tarnished frames. An hour, and another hour passed—

N

and still Marston paced this melancholy chamber, a prey
to his own fell passions and dark thoughts. He was not
a superstitious man, but, in the visions which haunted
him, perhaps, was something which made him unusually
excitable—for, he experienced a chill of absolute horror,
as, standing at the farther end of the room, with his face
turned towards the entrance, he beheld the door noiselessly and slowly pushed open, by a pale, thin hand, and
a figure dressed in a loose white robe, glide softly in.
He stood for some seconds gazing upon this apparition,
as it moved hesitatingly towards him from the dusky
extremity of the large apartment, before he perceived
that the form was that of Mrs. Marston.

"Hey, ha!—Mrs. Marston—what on earth has called
you hither?" he asked, sternly. " You ought to have
been at rest an hour ago; get to your chamber, and leave
me, I have business to attend to."

" Now, dear Richard, you must forgive me," she
said, drawing near, and looking up into his haggard face
with a sweet and touching look of timidity and love; " I
could not rest until I saw you again; your looks have
been all this night so unlike yourself; so strange and
terrible, that I am afraid some great misfortune threat-
ens you, which you fear to tell me of."

" My looks! why, curse it, must I give an account of
my looks?" replied Marston, at once disconcerted and
wrathful. " Misfortune! what misfortune can befal us
more? No, there is nothing, nothing, I say, but your
own foolish fancy; go to your room—go to sleep—my
looks, indeed; psha!"

" I came to tell you, dear Richard, that I will do, in
all respects, just as you desire. If you continue to wish

it, I will part with poor mademoiselle; though, indeed,
Richard, I shall miss her more than you can imagine;
and all your suspicions have wronged her deeply," said
Mrs. Marston.

Her husband darted a sudden flashing glance of suspicious scrutiny upon her face; but its expression was
frank, earnest, and noble. He was disarmed; he hung
his head gloomily upon his breast, and was silent for a
time. She came nearer, and laid her hand upon his
arm. He looked darkly into her upturned eyes, and a
feeling which had not touched his heart for many a day
—an emotion of pity, transient, indeed, but vivid, re-
visited him. He took her hand in his, and said, in
gentler terms than she had heard him use for a long
time—

" No, indeed, Gertrude, you have deceived yourself;
no misfortune has happened, and if I *am* gloomy, the
source of all my troubles is *within*. Leave me, Gertrude, for the present. As to the other matter, the
departure of Mademoiselle de Barras, we can talk of
that to-morrow—*now* I cannot; so let us part. Go to
your room; good night."

She was withdrawing, and he added, in a subdued
tone—

" Gertrude, I am very glad you came—*very* glad.
Pray for me to-night."

He had followed her a few steps toward the door, and
now stopped short, turned about, and walked dejectedly
back again.

" I *am* right glad she came," he muttered, as soon as
he was once more alone. " Wynston is provoking and
fiery, too. Were I, in my present mood, to seek a *tête-*

à-tête with him, who knows what might come of it?
Blood; my own heart whispers—*blood!* I'll not trust
myself."

He strode to the study door, locked it, and taking out
the key, shut it in the drawer of one of the cabinets.

" Now it will need more than accident or impulse to
lead me to him. I cannot go, at least, without reflection, without premeditation. Avaunt, fiend! I have
baffled you."

He stood in the centre of the room, cowering and
scowling as he said this, and looked round with a glance
half-defiant, half-fearful, as if he expected to see some
dreadful form in the dusky recesses of the desolate chamber. He sate himself by the smouldering fire, in sombre
and agitated rumination. He was restless; he rose
again, unbuckled his sword, which he had not loosed
since evening, and threw it hastily into a corner. He
looked at his watch, it was half-past twelve; he glanced
at the door, and thence at the cabinet in which he had
placed the key ; then he turned hastily, and sate down
again. He leaned his elbows on his knees, and his chin
upon his clenched hand; still he was restless and excited. Once more he arose, and paced up and down. He
consulted his watch again; it was now but a quarter to
one.   *   *   *   *   *   *

Sir Wynston's man having received the letters, and
his master's permission to retire to rest, got into his
bed, and was soon beginning to dose. We have already
mentioned that his and Sir Wynston's apartments were
separated by a small dressing-room, so that any ordinary
noise or conversasion could be heard but imperfectly
from one to the other. The servant, however, was

startled by a sound of something falling on the floor of
his master's apartment, and broken to pieces by the
violence of the shock. He sate up in his bed, listened,
and heard some sentences spoken vehemently, and gab-
bled very fast. He thought he distinguished the words
" wretch" and " God ;" and there was something so
strange in the tone in which they were spoken, that the
man got up and stole noiselessly through the dressing-
room, and listened at the door.

He heard him, as he thought, walking in his slippers
through the room, and making his customary arrangements previously to getting into bed. He knew that
his master had a habit of speaking when alone, and
concluded that the accidental breakage of some glass or
chimney-ornament had elicited the volley of words he
had heard. Well knowing that, except at the usual
hours, or in obedience to Sir Wynston's bell, nothing
more displeased his master than his presuming to enter
his sleeping-apartment while he was there, the servant
quietly retreated, and, perfectly satisfied that all was
right, composed himself to slumber, and was soon beginning to dose again.

The adventures of the night, however, were not yet
over. Waking, as men sometimes do, without any as-
certainable cause; without a start or an uneasy sensation; without even a disturbance of the attitude of repose, he opened his eyes and beheld Merton, the servant of whom we have spoken, standing at a little distance from his bed. The moonlight fell in a clear
flood upon this figure : the man was ghastly pale ; there
was a blotch of blood on his face ; his hands were clasped upon something which they nearly concealed ; and

his eyes, fixed on the servant who had just awakened, shone in the cold light with a wild and lifeless glitter. This spectre drew close to the side of the bed, and stood for a few moments there with a look of agony and menace, which startled the newly-awakened man, who rose upright, and said—

"Mr. Merton, Mr. Merton—in God's name, what is the matter?"

Merton recoiled at the sound of his voice; and, as he did so, dropped something on the floor, which rolled away to a distance; and he stood gazing silently and horribly upon his interrogator.

"Mr. Merton, I say, what *is* it?" urged the man. "Are you hurt? your face is bloody."

Merton raised his hand to his face mechanically, and Sir Wynston's man observed that it, too, was covered with blood.

"Why, man," he said, vehemently, and actually freezing with horror, "you are *all* bloody; hands and face; all over blood."

"My hand is cut to the bone," said Merton, in a harsh whisper; and speaking to himself, rather than addressing the servant—"I wish it was my neck; I wish to God I bled to death."

"You have hurt your hand, Mr. Merton," repeated the man, scarce knowing what he said.

"Ay," whispered Merton, wildly drawing toward the bedside again; "who told you I hurt my hand? It is cut to the bone, sure enough."

He stooped for a moment over the bed, and then cowered down toward the floor to search for what he had dropped.

"Why, Mr. Merton, what brings you here at this hour?" urged the man, after a pause of a few seconds. "It is drawing toward morning."

"Ay, ay," said Merton, doubtfully, and starting upright again, while he concealed in his bosom what he had been in search of. "Near morning, is it? Night and morning, it is all one to me. I believe I am going mad, by ——"

"But what do you want? what did you come here for at this hour?" persisted the man.

"*What!* ay, *that* is it; why, his boots and spurs, to be sure. I forgot them. His—his—Sir Wynston's boots and spurs; I forgot to take them, I say," said Merton, looking toward the dressing-room, as if about to enter it.

"Don't mind them to-night, I say; don't go in there," said the man, peremptorily, and getting out upon the floor. "I say, Mr. Merton, this is no hour to be going about searching in the dark for boots and spurs. You'll waken the master. I can't have it, I say; go down, and let it be for to-night."

Thus speaking, in a resolute and somewhat angry under-key, the valet stood between Merton and the entrance of the dressing-room; and, signing with his hand toward the other door of the apartment, continued—

"Go down, I say, Mr. Merton, go down; you may as well quietly, for, I tell you plainly, you shall neither go a step further, nor stay here a moment longer."

The man drew his shoulders up, and made a sort of shivering moan, and clasping his hands together, shook them, as it seemed, in great agony. He then turned abruptly, and hurried from the room by the door leading to the kitchen.

"By my faith," said the servant, "I am glad he is gone. The poor chap is turning crazy, as sure as I am a living man. I'll not have him prowling about here any more, however; that I am resolved on."

In pursuance of this determination, by no means an imprudent one, as it seemed, he fastened the door communicating with the lower apartments upon the inside. He had hardly done this, when he heard a step traversing the stable-yard, which lay under the window of his apartment. He looked out, and saw Merton walking hurriedly across, and into a stable at the farther end.

Feeling no very particular curiosity about his movements, the man hurried back to his bed. Merton's eccentric conduct of late had become so generally remarked and discussed among the servants, that Sir Wynston's man was by no means surprised at the oddity of the visit he had just had; nor, after the first few moments of doubt, before the appearance of blood had been accounted for, had he entertained any suspicions whatever connected with the man's unexpected presence in the room. Merton was in the habit of coming up every night to take down Sir Wynston's boots, whenever the baronet had ridden in the course of the day; and this attention had been civilly undertaken as a proof of good-will toward the valet, whose duty this somewhat soiling and ungentlemanlike process would otherwise have been. So far, the nature of the visit was explained; and the remembrance of the friendly feeling and good offices which had been mutually interchanged, as well as of the inoffensive habits for which Merton had earned a character for himself, speedily calmed the uneasiness, for a moment amounting to actual alarm, with which the servant had regarded his appearance.

We must now pass on to the morrow, and ask the reader's attention for a few moments to a different scene.

In contact with Gray Forest upon the northern side, and divided by a common boundary, lay a demesne, ih many respects presenting a very striking contrast to its grander neighbour. It was a comparatively modern place. It could not boast the towering timber which enriched and overshadowed the vast and varied expanse of its aristo-cratic rival; but, if it was inferior in the advantages of antiquity, and, perhaps, also in some of those of nature, its superiority in other respects was striking and impor-tant. Gray Forest was not more remarkable for its wild and neglected condition, than was Newton Park for the care and elegance with which it was kept. No one could observe the contrast, without, at the same time, divining its cause. The proprietor of the one was a man of wealth, fully commensurate with the extent and pre-tensions of the residence he had chosen; the owner of the other was a man of broken fortunes.

Under a green shade, which nearly met above, a very young man, scarcely one-and-twenty, of a frank and sensible, rather than a strictly handsome counte-nance, was walking, followed by half a dozen dogs of as many breeds and sizes. This young man was George Mervyn, the only son of the present proprietor of the place. As he approached the great gate, the clank of a horse's hoofs in quick motion upon the sequestered road which ran outside it, reached him; and hardly had he heard these sounds, when a young gentleman rode briskly by, directing his look into the demesne as he passed. He had no sooner seen him, than wheeling his horse about, he rode up to the iron gate, and dismounting, threw it open, and let his horse in.

"Ha! Charles Marston, I protest!" said the young man, quickening his pace to meet his friend. "Marston, my dear fellow," he called aloud, "how glad I am to see you."

There was another entrance into Newton Park, opening from the same road, about half a mile further on; and Charles Marston made his way lie through this. Thus the young people walked on, talking of a hundred things as they proceeded, in the mirth of their hearts.

Between the fathers of the two young men, who thus walked so affectionately together, there subsisted unhappily no friendly feelings. There had been several slight disagreements between them, touching their proprietary rights, and one of these had ripened into a formal and somewhat expensive litigation, respecting a certain right of fishing claimed by each. This legal encounter had terminated in the defeat of Marston. Mervyn, however, promptly wrote to his opponent, offering him the free use of the waters for which they had thus sharply contested, and received a curt and scarcely civil reply, declining the proposed courtesy. This exhibition of resentment on Marston's part had been followed by some rather angry collisions, where chance or duty happened to throw them together. It is but justice to say that, upon all such occasions, Marston was the aggressor. But Mervyn was a somewhat testy

in pride of his own, which
Thus, though near neigh-
young friends were more than
On Mervyn's side, however,
unalloyed with bitterness, and
ch the great moralist would have
pride." It did not include any
family, and Charles, as often as he
as, in truth, as often as his visits
special notice of his father, was a wel-
Newton Park.

respecting the mutual relation in which
ies stood, it was necessary to state, for the
making what follows perfectly clear. The
people had now reached the further gate, at
they were to part. Charles Marston, with a
beating happily in the anticipation of many a
ant meeting, bid him farewell for the present, and
few minutes more was riding up the broad, straight
venue, towards the gloomy mansion which closed in
the hazy and sombre perspective. As he moved onward,
he passed a labourer, with whose face, from his childhood, he had been familiar.

" How do you do, Tom ?" he cried.

"At your service, sir," replied the man, uncovering,
"and welcome home, sir."

here was something dark and anxious in the man's
which ill-accorded with the welcome he spoke, and
gested some undefined alarm.

naster, and mistress, and Miss Rhoda—are
he asked eagerly.

ll, sir, thank God," replied the man.

Marston spurred on, filled with

hensions, and observing the man still leaning upon his spade, and watching his progress with the same gloomy and curious eye.

At the hall-door he met with one of the servants, booted and spurred.

"Well, Daly," he said, as he dismounted, "how are all at home?"

This man, like the former, met his smile with a troubled countenance, and stammered—

"All, sir—that is, the master, and mistress, and Miss Rhoda—quite well, sir; but ——"

"Well, well," said Charles, eagerly, "speak on— what is it?"

"Bad work, sir," replied the man, lowering his voice. "I am going off this minute for ——"

"For what?" urged the young gentleman.

"Why, sir, for the coroner," replied he.

"The coroner—the coroner! Why, good God, what has happened?" cried Charles, aghast with horror.

"Sir Wynston," commenced the man, and hesitated.

"Well?" pursued Charles, pale and breathless.

"Sir Wynston—he—it is *he*," said the man.

"He? Sir Wynston? Is he dead, or *who* is?—who is dead?" demanded the young man, almost fiercely.

"Sir Wynston, sir; it is he that is dead. There is bad work, sir—very bad, I'm afraid," replied the man.

Charles did not wait to inquire further, but, with a feeling of mingled horror and curiosity, entered the house.

He hurried up the stairs, and entered his mother's sitting-room. She was there, perfectly alone, and so deadly pale, that she scarcely looked like a living being. In an instant they were locked in one another's arms.

" Mother—my dear mother, you are ill," said the young man, anxiously.

" Oh, no, no, dear Charles, but frightened, horrified ;" and as she said this, the poor lady burst into tears.

" What *is* this horrible affair? something about Sir Wynston. He is dead, I know, but is it—is it suicide ?" he asked.

" Oh, no, *not* suicide," said Mrs. Marston, greatly agitated.

"Good God! then he is murdered," whispered the young man, growing very pale.

" Yes, Charles—horrible—dreadful! I can scarcely believe it," replied she, shuddering while she wept.

" Where is my father ?" inquired the young man, after a pause. ·

" Why, why, Charles, darling—why do you ask for him ?" she said, wildly, grasping him by the arm, as she looked into his face with a terrified expression.

" Why—why, *he* could tell me the particulars of this horrible tragedy," answered he, meeting her agonized look with one of alarm and surprise, " as far as they have been as yet collected.   How is he, mother—is he well ?"

" Oh, yes, quite well, thank God," she answered, more collectedly—" quite well, but, of course, greatly, dreadfully shocked."

" I will go to him, mother ; I will see him," said he, turning towards the door.

" He has been wretchedly depressed and excited for some days," said Mrs. Marston, dejectedly, " and this dreadful occurrence will, I fear, affect him most deplorably."

The young man kissed her tenderly and affectionately,
and hurried down to the library, where his father usually
sat when he desired to be alone, or was engaged in business. He opened the door softly. His father was
standing at one of the windows, his face haggard as from
a night's watching, unkempt and unshorn, and with his
hands thrust into his pockets. At the sound of the
revolving door he started, and seeing his son, first recoiled a little, with a strange, doubtful expression, and
then rallying, walked quickly towards him with a smile,
which had in it something still more painful.

"Charles, I am glad to see you," he said, shaking
him with an agitated pressure by both hands, "Charles,
this is a great calamity, and what makes it still worse,
is, that the murderer has escaped ; it looks badly, you
know."

He fixed his gaze for a few moments upon his son,
turned abruptly, and walked a little way into the room
—then, in a disconcerted manner, he added, hastily
turning back—

"Not that it signifies to *us*, of course—but I would
fain have justice satisfied."

"And who is the wretch—the murderer ?" inquired
Charles.

"Who? Why, every one knows!—that scoundrel,
Merton," answered Marston, in an irritated tone—
"Merton murdered him in his bed, and fled last night ;
he is gone—escaped—and I suspect Sir Wynston's man
of being an accessory."

"Which was Sir Wynston's bed-room?" asked the
young man.

"The room that old Lady Mostyn had—the room
with the portrait of Grace Hamilton in it."

"I know—I know," said the young man, much excited. "I should wish to see it."

"Stay," said Marston; "the door from the passage is bolted on the inside, and I have locked the other; here is the key, if you choose to go, but you must bring Hughes with you, and do not disturb anything; leave all as it is; the jury ought to see, and examine for themselves."

Charles took the key, and, accompanied by the awe-struck servant, he made his way by the back stairs to the door opening from the dressing-room, which, as we have said, intervened between the valet's chamber and Sir Wynston's. After a momentary hesitation, Charles turned the key in the door, and stood

"In the dark chamber of white death."

The shutters lay partly open, as the valet had left them some hours before, on making the astounding discovery, which the partially-admitted light revealed. The corpse lay in the silk-embroidered dressing-gown, and other habiliments, which Sir Wynston had worn, while taking his ease in his chamber, on the preceding night. The coverlet was partially dragged over it. The mouth was gaping, and filled with clotted blood; a wide gash was also visible in the neck, under the ear; and there was a thickening pool of blood at the bedside, and quantities of blood, doubtless from other wounds, had saturated the bedclothes under the body. There lay Sir Wynston, stiffened in the attitude in which the struggle of death had left him, with his stern, stony face, and dim, terrible gaze turned up.

Charles looked breathlessly for more than a minute upon this mute and unchanging spectacle, and then silently suffered the curtain to fall back again, and stepped, with the light tread of awe, again to the door. There he turned back, and pausing for a minute, said, in a whisper, to the attendant—

" And Merton did this?"

" Troth, I'm afeard he did, sir," answered the man, gloomily.

" And has made his escape?" continued Charles.

" Yes, sir; he stole away in the night-time," replied the servant, "after the murder was done" (and he glanced fearfully toward the bed); "God knows where he's gone."

" The villain!" muttered Charles; "but what was his motive? why did he do all this—what does it mean?"

" I don't know exactly, sir, but he was very queer for a week and more before it," replied the man; "there was something bad over him for a long time."

" It is a terrible thing," said Charles, with a profound sigh; "a terrible and shocking occurrence."

He hesitated again at the door, but his feelings had sustained a terrible revulsion at sight of the corpse, and he was no longer disposed to prosecute his purposed examination of the chamber and its contents, with a view to conjecturing the probable circumstances of the murder.

" Observe, Hughes, that I have moved nothing in the chamber from the place it occupied when we entered," he said to the servant, as they withdrew.

He locked the door, and as he passed through the

hall, on his return, he encountered his father, and, re-
storing the key, said—

" I could not stay there ; I am almost sorry I have
seen it ; I am overpowered ; what a determined, fero-
cious murder it was ; the place is all in a pool of gore ;
he must have received many wounds."

" I can't say ; the particulars will be elicited soon
enough ; those details are for the inquest ; as for me, I
hate such spectacles," said Marston, gloomily ; " go,
now, and see your sister ; you will find her there."

He pointed to the small room where we have first
seen her and her fair governess ; Charles obeyed the
direction, and Marston proceeded himself to his wife's
sitting-room.

The young man, dispirited and horrified by the awful
spectacle he had just contemplated, hurried to the little
study occupied by his sister. Marston himself ascended,
as we have said, the great staircase leading to his wife's
private sitting-room.

" Mrs. Marston," he said, entering, " this is a hateful
occurrence, a dreadful thing to have taken place here ;
I don't mean to affect *grief* which I don't feel ; but the
thing is very shocking, and particularly so, as having
occurred under my roof ; but that cannot now be helped.
I have resolved to spare no exertions, and no influence,
to bring the assassin to justice ; and a coroner's jury
will, within a few hours, sift the evidence which we
have succeeded in collecting. But my purpose in seek-
ing you now is, to recur to the conversation we yesterday had, respecting a member of this establishment."

" Mademoiselle de Barras ?" suggested the lady.

" Yes, Mademoiselle de Barras," echoed Marston ;

o

"I wish to say, that, having reconsidered the circumstances affecting her, I am absolutely resolved that she shall not continue to be an inmate of this house."

He paused, and Mrs. Marston said—

"Well, Richard, I am sorry, very sorry for it; but your decision shall never be disputed by me."

"Of course," said Marston, drily; "and, therefore, the sooner you acquaint her with it, and let her know that she must go, the better."

Having said this, he left her, and went to his own chamber, where he proceeded to make his toilet with elaborate propriety, in preparation for the scene which was about to take place under his roof.

Mrs. Marston, meanwhile, suffered from a horrible uncertainty. She never harboured, it is true, one doubt as to her husband's perfect innocence of the ghastly crime which filled their house with fear and gloom; but at the same time that she thoroughly and indignantly scouted the possibility of his, under any circumstances, being accessory to such a crime, she experienced a nervous and agonising anxiety lest any one else should possibly suspect him, however obliquely and faintly, of any participation whatever in the foul deed. This vague fear tortured her; it had taken possession of her mind; and it was the more acutely painful, because it was of a kind which precluded the possibility of her dispelling it, as morbid fears so often are dispelled, by taking counsel upon its suggestions with a friend.

The day wore on, and strange faces began to fill the great parlour. The coroner, accompanied by a physician, had arrived. Several of the gentry in the immediate vicinity had been summoned as jurors, and now

began to arrive in succession. Marston, in a handsome
and sober suit, received these visiters with a stately and
melancholy courtesy, befitting the occasion. Mervyn
and his son had both been summoned, and, of course,
were in attendance.   There being now a sufficient number to form a jury, they were sworn, and immediately
proceeded to the chamber where the body of the murdered man was lying.

Marston accompanied them, and with a pale and stern
countenance, and in a clear and subdued tone, called their
attention successively to every particular detail which he
conceived important to be noted. Having thus employed
some minutes, the jury again returned to the parlour,
and the examination of the witnesses commenced.

Marston, at his own request, was first sworn and examined. He deposed merely to the circumstance of his
parting, on the night previous, with Sir Wynston, and
to the state in which he had seen the room and the
body in the morning. He mentioned also the fact, that
on hearing the alarm in the morning, he had hastened
from his own chamber to Sir Wynston's, and found, on
trying to enter, that the door opening upon the passage
was secured on the inside. This circumstance showed
that the murderer must have made his egress at least
through the valet's chamber, and by the back-stairs.
Marston's evidence went no further.

The next witness sworn was Edward Smith, the servant of the late Sir Wynston Berkley. His evidence
was a narrative of the occurrences we have already
stated. He described the sounds which he had overheard from his mater's room, the subsequent appearance of Merton, and the conversation which had passed

between them. He then proceeded to mention, that it
was his master's custom to have himself called at seven
o'clock, at which hour he usually took some medicine,
which it was the valet's duty to bring to him ; after
which he either settled again to rest, or rose in a short
time, if unable to sleep. Having measured and prepared
this dose in the dressing-room, the servant went on to
say, he had knocked at his master's door, and receiving
no answer, had entered the room, and partly unclosed
the shutters. He perceived the blood on the carpet,
and on opening the curtains, saw his master lying with
his mouth and eyes open, perfectly dead, and weltering
in gore. He had stretched out his hand, and seized
that of the dead man, which was quite stiff and cold ;
then, losing heart, he had run to the door communicating with the passage, but found it locked, and turned
to the other entrance, and ran down the back-stairs,
crying " murder." Mr. Hughes, the butler, and James
Carney, another servant, came immediately, and they all
three went back into the room. The key was in the
outer door, upon the inside, but they did not unlock it
until they had viewed the body. There was a great
pool of blood in the bed, and in it was lying a red-
handled caseknife, which was produced, and identified
by the witness. Just then they heard Mr. Marston
calling for admission, and they opened the door with
some difficulty, for the lock was rusty. Mr. Marston
had ordered them to leave the things as they were,
and had used very stern language to the witness. They
had then left the room, securing both doors.

This witness underwent a severe and searching examination, but his evidence was clear and consistent.

In conclusion, Marston produced a dagger, which was stained with blood, and asked the man whether he recognised it.

Smith at once stated this to have been the property of his late master, who, when travelling, carried it, together with his pistols, along with him. Since his arrival at Gray Forest, it had lain upon the chimney-piece in his bed-room, where he believed it to have been upon the previous night.

James Carney, one of Marston's servants, was next sworn and examined. He had, he said, observed a strange and unaccountable agitation and depression in Merton's manner for some days past; he had also been several times disturbed at night by his talking aloud to himself, and walking to and fro in his room. Their bed-rooms were separated by a thin partition, in which was a window, through which Carney had, on the night of the murder, observed a light in Merton's room, and, on looking in, had seen him dressing hastily. He also saw him twice take up, and again lay down, the red-hafted knife which had been found in the bed of the murdered man. He knew it by the handle being broken near the end. He had no suspicion of Merton having any mischievous intentions, and lay down again to rest. He afterwards heard him pass out of his room, and go slowly up the back-stairs leading to the upper story. Shortly after this he had fallen asleep, and did not hear or see him return. He then described, as Smith had already done, the scene which presented itself in the morning, on his accompanying him into Sir Wynston's bedchamber.

The next witness examined was a little Irish boy,

who described himself as "a poor scholar." His testimony was somewhat singular. He deposed that he had come to the house on the preceding evening, and had been given some supper, and was afterwards permitted to sleep among the hay in one of the lofts. He had, however, discovered what he considered a snugger berth. This was an unused stable, in the further end of which lay a quantity of hay. Among this he had lain down, and gone to sleep. He was, however, awakened in the course of the night by the entrance of a man, whom he saw with perfect distinctness in the moonlight, and his description of his dress and appearance tallied exactly with those of Merton. This man occupied himself for some time in washing his hands and face in a stable bucket, which happened to stand by the door; and, during the whole of this process, he continued to moan and mutter, like one in woful perturbation. He said, distinctly, twice or thrice, " by ——, I am done for;" and every now and then he muttered, " and nothing for it, after all." When he had done washing his hands, he took something from his coat-pocket, and looked at it, shaking his head; at this time he was standing with his back turned toward the boy, so that he could not see what this object might be. The man, however, put it into his breast, and then began to search hurriedly, as it seemed, for some hiding-place for it. After looking at the pavement, and poking at the chinks of the wall, he suddenly went to the window, and forced up the stone which formed the sill. Under this he threw the object which the boy had seen him examine with so much perplexity, and then he readjusted the stone, and removed the evidences of its having been recently stirred. The boy was a little frightened, but very curious about all that he saw; and when the man left the stable in which he lay, he got up, and following to the door, peeped after him. He saw him putting on an outside-coat and hat, near the yard gate; and then, with great caution, unbolt the wicket, constantly looking back towards the house, and so let himself out. The boy was uneasy, and sat in the hay, wide awake, until morning. He then told the servants what he had seen, and one of the men having raised the stone, which *he* had not strength to lift, they found the dagger, which Smith had identified as belonging to his master. This weapon was stained with blood; and some hair, which was found to correspond in colour with Sir Wynston's, was sticking in the crevice between the blade and the handle.

"It appears very strange that *one* man should have employed two distinct instruments of this kind," observed Mervyn, after a pause. A silence followed.

"Yes, strange; it *does* seem strange," said Marston, clearing his voice.

"Yet, it is clear," said another of the jury, "that the same hand *did* employ them. It is proved that the knife was in Merton's possession just as he left his chamber; and proved, also, that the dagger was secreted by him after he quitted the house."

"Yes," said Marston, with a grisly sort of smile, and glancing sarcastically at Mervyn, while he addressed the last speaker—"I thank you for recalling my attention to the facts. It certainly is not a very pleasant suggestion, that there still remains within my household an undetected murderer."

Mervyn ruminated for a time, and said he should wish to put a few more questions to Smith and Carney. They were accordingly recalled, and examined in great detail, with a view to ascertain whether any indication of the presence of a second person having visited the chamber with Merton was discoverable. Nothing, however, appeared, except that the valet mentioned the noise and the exclamations which he had indistinctly heard.

"You did not mention that before, sir," said Marston, sharply.

"I did not think of it, sir," replied the man, "the gentlemen were asking me so many questions; but I told you, sir, about it in the morning."

"Oh, ah—yes, yes—I believe you did," said Marston; "but you then said that Sir Wynston often talked when he was alone; eh, sir?"

"Yes, sir, and so he used, which was the reason I did not go into the room when I heard it," replied the man.

"How long afterwards was it when you saw Merton in your own room?" asked Mervyn.

"I could not say, sir," answered Smith; "I was soon asleep, and can't say how long I slept before he came."

"Was it an hour?" pursued Mervyn.

"I can't say," said the man, doubtfully.

"Was it five hours?" asked Marston.

"No, sir; I am sure it was not five."

"Could you swear it was more than half-an-hour?" persisted Marston.

"No, I could not swear that," answered he.

"I am afraid, Mr. Mervyn, you have found a mare's nest," said Marston, contemptuously.

"I have done my duty, sir," retorted Mervyn, cyni-

cally ; "which plainly requires that I shall have no
doubt, which the evidence of the witness can clear up,
unsifted and unsatisfied. I happened to think it of
some moment to ascertain, if possible, whether more
persons than one were engaged in this atrocious murder.
You don't seem to think the question so important a
one ; different men, sir, take different views."

" Views, sir, in matters of this sort, especially where
they tend to multiply suspicions, and to implicate others,
ought to be supported by something more substantial
than mere fancies," retorted Marston.

" I don't know what you call fancies," replied Mervyn, testily ; " but here are *two* deadly weapons, a knife
and a dagger, each, it would seem, employed in doing
this murder ; if you see nothing odd in that, I can't
enable you to do so."

" Well, sir," said Marston, grimly, "the *whole* thing
is, as you term it, *odd ;* and I can see no object in your
picking out this particular singularity for long-winded
criticism, except to cast scandal upon my household, by
leaving a hideous and vague imputation floating among
the members of it. Sir, sir, this is a foul way," he
cried, sternly, " to gratify a paltry spite."

" Mr. Marston," said Mervyn, rising, and thrusting
his hands into his pockets, while he confronted him to
the full as sternly, " the country knows in which of our
hearts the spite, if any there be between us, is harboured. I owe you no friendship, but, sir, I cherish no
malice, either ; and against the worst enemy I have on
earth I am incapable of perverting an opportunity like
this, and inflicting pain, under the pretence of discharg-
ing a duty."

Marston was on the point of retorting, but the coroner interposed, and besought them to confine their attention strictly to the solemn inquiry which they were summoned together to prosecute.

There remained still to be examined the surgeon who had accompanied the coroner, for the purpose of reporting upon the extent and nature of the injuries discoverable upon the person of the deceased. He, acccordingly, deposed, that having examined the body, he found no less than three deep wounds, inflicted with some sharp instrument ; two of them had actually penetrated the heart, and were, of course, supposed to cause instant death. Besides these, there were two contusions, one upon the back of the head, the other upon the forehead, with a slight abrasion of the eyebrow. There was a large lock of hair torn out by the roots at the front of the head, and the palm and fingers of the right hand were cut. This evidence having been taken, the jury once more repaired to the chamber where the body lay, and proceeded with much minuteness to examine the room, with a view to ascertain, if possible, more particularly the exact circumstances of the murder.

The result of this elaborate scrutiny was as follows:— The deceased, they conjectured, had fallen asleep in his easy chair, and, while he was unconscious, the murderer had stolen into the room, and, before attacking his victim, had secured the bedroom-door upon the inside. This was argued from the non-discovery of blood upon the handle, or any other part of the door. It was supposed that he had then approached Sir Wynston, with the view either of robbing, or of murdering him while he slept, and that the deceased had awakened just after he had

reached him; that a brief and desperate struggle
had ensued, in which the assailant had struck his victim with his fist upon the forehead, and having stunned
him, had hurriedly clutched him by the hair, and stabbed him with the dagger, which lay close by upon the
chimney-piece, forcing his head violently against the back
of the chair. This part of the conjecture was supported by
the circumstance of there being discovered a lock of
hair upon the ground at the spot, and a good deal of
blood. The carpet, too, was tumbled, and a water-
decanter, which had stood upon the table close by, was
lying in fragments upon the floor. It was supposed
that the murderer had then dragged the half-lifeless
body to the bed, where, having substituted the knife,
which he had probably brought to the room in the same
pocket from which the boy afterwards saw him take the
dagger, he despatched him; and either hearing some
alarm—perhaps the movement of the valet in the ad-
joining room, or from some other cause—he dropped
the knife in the bed, and was not able to find it again.
The wounds upon the hand of the dead man indicated
his having caught and struggled to hold the blade of
the weapon with which he was assailed. The impression of a bloody hand thrust under the bolster, where
it was Sir Wynston's habit to place his purse and watch,
when making his arrangements for the night, supplied
the motive of this otherwise unaccountable atrocity.

After some brief consultation, the jury agreed upon a
verdict of wilful murder against John Merton, a finding
of which the coroner expressed his entire approbation.

Marston, as a justice of the peace, had informations,
embodying the principal part of the evidence given be-

fore the coroner, sworn against Merton, and transmitted a copy of them to the Home Office. A reward for the apprehension of the culprit was forthwith offered, but for some months without effect.

Marston had, in the interval, written to several of Sir Wynston's many relations, announcing the catastrophe, and requesting that steps might immediately be taken to have the body removed. Meanwhile undertakers were busy in the chamber of death. The corpse was enclosed in lead, and that again in cedar, and a great oak shell, covered with crimson cloth and gold-headed nails, and with a gilt plate, recording the age, title, &c. &c., of the deceased, was screwed down firmly over all.

Nearly a fortnight elapsed before any reply to Marston's letters was received. A short epistle at last arrived from Lord H——, the late Sir Wynston's uncle, deeply regretting the " sad and inexplicable occurrence;" and adding, that the will, which, on receipt of the " distressing intelligence," was immediately opened and read, contained no direction whatever respecting the sepulture of the deceased, which had therefore better be completed as modestly and expeditiously as possible, in the neighbourhood ; and, in conclusion, he directed that the accounts of the undertakers, &c., employed upon the melancholy occasion, might be sent in to Mr. Skelton, who had kindly undertaken to leave London without any delay, for the purpose of completing these last arrangements, and who would, in any matter of business connected with the deceased, represent him, Lord H——, as executor of the late baronet.

This letter was followed, in a day or two, by the arrival of Skelton, a well-dressed, languid, impertinent

London tuft-hunter, a good deal faded, with a somewhat sallow and puffy face, charged with a pleasant combination at once of meanness, insolence, and sensuality—just such a person as Sir Wynston's parasite might have been expected to prove.

However well disposed to impress the natives with high notions of his extraordinary refinement and importance, he very soon discovered that, in Marston, he had stumbled upon a man of the world, and one thoroughly versed in the ways and characters of London life. After some ineffectual attempts, therefore, to overawe and astonish his host, Mr. Skelton became aware of the fruitlessness of the effort, and condescended to abate somewhat of his pretensions.

Marston could not avoid inviting this person to pass the night at his house, an invitation which was accepted, of course ; and next morning, after a late breakfast, Mr. Skelton observed, with a yawn—

"And now, about this body—poor Berkley !—what do you propose to do with him ?"

"I have no proposition to make," said Marston, drily. "It is no affair of mine, except that the body may be removed without more delay. I have no suggestion to offer."

"H——'s notion was to have him buried as near the spot as may be," said Skelton.

Marston nodded.

"There is a kind of vault, is not there, in the demesne, a family burial-place ?" inquired the visiter.

"Yes, sir," replied Marston, curtly.

"Well ?" drawled Skelton.

"Well, sir, what then ?" responded Marston.

"Why, as the wish of the parties is to have him buried—poor fellow!—as quietly as possible, I think he might just as well be laid *there* as anywhere else!"

"Had I desired it, Mr. Skelton, I should myself have made the offer," said Marston, abruptly.

". Then you don't wish it?" said Skelton.

"No, sir; certainly not—most peremptorily not," answered Marston, with more sharpness than, in his early days, he would have thought quite consistent with politeness.

"Perhaps," replied Skelton, for want of something better to say, and with a callous sort of levity; "perhaps you hold the idea—some people *do*—that murdered men can't rest in their graves until their murderers have expiated their guilt?"

Marston made no reply, but shot two or three lurid glances from under his brow at the speaker.

"Well, then, at all events," continued Skelton, indolently resuming his theme, "if you decline your assistance, may I, at least, hope for your advice? Knowing nothing of this country, I would ask you whither you would recommend me to have the body conveyed?"

"I don't care to advise in the matter," said Marston; "but if I were directing, I should have the remains buried in Chester. It is not more than twenty miles from this; and if, at any future time, his family should desire to remove the body, it could be effected more easily from thence. But you can decide."

"Egad! I believe you are right," said Skelton, glad to be relieved of the trouble of thinking about the matter; "and I shall take your advice."

In accordance with this declaration the body was,

within four-and-twenty hours, removed to Chester, and
buried there, Mr. Skelton attending on behalf of Sir
Wynston's numerous and afflicted friends and relatives.

There are certain heartaches for which time brings no
healing; nay, which grow but the sorer and fiercer as
days and years roll on. Of this kind, perhaps, were the
stern and bitter feelings which now darkened the face of
Marston with an almost perpetual gloom. His habits
became even more unsocial than before. The society of
his son he no longer seemed to enjoy. Long and solitary rambles in his wild and extensive demesne consumed
the listless hours of his waking existence; and when the
weather prevented this, he shut himself up, upon pretence of business, in his study.

He had not, since the occasion we have already mentioned, referred to the intended departure of Mademoiselle de Barras. Truth to say, his feelings with respect to that young lady were of a conflicting and mysterious kind; and as often as his dark thoughts wandered
to her (which, indeed, was frequently enough), his muttered exclamations seemed to imply some painful and
horrible suspicions respecting her.

"Yes," he would mutter, "I thought I heard your
light foot upon the lobby, on that *accursed* night. *Fancy!*
Well, it *may* have been, but assuredly a *strange* fancy.
I cannot comprehend that woman. She baffles my scrutiny. I have looked into her face with an eye she might
well understand, were it indeed as I sometimes suspect,
and she has been calm and unmoved. I have watched
and studied her; still—doubt, doubt, hideous doubt!—
is she what she seems, or—a TIGRESS?"

Mrs. Marston, on the other hand, procrastinated from

day to day the painful task of announcing to Mademoiselle de Barras the stern message with which she had
been charged by her husband. And thus several weeks
had passed, and she began to think that his silence upon
the subject, notwithstanding his seeing the young French
lady at breakfast every morning, amounted to a kind of
tacit intimation that the sentence of banishment was not
to be carried into immediate execution, but to be kept
suspended over the unconscious offender.

It was now six or eight weeks since the hearse carrying away the remains of the ill-fated Sir Wynston Berkley had driven down the dusky avenue; the autumn was
deepening into winter, and as Marston gloomily trod the
woods of Gray Forest, the withered leaves whirled drearily
along his pathway, and the gusts that swayed the mighty
branches above him were rude and ungenial. It was a
bleak and sombre day, and as he broke into a long and
picturesque vista, deep among the most sequestered
woods, he suddenly saw before him, and scarcely twenty
paces from the spot on which he stood, an apparition,
which for some moments absolutely froze him to the earth.

Travel-soiled, tattered, pale, and wasted, John Merton, the murderer, stood before him. He did not exhi-
bit the smallest disposition to turn about and make his
escape. On the contrary, he remained perfectly motionless, looking upon his former master with a wild and
sorrowful gaze. Marston twice or thrice essayed to
speak; his face was white as death, and had he beheld
the spectre of the murdered baronet himself, he could
not have met the sight with a countenance of ghastlier
horror.

"Take me, sir," said Merton, doggedly.

Still Marston did not stir.

"Arrest me, sir, in God's name ! here I am," he repeated, dropping his arms by his side ; "I'll go with you
wherever you tell me."

"Murderer !" cried Marston, with a sudden burst of
furious horror, "murderer—assassin—miscreant !—take
that !"

And, as he spoke, he discharged one of the pistols he
always carried about him full at the wretched man. The
shot did not take effect, and Merton made no other gesture but to clasp his hands together, with an agonized
pressure, while his head sunk upon his breast.

"Shoot me ; shoot me," he said hoarsely ; "kill me
like a dog : better for me to be dead than what I am."

The report of Marston's pistol had, however, reached
another ear ; and its ringing echoes had hardly ceased
to vibrate among the trees, when a stern shout was heard
not fifty yards away, and, breathless and amazed, Charles
Marston sprang to the place. His father looked from
Merton to him, and from him again to Merton, with a
guilty and stupified scowl, still holding the smoking
pistol in his hand.

"What—how ! Good God—Merton !" ejaculated
Charles.

"Ay, sir, Merton ; ready to go to gaol, or wherever
you will," said the man, recklessly.

"A murderer ; a madman ; don't believe him,"
muttered Marston, scarce audibly, with lips as white as
wax.

"Do you surrender yourself, Merton ?" demanded the
young man, sternly, advancing toward him.

"Yes, sir ; I desire nothing more ; God knows I wish

P

to die," responded he, despairingly, and advancing
slowly to meet Charles.

"Come, then," said young Marston, seizing him by
the collar, "come quietly to the house.   Guilty and unhappy man, you are now my prisoner, and, depend upon
it, I shall not let you go."

"I don't want to go, I tell you, sir.   I have travelled
fifteen miles to-day, to come here and give myself up to
the master."

"Accursed madman!" said Marston unconsciously,
gazing at the prisoner; and then suddenly rousing himself, he said, "Well, miscreant, you wish to die, and, by
——, you are in a fair way to *have* your wish."

"So best," said the man, doggedly.   "I don't want
to live; I wish I was in my grave; l wish I was dead a
year ago."

Some fifteen minutes afterwards, Merton, accompanied
by Marston and his son Charles, entered the hall of the
mansion which, not ten weeks before, he had quitted
under circumstances so guilty and terrible.   When they
reached the house, Merton seemed much agitated, and
wept bitterly on seeing two or three of his former fellow-
servants, who looked on him in silence as they passed,
with a gloomy and fearful curiosity.   These, too, were
succeeded by others, peeping and whispering, and upon
one pretence or another crossing and re-crossing the
hall, and stealing hurried glances at the criminal.   Merton sate with his face buried in his hands, sobbing, and
taking no note of the humiliating scrutiny of which he
was the subject.   Meanwhile Marston, pale and agitated,
made out his committal, and having sworn in several of
his labourers and servants as special constables, de-

spatched the prisoner in their charge to the county gaol, where, under lock and key, we leave him in safe custody for the present.

After this event Marston became excited and restless. He scarcely ate or slept, and his health seemed now as much shattered as his spirits had been before. One day he glided into the room in which, as we have said, it was Mrs. Marston's habit frequently to sit alone. His wife was there, and, as he entered, she uttered an exclamation of doubtful joy and surprise. He sate down near her in silence, and for some time looked gloomily on the ground. She did not care to question him, and anxiously waited until he should open the conversation. At length he raised his eyes, and, looking full at her, asked abruptly—

" Well, what about mademoiselle ?"

Mrs. Marston was embarrassed, and hesitated.

" I told you what I wished with respect to that young lady some time ago, and commissioned you to acquaint her with my pleasure ; and yet I find her still here, and apparently as much established as ever."

Again Mrs. Marston hesitated. She scarcely knew how to confess 'to him that she had not conveyed his message.

" Don't suppose, Gertrude, that I wish to find fault. I merely wanted to know whether you had told Mademoiselle de Barras that we were agreed as to the necessity or expediency, or what you please, of dispensing henceforward with her services. I perceive by your manner that you have not done so. I have no doubt your motive was a kind one, but my decision remains unaltered ; and I now assure you again that I wish you to speak to her; I wish you explicitly to let her know my wishes and yours."

"Not *mine*, Richard," she answered faintly.

"Well, *mine*, then," he replied, roughly; "we shan't quarrel about that."

"And when—how soon—do you wish me to speak to her on this, to both of us, most painful subject?" asked she, with a sigh.

"To-day—this hour—this minute, if you can; in short the sooner the better," he replied, rising. "I see no reason for holding it back any longer. I am sorry my wishes were not complied with immediately. Pray, let there be no further hesitation or delay. I shall expect to learn this evening that all is arranged."

Marston having thus spoken, left her abruptly, went down to his study with a swift step, shut himself in, and throwing himself into a great chair, gave a loose to his agitation, which was extreme.

Meanwhile Mrs. Marston had sent for Mademoiselle de Barras, anxious to get through her painful task as speedily as possible. The fair French girl quickly presented herself.

"Sit down, mademoiselle," said Mrs. Marston, taking her hand kindly, and drawing her to the priediéu chair beside herself.

Mademoiselle de Barras sate down, and, as she did so, read the countenance of her patroness with one rapid glance of her flashing eyes. These eyes, however, when Mrs. Marston looked at her the next moment, were sunk softly and sadly upon the floor. There was a heightened colour, however, in her cheek, and a quicker heaving of her bosom, which indicated the excitement of an antici-

pated and painful disclosure. The outward contrast of
the two women, whose hands were so lovingly locked together, was almost as striking as the moral contrast of
their hearts. The one, so chastened, sad, and gentle ;
the other, so capable of pride and passion ; so darkly
exciteable, and yet so mysteriously beautiful. The one,
like a Niobe seen in the softest moonshine; the other, a
Venus, lighted in the glare of distant conflagration.

"Mademoiselle, dear mademoiselle, I am so much
grieved at what I have to say, that I hardly know how to
speak to you," said poor Mrs. Marston, pressing her
hand ; "but Mr. Marston has twice desired me to tell
you, what you will hear with far less pain than it costs
me to say it."

Mademoiselle de Barras stole another flashing glance
at her companion, but did not speak.

" Mr. Marston still persists, mademoiselle, in desiring
that we shall part."

"*Est il possible ?*" cried the Frenchwoman, with a
genuine start.

"Indeed, mademoiselle, you may well be surprised,"
said Mrs. Marston, encountering her full and dilated
gaze, which, however, dropped again in a moment to the
ground. " You may, indeed, naturally be surprised and
shocked at this, to me, most severe decision."

"When did he speak last of it ?" said she, rapidly.

" But a few moments since," answered Mrs. Marston.

" Ha !" said mademoiselle, and remained silent and
motionless for more than a minute.

" Madame," she cried at last, mournfully, " I suppose,
then, I must go ; but it tears my heart to leave you and
dear Miss Rhoda. I would be very happy if, before de-

parting, you would permit me, dear madame, once more
to assure Mr. Marston of my innocence, and, in his presence, to call heaven to witness how unjust are all his
suspicions."

"Do so, mademoiselle, and I will add my earnest assurances again; though, heaven knows," she said,
despondingly, "I anticipate little success; but it is well
to leave no chance untried."

Marston was sitting, as we have said, in his library.
His agitation had given place to a listless gloom, and he
leaned back in his chair, his head supported by his hand,
and undisturbed, except by the occasional fall of the em-
bers upon the hearth. There was a knock at the chamber
door. His back was towards it, and, without turning
or moving, he called to the applicant to enter. The door
opened—closed again: a light tread was audible—a tall
shadow darkened the wall: Marston looked round, and
Mademoiselle de Barras was standing before him. Without knowing how or why, he rose, and stood gazing upon
her in silence.

"Mademoiselle de Barras!" he said, at last, in a tone
of cold surprise.

"Yes, poor Mademoiselle de Barras," replied the
sweet voice of the young Frenchwoman, while her lips
hardly moved as the melancholy tones passed them.

"Well, mademoiselle, what do you desire?" he asked,
in the same cold accents, and averting his eyes.

"Ah, monsieur, do you ask?—can you pretend to be
ignorant? Have you not sent me a message, a cruel,
cruel message?"

She spoke so low and gently, that a person at the other
end of the room could hardly have heard her words.

"Yes, Mademoiselle de Barras, I *did* send you a message," he replied, doggedly. "A cruel one you will scarcely presume to call it, when you reflect upon your own conduct, and the circumstances which have provoked the measures I have taken."

"What have I done, Monsieur?—what circumstances do you mean?" asked she, plaintively.

"What have you done! A pretty question, truly. Ha, ha!" he repeated, bitterly, and then added, with suppressed vehemence, "ask your own heart, mademoiselle."

"I have asked, I do ask, and my heart answers—*nothing*," she replied, raising her fine melancholy eyes for a moment to his face."

"It lies, then," he retorted, with a fierce scoff.

"Monsieur, before heaven I swear, you wrong me foully," she said, earnestly, clasping her hands together.

"Did ever woman say she was accused *rightly*, mademoiselle?" retorted Marston, with a sneer.

"I don't know—I don't care. I only know that *I* am innocent," continued she, piteously. I call heaven to witness you have wronged me."

"Wronged you!—why, after all, with what have I charged you?" said he, scoffingly; "but let that pass. I have formed my opinions, arrived at my conclusions. If I have not named them broadly, you at least seem to understand their nature thoroughly. I know the world. I am no novice in the arts of women, mademoiselle. Reserve your vows and attestations for schoolboys and simpletons : they are sadly thrown away upon me."

Marston paced to and fro, with his hands thrust into his pockets, as he thus spoke.

"Then you don't, or rather you will not believe what I tell you?" said she, imploringly.

"No," he answered, drily and slowly, as he passed her. "I don't, and I won't (as you say) believe one word of it ; so, pray spare yourself further trouble about the matter."

She raised her head, and darted after him a glance that seemed absolutely to blaze, and at the same time smote her little hand fast clenched upon her breast. The words, however, that trembled on her pale lips were not uttered ; her eyes were again cast down, and her fingers played with the little locket that hung round her neck.

"I must make, before I go," she said, with a deep sigh and a melancholy voice, "one confidence—one last confidence : judge me by it. You cannot choose but believe me now : it is a secret, and it must even here be *whispered, whispered, whispered !*"

As she spoke, the colour fled from her face, and her tones became so strange and resolute, that Marston turned short upon his heel, and stopped before her. She looked in his face ; he frowned, but lowered his eyes. She drew nearer, laid her hand upon his shoulder, and whispered for a few moments in his ear. He raised his face suddenly : its features were sharp and fixed ; its hue was changed ; it was livid and moveless, like a face cut in gray stone. He staggered back a little and a little more, and then a little more, and fell backward. Fortunately, the chair in which he had been sitting received him, and he lay there insensible as a corpse. When at last his eyes opened, there was no gleam of triumph, no shade of anger, nothing perceptible of guilt or menace, in the young woman's countenance.

The flush had returned to her cheeks; her dimpled chin had sunk upon her full white throat; sorrow, shame, and pride seemed struggling in her handsome face: and she stood before him like a beautiful penitent, who has just made a strange and humbling shrift to her father confessor.

Next day, Marston was mounting his horse for a solitary ride through his park, when Doctor Danvers rode abruptly into the court-yard from the back entrance. Marston touched his hat, and said—

"I don't stand on forms with you, doctor, and you, I know, will waive ceremony with me. You will find Mrs. Marston at home."

"Nay, my dear sir," interrupted the clergyman, sitting firm in his saddle, "my business lies with *you* to-day."

"The devil it does!" said Marston, with discontented surprise.

"Truly it does, sir," repeated he, with a look of gentle reproof, for the profanity of Marston's ejaculation, far more than the rudeness of his manner, offended him; "and I grieve that your surprise should have somewhat carried you away ——"

"Well, then, Doctor Danvers," interrupted Marston, drily, and without heeding his concluding remark, "if you really *have* business with me, it is, at all events, of no very pressing kind, and may be as well told after supper as now. So, pray, go into the house and rest yourself: we can talk together in the evening."

"My horse is not tired," said the clergyman, patting his steed's neck; and if you do not object, I will ride

by your side for a short time, and as we go, I can say
out what I have to tell."

"Well, well, be it so," said Marston, with suppressed
impatience, and without more ceremony, he rode slowly
along the avenue, and turned off upon the soft sward in
the direction of the wildest portion of his wooded demesne, the clergyman keeping close beside him. They
proceeded some little way at a walk before Doctor Danvers spoke.

"I have been twice or thrice with that unhappy man,"
at length he said.

"*What* unhappy man? Unhappiness is no distin-
guishing singularity, is it?" said Marston, sharply.

"No, trúly, you have well said," replied Doctor Danvers. "True it is that man is born unto trouble as the
sparks fly upward. I speak, however, of your servant,
Merton—a *most* unhappy wretch."

"Ha! you have been with *him*, you say?" replied
Marston, with evident interest and anxiety.

"Yes, several times, and conversed with him long
and gravely," continued the clergyman.

"Humph! I thought that had been the chaplain's
business, not yours, my good friend," observed Marston.

"He has been unwell," replied Dr. Danvers; "and
thus, for a day or two, I took his duty, and this poor man,
Merton, having known something of me, preferred seeing me rather than a stranger; and so, at the chaplain's
desire and his, I continued my visits."

"Well, and you have taught him to pray and sing
psalms, I suppose; and what has come of it all?" demanded Marston, testily.

" He does pray, indeed, poor man! and I trust his prayers are heard with mercy at the throne of grace," said his companion, in his earnestness disregarding the sneering tone of his companion. " He is full of compunction, and admits his guilt."

" Ho! that is well—well for *himself*—well for his *soul*, at least; you are sure of it; he confesses; confesses his guilt?"

Marston put his question so rapidly and excitedly, that the clergyman looked at him with a slight expression of surprise; and recovering himself, he added, in an unconcerned tone—

" Well, well—it was just as well he did so; the evidence is too clear for doubt or mystification; he knew he had no chance, and has taken the seemliest course; and, doubtless, the best for his hopes hereafter."

" I did not question him upon the subject," said Doctor Danvers; " I even declined to hear him speak upon it at first; but he told me he was resolved to offer no defence, and that he saw the finger of God in the fate which had overtaken him."

" He will plead guilty, then, I suppose?" suggested Marston, watching the countenance of his companion with an anxious and somewhat sinister eye.

" His words seem to imply so much," answered he; " and having thus frankly owned his guilt, and avowed his resolution to let the law take its due course in his case, without obstruction or evasion, I urged him to complete the grand work he had begun, and to confess to you, or to some other magistrate fully, and in detail, every circumstance connected with the perpetration of the dreadful deed."

Marston knit his brows, and rode on for some minutes
in silence.   At length he said, abruptly—

" In *this*, it seems to me, sir, you a little exceeded
your commission."

" How so, my dear sir ?" asked the clergyman.

" Why, sir," answered Marston, " the man may possibly change his mind before the day of trial, and it is
the hangman's office, not yours, my good sir, to fasten
the halter about his neck. You will pardon my freedom ;
but, were this deposition made as you suggest, it would
undoubtedly hang him."

" God forbid, Mr. Marston," rejoined Danvers, "that
I should induce the unhappy man to forfeit his last
chances of escape, and to shut the door of human mercy
against himself, but on this he seems already resolved ;
he says so ; he has solemnly declared his resolution to
me ; and even against my warning, again and again reite-
rated the same declaration."

" *That* I should have thought quite enough, were *I*
in your place, without inviting a detailed description of
the whole process by which this detestable butchery was
consummated.   What more than the simple knowledge
of the man's guilt does any mortal desire ; guilty, or not
guilty, is the plain question which the law asks, and no
more ; take my advice, sir, as a poor Protestant layman,
and leave the arts of the confessional and inquisition to
Popish priests."

" Nay, Mr. Marston, you greatly misconceive me ;
as matters stand, there exists among the coroner's jury,
and thus among the public, some faint and unfounded
suspicion of the possibility of Merton's having had an
accessory or accomplice in the perpetration of this foul
murder."

"It is a lie, sir—a malignant, d—d lie—the jury believe no such thing, nor the public neither," said Marston, starting in his saddle, and speaking in a voice of thunder; "you have been crammed with lies, sir; malicious, unmeaning, vindictive lies; lies invented to asperse my family, and torture my feelings; suggested in my presence by that scoundrel Mervyn, and scouted by the common sense of the jury."

"I do assure you," replied Doctor Danvers, in a voice which seemed scarcely audible, after the stunning and passionate explosion of Marston's wrath, "I did not imagine that you could feel thus sorely upon the point; nay, I thought that you yourself were not without such painful doubts."

"Again, I tell you, sir," said Marston, in a tone somewhat calmer, but no less stern, "such doubts as you describe have *no* existence; your unsuspecting ear has been alarmed by a vindictive wretch, an old scoundrel who has scarce a passion left but spite towards me; few such there are, thank God; few such villains as would, from a man's very calamities, distil poison to kill the peace and character of his family."

"I am sorry, Mr. Marston," said the clergyman, "you have formed so ill an opinion of a neighbour, and I am very sure that Mr. Mervyn meant *you* no ill in frankly expressing whatever doubts still rested on his mind, after the evidence was taken."

"He did—the scoundrel!" said Marston, furiously striking his hand, in which his whip was clutched, upon his thigh; he *did* mean to wound and torture me; and with the same object he persists in circulating what he calls his doubts. Meant me no ill, forsooth! why, my

great God, sir, could any man be so stupid as not to
perceive that the suggestion of such suspicions—absurd,
contradictory, incredible as they were—was precisely
the thing to exasperate feelings sufficiently troubled
already; and not content with raising the question,
where it was scouted, as I said, as soon as named, the
vindictive slanderer proceeds to propagate and publish
his pretended surmises—d——n him!"

"Mr. Marston, you will pardon me when I say that,
as a Christian minister, I cannot suffer a spirit so ill as
that you manifest, and language so unseemly as that you
have just uttered, to pass unreproved," said Danvers,
solemnly. "If you will cherish those bitter and un-
christian feelings, at least for the brief space that I am
with you, command your fierce, unbecoming words."

Marston was about to make a sneering retort, but
restrained himself, and turned his head away.

"The wretched man himself appears now very anxious to make some further disclosures," resumed Doctor
Danvers, after a pause, "and I recommended him to
make them to *you*, Mr. Marston, as the most natural
depository of such a statement."

"Well, Mr. Danvers, to cut the matter short, as it
appears that a confession of some sort is to be made, be
it so. I will attend and receive it. The judges will not
be here for eight or ten weeks to come, so there is no
great hurry about it. I shall ride down to the town,
and see him in the jail some time in the next week."

With this assurance Marston parted from the old
clergyman, and rode on alone through the furze and fern
of his wild and sombre park.

After supper that evening Marston found himself

alone in the parlour with his wife. Mrs. Marston availed herself of the opportunity to redeem her pledge to
Mademoiselle de Barras.   She was not aware of the
strange interview which had taken place between him
and the lady for whom she pleaded.   The result of her
renewed entreaties perhaps the reader has anticipated.
Marston listened, doubted—listened, hesitated again—put
questions, pondered the answers; debated the matter
inwardly, and at last gruffly consented to give the young
lady another trial, and permit her to remain some
time longer.   Poor Mrs. Marston, little suspecting the
dreadful future, overwhelmed her husband with gratitude
for granting to her entreaties (as he had predetermined
to do) this fatal boon.   Not caring to protract this
scene—either from a disinclination to listen to expres-
sions of affection, which had long lost their charm for
him, and had become even positively distasteful, or perhaps from some instinctive recoil from the warm expression of gratitude from lips which, were the truth revealed, might justly have trembled with execration and reproach—he abruptly left the room, and Mrs. Marston,
full of her good news, hastened, in the kindness of her
heart, to communicate the fancied result of her advocacy
to Mademoiselle de Barras.
    It was about a week after this, that Marston was one
evening surprised in his study by the receipt of the following letter from Dr. Danvers :—

    " MY DEAR SIR,—You will be shocked to hear that
Merton is most dangerously ill, and at this moment in
imminent peril.   He is thoroughly conscious of his
situation, and himself regards it as a merciful interposition of Providence to spare him the disgrace and terror

of the dreadful fate which he anticipated. The unhappy
man has twice repeated his anxious desire, this day, to
state some facts connected with the murder of the late
Sir Wynston Berkley, which, he says, it is of the utmost
moment that you should hear. He says that he could
not leave the world in peace without having made this
disclosure, which he especially desires to make to yourself, and entreats that you will come to receive his communication as early as you can in the morning. This
is indeed needful, as the physician says that he is fast
sinking. I offer no apology for adding my earnest solicitations to those of the dying man ; and am, dear sir,
your very obedient servant,

"J. DANVERS."

"He regards it as a merciful interposition of Providence," muttered Marston, as he closed the letter, with
a sneer. "Well, some men have odd notions of mercy
and providence, to be sure; but if it pleases *him*, certainly *I* shall not complain for one."

Marston was all this evening in better spirits than he
had enjoyed for months, or even years. A mountain
seemed to have been lifted from his heart. He joined in
the conversation during and after supper, listened with
apparent interest, talked with animation, and even
laughed and jested. It is needless to say all this
flowed not from the healthy cheer of a heart at ease,
but from the excited and almost feverish sense of sudden
relief.

Next morning, Marston rode into the old-fashioned
town, at the further end of which the dingy and grated
front of the jail looked warningly out upon the rustic
passengers. He passed the sentries, and made his inquiries of the official at the hatch. He was relieved
from the necessity of pushing these into detail, however,

by the appearance of the physician, who at that moment passed from the interior of the prison.

"Dr. Danvers told me he expected to see you here this morning," said the medical man, after the customary salutation had been interchanged. "Your call, I believe, is connected with the prisoner, John Merton?"

"Yes, sir, so it is," said Marston. "Is he in a condition, pray, to make a statement of considerable length?"

"Far from it, Mr. Marston; he has but a few hours to live," answered the physician, "and is now insensible; but I believe he last night saw Dr. Danvers, and told him whatever was weighing upon his mind."

"Ha!—and can you say where Dr. Danvers now is?" inquired Marston, anxiously and hurriedly. "Not *here*, is he?"

"No; but I saw him, as I came here, not ten minutes since, ride into the town. It is market-day, and you will probably find him somewhere in the high street for an 'hour or two to come," answered he.

Marston thanked him, and, lost in abstraction, rode down to the little inn, entered a sitting-room, and wrote a hurried line to Dr. Danvers, entreating his attendance *there*, as a place where they might converse less interruptedly than in the street; and committing this note to the waiter, with the injunction to deliver it at once, and an intimation of where Dr. Danvers was probably to be found, he awaited, with intense and agitating anxiety, the arrival of the clergyman.

It was not for nearly ten minutes, however, which his impatience magnified into an eternity, that the well-known voice of Dr. Danvers reached him from the little hall. It was in vain that Marston strove to curb his violent agitation: his heart swelled as if it would smother him; he felt, as it were, the chill of death pervade his frame, and he could scarcely see the door through which he momentarily expected the entrance of the clergyman.

A few minutes more, and Dr. Danvers entered the little apartment.

"My dear sir," said he, gravely and earnestly, as he grasped the cold hand of Marston, "I am rejoiced to see you. I have matters of great moment and the strangest mystery to lay before you."

"I dare say—I was sure—that is, I suspected so much," answered Marston, breathing fast, and looking very pale. "I heard at the prison that the murderer, Merton, was fast dying, and now is in an unconscious state; and from the physician, that you had seen him, at his urgent entreaty, last night. My mind misgives me, sir. I fear I know not what. I long, yet dread, to hear the wretched man's confession. For God's sake tell me, does it implicate anybody else in the guilt?"

"No; no one specifically; but it has thrown a hideous additional mystery over the occurrence. Listen to me, my dear sir, and the whole narrative, as he stated it to me, shall be related now to you," said Dr. Danvers.

Marston had closed the door carefully, and they sate down together at the further end of the apartment. Marston, breathless and ghastly pale; his lips compressed—his brows knit—and his dark, dilated gaze fixed immoveably upon the speaker. Dr. Danvers, on the other hand, tranquil and solemn, and with, perhaps, some shade of awe overcasting the habitual sweetness of his countenance.

"His confession was a strange one," renewed Dr. Danvers, shaking his head gravely. "He said that the first idea of the crime was suggested by Sir Wynston's man accidentally mentioning, a few days after their arrival, that his master slept with his bank-notes, to the amount of some hundreds of pounds, in a pocket-book under his pillow. He declared that as the man mentioned this circumstance, something muttered the infernal suggestion in his ear, and from that moment he was the slave of that one idea; it was ever present with him. He contended against it in vain; he dreaded and abhorred it; but still it possessed him; he felt his power of resistance yielding. This horrible stranger which had stolen into his heart, waxed in power and importunity, and tormented him day and night. He resolved to fly from the house. He gave notice to you and Mrs. Marston of his intended departure; but accident protracted his stay until that fatal night which sealed his doom. The influence which had mastered him forced him to rise from his bed, and take the knife—the discovery of which afterwards helped to convict him—and led him to Sir Wynston's chamber; he entered; it was a moonlight night."

Here the clergyman, glancing round the room, lowered his voice, and advanced his lips so near to Marston, that their heads nearly touched. In this tone and attitude he continued his narrative for a few minutes. At the end of this brief space, Marston rose up slowly, and with a movement backward, every feature strung with horror,

and saying, in a long whisper, the one word, "yes,"
which seemed like the hiss of a snake before he makes
his last deadly spring. Both were silent for a time. At
last Marston broke out with hoarse vehemence—

"Dreadful—horrible—oh, God! God!—my God!
how frightful!"

And throwing himself into a chair, he clasped his
hands across his eyes and forehead, while the sweat of
agony literally poured down his pale face.

"Truly it is so," said the clergyman, scarcely above
his breath; and, after a long interval—"horrible indeed!"

"Well," said Marston, rising suddenly to his feet,
wiping the dews of horror from his face, and looking
wildly round, like one newly waked from a nightmare,
"I must make the most of this momentous and startling
disclosure. I shall spare no pains to come at the truth,"
said he, energetically. "Meanwhile, my dear sir, for
the sake of justice and of mercy, observe secrecy. Leave
me to sift this matter; give no note anywhere that we
suspect. Observe this reserve and security, and with it
detection will follow. Breathe but one word, and you
arm the guilty with double caution, and turn licentious
gossip loose upon the fame of an innocent and troubled
family. Once more I entreat—I expect—I implore
silence—silence, at least, for the present—*silence!*"

"I quite agree with you, my dear Mr. Marston,"
answered Dr. Danvers. "I have not divulged one syllable of that poor wretch's confession, save to yourself
alone. You, as a magistrate, a relative of the murdered
gentleman, and the head of that establishment among
whom the guilt rests, are invested with an interest in

detecting, and powers of sifting the truth in this matter, such as none other possesses. I clearly see, with you, too, the inexpediency and folly of talking, for talking's sake, of this affair. I mean to keep my counsel, and shall most assuredly, irrespectively even of your request —which should, however, of course, have weight with me—maintain a strict and cautious silence upon this subject."

Some little time longer they remained together, and Marston, buried in strange thoughts, took his leave, and rode slowly back to Gray Forest.

Months passed away—a year, and more—and though no new character appeared upon the stage, the relations which had subsisted among the old ones became, in some respects, very materially altered. A gradual and disagreeable change came over Mademoiselle de Barras' manner; her affectionate attentions to Mrs. Marston became less and less frequent; nor was the change merely confined to this growing coldness; there was something of a positive and still more unpleasant kind in the alteration we have have noted. There was a certain independence and carelessness, conveyed in a hundred intangible but significant little incidents and looks—a something which, without being open to formal rebuke or remonstrance, yet bordered, in effect, upon impertinence, and even insolence. This indescribable and provoking self-assertion, implied in glances, tones, emphasis, and general bearing, surprised Mrs. Marston far more than it irritated her. As often as she experienced one of these studied slights or insinuated impertinences, she revolved in her own mind all the incidents of their past intercourse, in the vain endeavour to recollect some one among them which could possibly account for the offensive change so manifest in the conduct of the young Frenchwoman.

Mrs. Marston, although she sometimes rebuked these artful affronts by a grave look, a cold tone, or a distant manner, yet had too much dignity to engage in a petty warfare of annoyance, and had, in reality, no substantial and well-defined ground of complaint against her, such as would have warranted her either in taking the young lady herself to task, or in bringing her conduct under the censure of Marston.

One evening it happened that Mrs. Marston and Mademoiselle de Barras had been left alone together, after the supper-party had dispersed. They had been for a long time silent, and Mrs. Marston resolved to improve the *tête-à-tête*, for the purpose of eliciting from mademoiselle an explanation of her strange behaviour.

"Mademoiselle," said she, "I have lately observed a very marked change in your conduct to me."

"*Indeed!*" said the Frenchwoman.

"Yes, mademoiselle; you must be yourself perfectly aware of that change ; it is a studied and intentional one," continued Mrs. Marston, in a gentle but dignified tone; "and although I have felt some doubt as to whether it were advisable, so long as you observe toward me the forms of external respect, and punctually discharge the duties you have undertaken, to open any discussion whatever upon the subject ; yet I have thought it better to give you a fair opportunity of explaining frankly, should you desire to do so, the feelings and impressions under which you are acting."

"Ah, you are very obliging, madame," said she, coolly.

"It is quite clear, mademoiselle, that you have either

misunderstood me, or that you are dissatisfied with your situation among us : your conduct cannot otherwise be accounted for," said Mrs. Marston, gravely.

"My conduct—*ma foi !* what conduct?" retorted the handsome Frenchwoman, confidently, and with a disdainful glance.

"If you question the fact, mademoiselle," said the elder lady, "it is enough. Your ungracious manner and ungentle looks, I presume, arise from what appears to you a asufficient and well-defined cause, of which, however, I know nothing."

"I really was not aware," said Mademoiselle de Barras, with a supercilious smile, "that my looks and my manner were subjected to so strict a criticism, or that it was my duty to regulate both according to so nice and difficult a standard."

"Well, mademoiselle," continued Mrs. Marston, "it is plain that whatever may be the cause of your dissatisfaction, you are resolved against confiding it to me. I only wish to know frankly from your own lips, whether you have formed a wish to leave this situation : if so, I entreat of you to declare it freely."

"You are very obliging, indeed, madame," said the pretty foreigner, drily; "but I have no such wish, at least at present."

"Very well, mademoiselle," replied Mrs. Marston, with gentle dignity ; "I regret your want of candour, on your own account. You would, I am sure, be much happier, were you to deal frankly with me."

"May I now have your permission, madame, to retire to my room ?" asked the French girl, rising, and making

a low courtesy—"that is, if madame has nothing further
to censure."

"Certainly, mademoiselle ; I have nothing further to
say," replied the elder lady.

The Frenchwoman made another and a deeper courtesy, and withdrew. Mrs. Marston, however, heard, as
she was designed to do, the young lady tittering and
whispering to herself, as she lighted her candle in the
hall. This scene mortified and grieved poor Mrs. Marston inexpressibly. She was little, if at all, accessible
to emotions of anger, and certainly none such mingled
in the feelings with which she regarded Mademoiselle
de Barras. But she had found in this girl a companion,
and even a confidante in her melancholy solitude ; she
had believed her affectionate, sympathetic, tender, and
the disappointment was as bitter as unimagined.

The annoyances which she was fated to receive from
Mademoiselle de Barras were destined, however, to grow
in number and in magnitude. The Frenchwoman sometimes took a fancy, for some unrevealed purpose, to talk
a good deal to Mrs. Marston, and on such occasions
would persist, notwithstanding that lady's marked reserve and discouragement, in chatting away, as if she
were conscious that her conversation was the most welcome entertainment possible to her really unwilling audi-
tor. No one of their interviews did she ever suffer to
close without in some way or other suggesting or insinuating something mysterious and untold to the prejudice
of Mr. Marston. Those vague and intangible hints, the
meaning of which, for an instant legible and terrific, seemed in another moment to dissolve and disappear, tortured

Mrs. Marston like the intrusions of a spectre ; and this, along with the portentous change, rather *felt* than visible, in mademoiselle's conduct toward her, invested the beautiful Frenchwoman, in the eyes of her former friend and patroness, with an indefinable character that was not only repulsive but formidable.

Mrs. Marston's feelings with respect to this person were still further disturbed by the half-conveyed hints and inuendoes of her own maid, who never lost an opportunity of insinuating her intense dislike of the Frenchwoman, and appeared perpetually to be upon the very verge of making some explicit charges, or some shocking revelations, respecting her, which, however, she as invariably evaded ; and even when Mrs. Marston once or twice insisted upon her explaining her meaning distinctly, she eluded her mistress's desire, and left her still in the same uneasy uncertainty.

Marston, on his part, however much his conduct might tend to confirm suspicion, certainly did nothing to dissipate the painful and undefined apprehensions respecting himself, which Mademoiselle de Barras, with such malign and mysterious industry, laboured to raise. His spirits and temper were liable to strange fluctuations. In the midst of that excited gaiety, to which, until lately, he had been so long a stranger, would sometimes intervene paroxyms of the blackest despair, all the ghastlier for the contrast, and with a suddenness so abrupt and overwhelming, that one might have fancied him crossed by the shadow of some terrific apparition. Sometimes for a whole day, or even more, he would withdraw himself from the society of his family, and, in morose and moody solitude, take his meals alone in his library, and steal

out unattended to wander among the thickets and glades
of his park.   Sometimes, again, he would sit for hours
in the room which had been Sir Wynston's, and, with a
kind of horrible resolution, often loiter there till after
nightfall.   In such hours, the servants would listen
with curious awe, as they heard his step, pacing to and
fro, in that deserted and inauspicious chamber, while his
voice, in broken sentences, was also imperfectly audible, as
if maintaining a muttered dialogue.   These eccentric practices gradually invested him, in the eyes of his domestics,
with a certain preternatural mystery, which enhanced the
fear with which they habitually regarded him, and was
subsequently confirmed by his giving orders to have the
furniture taken out of the ominous suite of rooms, and
the doors nailed up and secured.   He gave no reason for
this odd and abrupt measure, and gossip of course reported that the direction had originated in his having
encountered the spectre of the murdered baronet, in one
of these strange and unseasonable visits to the scene of
the fearful catastrophe.

In addition to all this, Marston's conduct towards his
wife became strangely capricious.   He avoided her society more than ever ; and when he did happen to exchange a few words with her, they were sometimes
harsh and violent, and at others remorsefully gentle and
sad, and this without any changes of conduct upon her
part to warrant the wayward uncertainty of his treatment.   Under all these circumstances, Mrs. Marston's
unhappiness and uneasiness greatly increased.   Mademoiselle de Barras, too, upon several late occasions, had
begun to assume a tone of authority and dictation,
which justly offended the mistress of the establishment.

Meanwhile Charles Marston had returned to Cambridge ; and Rhoda, no longer enjoying happy walks with her brother, pursued her light and easy studies with Mademoiselle de Barras, and devoted her leisure hours to the loved society of her mother.

One day Mrs. Martson, sitting in her room with Rhoda, had happened to call her own maid, to take down and carefully dust some richly-bound volumes which filled a bookcase in the little chamber.

"You have been crying, Willett," said Mrs. Marston, observing that the young woman's eyes were red and swollen.

"Indeed, and I was, ma'am," she replied, reluctantly, "and I could not help it, so I could not."

"Why, what has happened to vex you ? has any one ill-treated you ?" said Mrs. Marston, who had an esteem for the poor girl. "Come, come, you must not fret about it; only tell me what has vexed you."

"Oh ! ma'am, no one has ill-used me, ma'am ; but I can't but he vexed sometimes, ma'am, and fretted to see how things is going on. I have one wish, just one wish, ma'am, and if I got that, I'd ask no more," said the girl.

"And what is it ?" asked Mrs. Marston ; "what do you wish for ? speak plainly, Willett ; what is it ?"

"Ah ! ma'am, if I said it, maybe you might not be pleased. Don't ask me, ma'am," said the girl, dusting the books very hard, and tossing them down again with angry emphasis. "I don't desire anybody's harm, God knows ; but, for all that, I wish what I wish, and that is the truth."

"Why, Willett, I really cannot account for your strange habit of lately hinting, and insinuating, and al-

ways speaking riddles, and refusing to explain your
meaning. What *do* you mean? speak plainly. If
there are any dishonest practices going on, it is your
duty to say so distinctly."

"Oh! ma'am, it is just a wish I have. I wish ——;
but it's no matter. If I could once see the house clear
of that Frenchwoman ——"

"If you mean Mademoiselle de Barras, she is *a
lady,*" interrupted Mrs. Marston.

"Well, ma'am, I beg pardon," continued the woman;
"lady or no lady, it is all one to me; for I am very
sure, ma'am, she'll never leave the house till there is
something bad comes about; and—and ——. I can't
bring myself to talk to you about her, ma'am. I can't
say what I want to tell you; but—but ——. Oh, ma'am,
for God's sake, try and get her out, any way, no matter
how; try and get rid of her."

As she said this, the poor girl burst into a passionate
agony of tears, and Mrs. Marston and Rhoda looked on
in silent amazement, while she for some minutes continued to sob and weep.

The party were suddenly recalled from their various
reveries by a knock at the chamber-door. It opened,
and the subject of the girl's deprecatory entreaty entered. There was something unusually excited and assured in Mademoiselle de Barras' air and countenance;
perhaps she had a suspicion that she had been the topic
of their conversation. At all events, she looked round
upon them with a smile, in which there was something
supercilious, and even defiant; and, without waiting to
be invited, sate herself down, with a haughty air.

"I was about to ask you to sit down, mademoiselle,

but you have anticipated me," said Mrs. Marston, gravely. "You have something to say to me, I suppose; I am quite at leisure, so pray let me hear it now."

"Thank you, thank you, madame," replied she, with a sharp, and even scornful glance; "I ought to have asked your permission to sit; I forgot; but you have condescended to give it without my doing so; that was very kind, very kind, indeed."

"But I wish to know, mademoiselle, whether you have anything very particular to say to me?" said Mrs. Marston.

"You wish to know!—and why, pray, madame?" asked Mademoiselle de Barras, sharply.

"Because, unless it is something very urgent, I should prefer your talking to me some other time; as, at present, I desire to be alone with my daughter."

"Oh, ho! I ought to ask pardon, again," said mademoiselle, with the same glance, and the same smile. "I find I am *de trop*—quite in the way. Helas! I am very unfortunate to-day."

Mademoiselle de Barras made not the slightest movement, and it was evident that she was resolved to prolong her stay, in sheer defiance of Mrs. Marston's wishes.

"Mademoiselle, I conclude from your silence that you have nothing very pressing to say, and, therefore, must request that you will have the goodness to leave me for the present," said Mrs. Marston, who felt that the spirit of the French girl's conduct was too apparent not to have been understood by Rhoda and the servant, and that it was of a kind, for example sake, impossible to be submitted to, or tolerated.

Mademoiselle de Barras darted a fiery and insolent glance at Mrs. Marston, and was, doubtless, upon the point of precipitating the open quarrel which was impending, by setting her authority at defiance ; but she checked herself, and changed her line of operations.

"We are *not* alone madame," she said, with a heightened colour, and a slight toss of the head. "I was about to speak of Mr. Marston. I had something, not much, I confess, to say ; but before servants I shan't speak ; nor, indeed, *now* at all. So, madame, as you desire it, I shall no further interrupt you. Come, Miss Rhoda, come to the music-room, if you please, and finish your practice for to-day."

"You forget, mademoiselle, that I wish to have my daughter with me at present," said Mrs. Marston.

"I am very sorry, madame," said the French lady, with the same heightened colour and unpleasant smile, and her finely-pencilled brows just discernibly knit, so as to give a novel and menacing expression to her beautiful face—"I am very sorry, madame, but she must, so long as I remain accountable for her education, complete her allotted exercises at the appointed hours ; and nothing shall, I assure you, with my consent, interfere with these duties. Come, Miss Rhoda, precede me, if you please, to the music-room. Come, come."

"Stay where you are, Rhoda," said Mrs. Marston, firmly and gently, and betraying no symptom of excitement, except in a slight tremor of her voice, and a faint flush upon her cheek—"Stay where you are, my dear child. I am your *mother*, and, next to your father, have the first claim upon your obedience. Mademoiselle," she continued, addressing the Frenchwoman, calmly but firmly, "my daughter will remain here for some time longer, and you will have the goodness to withdraw. I insist upon it, Mademoiselle de Barras."

"I will not leave the room, I assure you, madame, without my pupil," retorted mademoiselle, with resolute insolence. "Your husband, madame, has invested me with this authority, and she *shall* obey me. Miss Rhoda, I say again, go down to the music-room."

"Remain where you are, Rhoda," said Mrs. Marston again. "Mademoiselle, you have long been acting as if your object were to provoke me to part with you. I find it impossible any longer to overlook this grossly disrespectful conduct; conduct of which I had, indeed, believed you absolutely incapable. Willett," she continued, addressing the maid, who was evidently bursting with rage at the scene she had just witnessed, "your master is, I believe, in the library; go down, and tell him that I entreat him to come here immediately."

The maid started on her mission with angry alacrity, darting a venomous glance at the handsome Frenchwoman as she passed.

Mademoiselle de Barras, meanwhile, sate, listless and defiant, in her chair, and tapping her little foot with angry excitement upon the floor. Rhoda sate close by her mother, holding her hand fast, and looking frightened, perplexed, and as if she were on the point of weeping. Mrs. Marston, though flushed and excited, yet maintained her dignified and grave demeanour. And thus, in silence, did they all three await the arrival of the arbiter to whom Mrs. Marston had so promptly appealed.

A few minutes more, and Marston entered the room.

Mademoiselle's expression changed as he did so to one
of dejected and sorrowful submission; and, as Marston's
eye lighted upon her, his brow darkened and his face
grew pale.

"Well, well—what is it?—what is all this?" he said,
glancing with a troubled eye from one to the other.
"Speak, some one. Mrs. Marston, *you* sent for me;
what is it?"

"I want to know, Mr. Marston, from your own lips,"
said the lady, in reply, "whether Rhoda is to obey me
or Mademoiselle de Barras?"

"Bah!—a question of women's prerogative," said
Marston, with muttered vehemence.

"Of a *wife's* and a *mother's* prerogative, Richard,"
said Mrs. Marston, with gentle emphasis. "A very
simple question, and one I should have thought needing
no deliberation to decide it."

"Well, child," said he, turning to Rhoda, with angry
irony, "pray what is all this fuss about? You are a
very ill-used young lady, I dare aver. Pray what
cruelties does Mademoiselle de Barras propose inflicting
upon you, that you need to appeal thus to your mother
for protection?"

"You quite mistake me, Richard," interposed Mrs.
Marston; "Rhoda is perfectly passive in the matter.
I simply wish to learn from you, in mademoiselle's pre-
sence, whether I or she is to command my daughter?"

"*Command!*" said Marston, evading the direct appeal; "and pray what is all this *commanding* about?—
what do you want the girl to do?"

"*I* wish her to remain here with me for a little time,
and mademoiselle, knowing this, desires her instantly to

go to the music-room, and leave me. That is all," said
Mrs. Marston.

"And pray, is there nothing to make her going to
the music-room advisable or necessary? Has she no
music to learn, or studies to pursue? Psha! Mrs.
Marston, what needs all this noise about nothing? Go,
miss," he added, sharply and peremptorily, addressing
Rhoda, "go this moment to the music-room."

The girl glided from the room, and mademoiselle, as
she followed, shot a glance at Mrs. Marston which
wounded and humbled her in the dust.

"Oh! Richard, Richard, if you knew all, you would
not have subjected me to this indignity," she said; and
throwing her arms about his neck, she wept, for the
first time for many a long year, upon his breast.

Marston was embarrassed and agitated. He disen-
gaged her arms from his neck, and placed her gently in
a chair. She sobbed on for some time in silence—a
silence which Marston himself did not essay to break.
He walked to the door, apparently with the intention of
leaving her. He hesitated, however, and returned;
took a hurried turn through the room; hesitated again;
sat down; then returned to the door, not to depart, but
to close it carefully, and walked gloomily to the window,
whence he looked forth, buried in agitating and absorbing thoughts.

"Richard, to you this seems a trifling thing; but, indeed, it is not so," said Mrs. Marston, sadly.

"You are very right, Gertrude," he said, quickly,
and almost with a start; "it is very far from a trifling
thing; it is very important."

"You don't blame me, Richard?" said she.

R

"I blame nobody," said he.

"Indeed, I never meant to offend you, Richard," she urged.

"Of course not; no, no; I never said so," he interrupted, sarcastically; "what could you gain by that?"

"Oh! Richard, better feelings have governed me," she said, in a melancholy and reproachful tone.

"Well, well, I suppose so," he said; and after an interval, he added, abstractedly, "This cannot, however, go on; no, no — it *cannot*. Sooner or later it must have come; better at once—better *now*."

"What do you mean, Richard?" she said, greatly alarmed, she knew not why. "What are you resolving upon? Dear Richard, in mercy tell me. I implore of you, tell me."

"Why, Gertrude, you seem to me to fancy that, because I don't talk about what is passing, that I don't *see* it either. Now this is quite a mistake," said Marston, calmly and resolutely. "I have long observed your growing dislike of Mademoiselle de Barras. I have thought it over; this *fracas* of to-day has determined me; it is decisive. I suppose you now wish her to *go*, as earnestly as you once wished her to stay. You need not answer. I know it. I neither ask nor care to whose fault I am to attribute these changed feelings— female caprice accounts sufficiently for it; but whatever the cause, the effect is undeniable; and the only way to deal satisfactorily with *it* is, to dismiss mademoiselle at once. You need take no part in the matter; I take it all upon myself. To-morrow morning she shall have left this house. I have said it, and am perfectly resolved."

As he thus spoke, as if to avoid the possibility of any further discussion, he turned abruptly from her, and left the room.

The extreme agitation which she had just undergone combined with her physical delicacy to bring on an hysterical attack; and poor Mrs. Marston, with an aching head and a heavy heart, lay down upon her bed. She had swallowed an opiate, and before ten o'clock upon that night, an eventful one as it proved, she had sunk into a profound slumber.

Some hours after this, she became in a confused way conscious of her husband's presence in the room. He was walking, with an agitated mien, up and down the chamber, and casting from time to time looks of great trouble toward the bed where she lay. Though the presence of her husband was a strange and long un-wonted occurrence there, at such an hour, and though she felt the strangeness of the visit, the power of the opiate overwhelmed her so, that she could only see this apparition gliding slowly back and forward before her, with the passive wonder and curiosity with which one awaits the issue of an interesting dream.

For a time she lay once more in an uneasy sleep; but still, throughout even this, she was conscious of his pre-sence; and when, a little while after, she again saw him, he was not walking to and fro before the foot of the bed, but sitting beside her, with one hand laid upon the pillow on which her head was resting, the other sup-porting his chin. He was looking steadfastly upon her, with a changed face, an expression of bitter sorrow, compunction, and tenderness. There was not one trace of sternness; all was softened. The look was what she

fancied he might have turned upon her had she lain
there dead, ere yet the love of their early and ill-fated
union had grown cold in his heart. There was something in it which reminded her of days and feelings
gone, never to return. And while she looked in his
face with a sweet and mournful fascination, tears unconsciously wet the pillow on which her poor head was
resting. Unable to speak, unable to move, she heard
him say—

"It was not your fault, Gertrude—it was not yours,
nor mine. There is a destiny in these things too strong
for us. Past is past—what is done, is done for ever;
and even were it all to do over again, what power have
I to mend it? No, no; how could I contend against
the combined power of passions, circumstances, influences—in a word, of FATE? You have been good and
patient, while I——; but no matter. Your lot, Gertrude, is a happier one than mine."

Mrs. Marston heard him and saw him, but she had
not the power, nor even the will, herself to speak or
move. He appeared before her passive sense like the
phantasm of a dream. He stood up at the bedside, and
looked on her steadfastly, with the same melancholy
expression. For a moment he stooped over her, as if
about to kiss her face, but checked himself, stood erect
again at the bedside, then suddenly turned; the curtain
fell back into its place, and she saw him no more.

With a strange mixture of sweet and bitter feelings
this vision rested upon the memory of Mrs. Marston,
until, gradually, deep slumber again overcame her senses,
and the incident and all its attendant circumstances faded
into oblivion.

It was past eight o'clock when Mrs. Marston awoke next morning. The sun was shining richly and cheerily in at the windows; and as the remembrance of Marston's visit to her chamber, and the unwonted manifestations of tenderness and compunction which accompanied it, returned, she felt something like hope and happiness, to which she had long been a stranger, flutter her heart. The pleasing reverie to which she was yielding was, however, interrupted. The sound of stifled sobbing in the room reached her ear, and, pushing back the bed-curtains, and leaning forward to look, she saw her maid, Willett, sitting with her back to the wall, crying bitterly, and striving, as it seemed, to stifle her sobs with her apron, which was wrapped about her face.

"Willett, Willett, is it *you* who are sobbing? What is the matter with you, child?" said Mrs. Marston, anxiously.

The girl checked herself, dried her eyes hastily, and walking briskly to a little distance, as if engaged in arranging the chamber, she said, with an affectation of carelessness—

"Oh, ma'am, it is nothing; nothing at all, indeed, ma'am."

Mrs. Marston remained silent for a time, while all her vague apprehensions returned. Meantime the girl continued to shove the chairs hither and thither, and to arrange and disarrange everything in the room with a fidgety industry, intended to cover her agitation. A few minutes, however, served to weary her of this, for she abruptly stopped, stood by the bedside, and, looking at her mistress, burst into tears.

"Good God! what is it?" said Mrs. Marston, shocked

and even terrified, while new alarms displaced her old ones. "Is Miss Rhoda—can it be—is she—is my darling well?"

"Oh, yes, ma'am," answered the maid, "very well, ma'am; she is up, and out walking, and knows nothing of all this."

"All *what?*" urged Mrs. Marston. Tell me, tell me, Willett, what has happened. What is it? Speak, child; say what it is?"

"Oh, ma'am! oh, my poor dear mistress!" continued the girl, and stopped, almost stifled with sobs.

"Willett, you must speak; you must say what is the matter. I implore of you—I desire you!" urged the distracted lady. Still the girl, having made one or two ineffectual efforts to speak, continued to sob.

"Willett, you will drive me mad. For mercy's sake, for God's sake, speak—tell me what it is!" cried the unhappy lady.

"Oh, ma'am, it is—it is about the master," sobbed the girl.

"Why he can't—he has not—oh, merciful God! he has not hurt himself!" she almost screamed.

"No, ma'am, no; not *himself;* no, no, but——" and again she hesitated.

"But *what?* Speak out, Willett; dear Willett have mercy on me, and speak out," cried her wretched mistress.

"Oh, ma'am, don't be fretted; don't take it to heart, ma'am," said the maid, clasping her hands together in anguish.

"Anything, anything, Willett; only speak at once," she answered.

"Well, ma'am, it is soon said—it is easy told. The master, ma'am—the master is gone with the French-woman; they went in the travelling coach last night, ma'am; he is gone away with her, ma'am; that is all."

Mrs. Marston looked at the girl with a gaze of stupi-fied, stony terror; not a muscle of her face moved; not one heaving respiration showed that she was living. Motionless, with this fearful look fixed upon the girl, and her thin hands stretched towards her, she remained, second after second. At last her outstretched hands began to tremble more and more violently; and as if for the first time the knowledge of his calamity had reached her, with a cry, as though body and soul were parting, she fell back motionless in her bed.

Several hours had passed before Mrs. Marston was restored to consciousness. To this state of utter insen-sibility, one of silent, terrified stupor succeeded; and it was not until she saw her daughter Rhoda standing at her bedside, weeping, that she found voice and recollec-tion to speak.

"My child; my darling, my poor child," she cried, sob-bing piteously, as she drew her to her heart and looked in her face alternately—" my darling, my darling child!"

Rhoda could only weep, and return her poor mother's caresses in silence. Too young and inexperienced to un-derstand the full extent and nature of this direful cala-mity, the strange occurrence, the general and apparent consternation of the whole household, and the spectacle of her mother's agony, had filled her with fear, perplex-ity, and anguish. Scared and stunned with a vague sense of danger, like a young bird that, for the first time, cowers under a thunder-storm, she nestled in her

mother's bosom ; there, with a sense of protection, and
of boundless love and tenderness, she lay frightened,
wondering, and weeping.

Two or three days passed, and Dr. Danvers came and
sate for several hours with poor Mrs. Marston. To
comfort and console were, of course, out of his power.
The nature of the bereavement, far more terrible than
death—its recent occurrence—the distracting consciousness of all its complicated consequences—rendered this a
hopeless task. She bowed herself under the blow with
the submission of a broken heart. The hope to which
she had clung for years had vanished ; the worst that
ever her imagination feared had come in earnest.

One idea was now constantly present in her mind.
She felt a sad, but immoveable assurance, that she should
not live long, and the thought, " what will become of my
darling when I am gone ; who will guard and love my
child when I am in my grave ; to whom is she to look
for tenderness and protection then?" perpetually haunted
her, and superadded the pangs of a still wilder despair
to the desolation of a broken heart.

It was not for more than a week after this event, that
one day Willett, with a certain air of anxious mystery,
entered the silent and darkened chamber where Mrs.
Marston lay. She had a letter in her hand ; the seal
and hand-writing were Mr. Marston's. It was long before the injured wife was able to open it ; when she did
so, the following sentences met her eye :—

" GERTRUDE,—You can be ignorant neither of the
nature nor of the consequences of the decisive step I have
taken : I do not seek to excuse it. For the censure of

the world, its meddling and mouthing hypocrisy, I'care absolutely nothing; I have long set *it* at defiance. And you yourself, Gertrude, when you deliberately reconsider the circumstances of estrangement and coldness under which, though beneath the same roof, we have lived for years, without either sympathy or confidence, can scarcely, if at all, regret the rupture of a tie which had long ceased to be anything better than an irksome and galling formality. I do not desire to attribute to you the smallest blame. There was an incompatibility, not of temper but of feelings, which made us *strangers*, though calling one another man and wife. Upon this fact I rest my own justification; our living together under these circumstances was, I dare say, equally undesired by us both. It was, in fact, but a deference to the formal hypocrisy of the world. At all events, the irrevocable act which separates us for ever is done, and I have now merely to state so much of my intentions as may relate in anywise to your future arrangements. I have written to your cousin, and former guardian, Mr. Lattimer, telling him how matters stand between us. You, I told him, shall have, without opposition from me, the whole of your own fortune to your own separate use, together with whatever shall be mutually agreed upon as reasonable, from my income, for your support and that of my daughter. It will be necessary to complete your arrangements with expedition, as I purpose returning to Gray Forest in about three weeks ; and as, of course, a meeting between you and those by whom I shall be accompanied is wholly out of the question, you will see the expediency of losing no time in adjusting everything for your's and my daughter's departure. In the details, of course, I shall not interfere. I think I have made myself clearly intelligible, and would recommend your communicating at once with Mr. Lattimer, with a view. to completing temporary arrangements, until your final plans shall have been decided upon.

" RICHARD MARSTON."

The reader can easily conceive the feelings with which this letter was perused. We·shall not attempt to describe them; nor shall we weary his patience by a detail of all the circumstances attending Mrs. Marston's departure. Suffice it to mention that, in less than a fortnight after the receipt of the letter which we have just copied, she had for ever left the mansion of Gray Forest.

In a small house, in a sequestered part of the rich county of Warwick, the residence of Mrs. Marston and her daughter was for the present fixed. And there, for a time, the heartbroken and desolate lady enjoyed, at least, the privilege of an immunity from the intrusions of all external trouble. But the blow, under which the feeble remains of her health and strength were gradually to sink, had struck too surely home; and, from month to month—almost from week to week—the progress of decay was perceptible.

Meanwhile, though grieved and humbled, and longing to comfort his unhappy mother, Charles Marston, for the present absolutely dependant upon his father, had no choice but to remain at Cambridge, and to pursue his studies there.

At Gray Forest Marston and the partner of his guilt continued to live. The old servants were all gradually dismissed, and new ones hired by Mademoiselle de Barras. There they dwelt, shunned by everybody, in a stricter and more desolate seclusion than ever. The novelty of the unrestraint and licence of their new mode of life speedily passed away, and with it the excited and guilty sense of relief which had for a time produced a false and hollow gaiety. The sense of security prompted in mademoiselle a hundred indulgences which, in her former precarious position, she would not have dreamed of. Outbreaks of temper, sharp and sometimes violent, began to manifest themselves on her part, and renewed disappointment and blacker remorse to darken the soul of Marston himself. Often, in the dead of night, the servants would overhear their bitter and fierce altercations ringing through the melancholy mansion, and often the reckless use of terrible and mysterious epithets of crime. Their quarrels increased in violence and in frequency; and, before two years had passed, feelings of bitterness, hatred, and dread, alone seemed to subsist between them. Yet upon Marston she continued to exercise a powerful and mysterious influence. There was a dogged, apathetic submission on his part, and a growing insolence upon hers, constantly more and more strikingly visible. Neglect, disorder, and decay, too, were more than ever apparent in the dreary air of the place.

Doctor Danvers, save by rumour and conjecture, knew nothing of Marston and his abandoned companion. He had, more than once, felt a strong disposition to visit Gray Forest, and expostulate, face to face, with its guilty proprietor. This idea, however, he had, upon consideration, dismissed; not on account of any shrinking from the possible repulses and affronts to which the attempt might subject him, but from a thorough conviction that the endeavour would be utterly fruitless for good, while it might, very obviously, expose him to painful misinterpretation and suspicion, and leave it to be imagined that he had been influenced, if by no meaner motive, at least by the promptings of a coarse curiosity.

Meanwhile he maintained a correspondence with Mrs.

Marston, and had even once or twice since her departure
visited her.   Latterly, however, this correspondence
had been a good deal interrupted, and its intervals had
been supplied occasionally by Rhoda, whose letters, although she herself appeared unconscious of the mournful
event the approach of which they too plainly indicated,
were painful records of the rapid progress of mortal
decay.

He had just received one of those ominous letters, at
the little post-office in the town we have already mentioned, and, full of the melancholy news it contained, Dr.
Danvers was returning slowly towards his home.   As he
rode into a lonely road, traversing an undulating tract of
some three miles in length, the singularity, it may be, of
his costume attracted the eye of another passenger, who
was, as it turned out, no other than Marston himself.
For two or three miles of this desolate road, their ways
happened to lie together.   Marston's first impulse was
to avoid the clergyman; his second, which he obeyed,
was to join company, and ride along with him, at all
events, for so long as would show that he shrank from no
encounter which fortune or accident presented.   There
was a spirit of bitter defiance in this, which cost him a
painful effort.

"How do you do, Parson Danvers?" said Marston,
touching his hat with the handle of his whip.

Danvers thought he had seldom seen a man so changed
in so short a time.   His face had grown sallow and
wasted, and his figure slightly stooped, with an appearance almost of feebleness.

"Mr. Marston," said the clergyman, gravely, and almost sternly, though with some embarrassment, "it is

a long time since you and I have seen one another, and many and painful events have passed in the interval. I scarce know upon what terms we meet. I am prompted to speak to you, and in a tone, perhaps, which you will hardly brook ; and yet, if we keep company, as it seems likely we may, I cannot, and I ought not, to be silent."

" Well, Mr. Danvers, I accept the condition—speak what you will," said Marston, with a gloomy promptitude. " If you exceed your privilege, and grow uncivil, I need but use my spurs, and leave you behind me preaching to the winds."

" Ah ! Mr. Marston," said Dr. Danvers, almost sadly, after a considerable pause, " when I saw you close beside me, my heart was troubled within me."

" You looked on me as something from the nether world, and expected to see the cloven hoof," said Marston, bitterly, and raising his booted foot a little as he spoke; " but, after all, I am but a vulgar sinner of flesh and blood, without enough of the preternatural about me to frighten an old nurse, much less to agitate a pillar of the Church."

" Mr. Marston, you talk sarcastically ; but you *feel* that recent circumstances, as well as old recollections, might well disturb and trouble me at sight of you," answered Dr. Danvers.

" Well—yes—perhaps it is so," said Marston, hastily and sullenly, and became silent for a while.

" My heart is full, Mr. Marston ; charged with grief, when I think of the sad history of those with whom, in my mind, you must ever be associated," said Doctor Danvers.

"Ay, to be sure," said Marston, with stern impatience ;

" but, then, you have much to console you. You have
got your comforts and your respectability ; all the dearer, too, from the contrast of other people's misfortunes
and degradations ; then you have your religion moreover ——"

" Yes," interrupted Danvers, earnestly, and hasten-
ing to avoid a sneer upon this subject ; "God be blessed, I am an humble follower of his gracious Son, our
Redeemer ; and though, I trust, I should bear with
patient submission whatever chastisement in his wisdom
and goodness he might see fit to inflict upon me, yet I
do praise and bless him for the mercy which has hitherto
spared me, and I do feel that mercy all the more profoundly, from the afflictions and troubles with which I
daily see others overtaken."

" And in the matter of piety and decorum, doubtless, you bless God also," said Marston, sarcastically,
" that you are not as other men are, nor even as this
publican."

" Nay, Mr. Marston ; God forbid I should harden my
sinful heart with the wicked pride of the Pharisee. Evil
and corrupt am I already—over much. Too well I know
the vileness of my heart, to make myself righteous in
my own eyes," replied Dr. Danvers, humbly. " But,
sinner as I am, I am yet a messenger of God, whose
mission is one of authority to his fellow-sinners ; and
woe is me if I speak not the truth at all seasons, and in
all places where my words may be profitably heard."

" Well, Doctor Danvers, it seems you think it your
duty to speak to me, of course, respecting my conduct
and my spiritual state. I shall save you the pain and
trouble of opening the subject ; I shall state the case for

you in two words," said Marston, almost fiercely. "I
have put away my wife without just cause, and am living
in sin with another woman. Come, what have you to say
on this theme? Speak out. Deal with me as roughly
as you will, I will hear it, and answer you again."

"Alas, Mr. Marston! and do not these things trouble
you?" exclaimed Dr. Danvers, earnestly. "Do they
not weigh heavy upon your conscience? Ah, sir, do
you not remember that, slowly and surely, you are
drawing towards the hour of death, and the day of
judgment?"

"The hour of death! Yes, I know it is coming, and
I await it with indifference. But, for the day of judgment, with its books and trumpets! my dear doctor,
pray don't expect to frighten me with that."

Marston spoke with an angry scorn, which had the
effect of interrupting the conversation for some moments.

They rode on, side by side, for a long time, without
speaking. At length, however, Marston unexpectedly
broke the silence—

"Doctor Danvers," said he, "you asked me some
time ago if I feared the hour of death, and the day of
judgment. I answered you truly, I do *not* fear them;
nay *death*, I think, I could meet with a happier and a
quieter heart than any other chance that can befal me;
but there are other fears; fears that *do* trouble me
much."

Doctor Danvers looked inquiringly at him; but neither
spoke for a time.

"You have not seen the catastrophe of the tragedy
yet," said Marston, with a stern, stony look, made more

horrible by a forced smile and something like a shudder.
"I wish I could tell you—*you*, Doctor Danvers—for
you are honourable and gentle-hearted. I wish I durst
tell you what I fear; the only, *only* thing I really do
fear. No mortal knows it but myself, and I see it com·
ing upon me with slow, but unconquerable power. Oh,
God—dreadful Spirit—spare me!"

Again they were silent, and again Marston resumed—

"Doctor Danvers, don't mistake me," he said, turning sharply, and fixing his eyes with a strange expression
upon his companion. "I dread nothing *human;* I fear
neither death, nor disgrace, nor eternity; I have no
secrets to keep—no exposures to apprehend; but I
dread—I dread ——"

He paused, scowled darkly, as if stung with pain,
turned away, muttering to himself, and gradually became much excited.

"I can't tell you now, sir, and I won't," he said, abruptly and fiercely, and with a countenance darkened
with a wild and appalling rage that was wholly unaccountable. "I see you searching me with your eyes.
Suspect what you will, sir, you shan't inveigle me into
admissions. Ay, pry—whisper—stare—question, conjecture, sir—I suppose I must endure the world's impertinence, but d—n me if I gratify it."

It would not be easy to describe Dr. Danvers' astonishment at this unaccountable explosion of fury. He was
resolved, however, to bear his companion's violence with
temper.

They rode on slowly for fully ten minutes in utter
silence, except that Marston occasionally muttered to
himself, as it seemed, in excited abstraction. Danvers

had at first felt naturally offended at the violent and
insulting tone in which he had been so unexpectedly and
unprovokedly addressed; but this feeling of irritation
was but transient, and some fearful suspicions as to Marston's sanity flitted through his mind.   In a calmer and
more dogged tone, his companion now addressed him :—

"There is little profit you see, doctor, in worrying
me about your religion," said Marston.   "It is but
sowing the wind, and reaping the whirlwind ; and, to
say the truth, the longer you pursue it, the less I am in
the mood to listen.   If ever *you* are cursed and perse-
cuted as I have been, you will understand how little
tolerant of gratuitous vexations and contradictions a man
may become.   We have squabbled over religion long
enough, and each holds his own faith still.   Continue
to sun yourself in your happy delusions, and leave me
untroubled to tread the way of my own dark and cheer-
less destiny."

Thus saying, he made a sullen gesture of farewell,
and spurring his horse, crossed the broken fence at the
roadside, and so, at a listless pace, through gaps and
by farm-roads, penetrated towards his melancholy and
guilty home.

Two years had now passed since the decisive event
which had for ever separated Marston from her who
had loved him so devotedly and so fatally ; two years to
him of disappointment, abasement, and secret rage ; two
years to her of gentle and heart-broken submission to
the chastening hand of heaven.   At the end of this time
she died.   Marston read the letter that announced the
event with a stern look, and silently, but the shock he
felt was terrific.   No man is so self-abandoned to de-

s

spair and degradation, that at some casual moment
thoughts of amendment—some gleams of hope, however
faint and transient, from the distant future—will not
visit him. With Marston, those thoughts had somehow ever been associated with vague ideas of a reconci-
liation with the being whom he had forsaken—good
and pure, and looking at her from the darkness and
distance of his own fallen state, almost angelic as she
seemed. But she was now dead; he could make her
no atonement; she could never smile forgiveness upon
him. This long-familiar image—the last that had reflected for him one ray of the lost peace and love of
happier times—had vanished, and henceforward there
was before him nothing but storm and fear.

Marston's embarrassed fortunes made it to him an
object to resume the portion of his income heretofore
devoted to the separate maintenance of his wife and
daughter. In order to effect this, it became, of course,
necessary to recall his daughter, Rhoda, and fix her
residence once more at Gray Forest. No more dreadful
penalty could have been inflicted upon the poor girl—
no more agonising ordeal than that she was thus doomed
to undergo. She had idolised her mother, and now
adored her memory. She knew that Mademoiselle de
Barras had betrayed and indirectly *murdered* the parent
she had so devotedly loved; she knew that that woman
had been the curse, the fate of her family, and she regarded her naturally with feelings of mingled terror and
abhorrence, the intensity of which was indescribable.

The few scattered friends and relatives, whose sym-
pathies had been moved by the melancholy fate of poor
Mrs. Marston, were unanimously agreed that the in-

tended removal of the young and innocent daughter to the polluted mansion of sin and shame, was too intolerably revolting to be permitted. But each of these virtuous individuals unhappily thought it the duty of the *others* to interpose ; and with a running commentary of wonder and reprobation, and much virtuous criticism, events were suffered uninterruptedly to take their sinister and melancholy course.

It was about two months after the death of Mrs. Marston, and on a bleak and ominous night at the wintry end of autumn, that poor Rhoda, in deep mourning, and pale with grief and agitation, descended from a chaise at the well-known door of the mansion of Gray Forest. Whether from consideration for her feelings, or, as was more probable, from pure indifference, Rhoda was conducted, on her arrival, direct to her own chamber, and it was not until the next morning that she saw her father. He entered her room unexpectedly ; he was very pale, and as she thought, greatly altered, but he seemed perfectly collected, and free from agitation. The marked and even shocking change in his appearance, and perhaps even the trifling though painful circumstance that he wore no mourning for the beloved being who was gone, caused her, after a moment's mute gazing in his face, to burst into an irrepressible flood of tears.

Marston waited stoically until the paroxysm had subsided, and then taking her hand, with a look in which a dogged sternness was contending with something like shame, he said :—

"There, there ; you can weep when I am gone. I shan't say very much to you at present, Rhoda, and

only wish you to attend to me for one minute. Listen,
Rhoda ; the lady whom you have been in the habit
(here he slightly averted his eyes) of calling Mademoiselle de Barras, is no longer so ; she is married ; she is
my wife, and consequently you will treat her with the
respect due to"—he would have said "a mother," but
could not, and supplied the phrase by adding, " to that
relation."

Rhoda was unable to speak, but almost unconsciously
bowed her head in token of attention and submission,
and her father pressed her hand more kindly, as he continued :—

" I have always found you a dutiful and obedient
child, Rhoda, and expected no other conduct from you.
Mrs. Marston will treat you with proper kindness and consideration, and desires me to say that you can, whenever
you please, keep strictly to yourself, and need not, unless
you feel so disposed, attend the regular meals of the
family. This privilege may suit your present depressed
spirits, and you must not scruple to use it."

After a few words more, Marston withdrew, leaving
his daughter to her reflections, and bleak and bitter
enough they were.

Some weeks passed away, and perhaps we shall best
consult our readers' ease by substituting for the formal
precision of narrative, a few extracts from the letters
which Rhoda wrote to her brother, still at Cambridge.
These will convey her own impressions respecting the
scenes and personages among whom she was now to
move.

" The house and place are much neglected, and the
former in some parts suffered almost to go to decay.
The windows broken in the last storm, nearly eight

months ago, they tell me, are still unmended, and the
roof, too, unrepaired. The pretty garden, near the
well, among the lime-trees, that our darling mother was
so fond of, is all but obliterated with weeds and grass,
and since my first visit I have not had heart to go near
it again. All the old servants are gone ; new faces
everywhere.

"I have been obliged several times, through fear of
offending my father, to join the party in the drawing-
room. You may conceive what I felt at seeing mademoiselle in the place once filled by our dear mamma. I
was so choked with sorrow, bitterness, and indignation,
and my heart so palpitated, that I could not speak, and
I believe they thought I was going to faint. Mademoiselle looked very angry, but my father pretending to
show me, heaven knows what, from the window, led me
to it, and the air revived me a little. Mademoiselle (for
I cannot call her by her new name) is altered a good
deal—more, however, in the character than in the con-
tour of her face and figure. Certainly, however, she has
grown a good deal fuller, and her colour is higher ; and
whether it is fancy or not, I cannot say, but certainly to
me it seems that the expression of her face has acquired
something habitually lowering and malicious, and which,
I know not how, inspires me with an undefinable dread.
She has, however, been tolerably civil to me, but seems
contemptuous and rude to my father, and I am afraid he
is very wretched. I have seen them exchange such
looks, and overheard such intemperate and even appalling
altercations between them, as indicate something worse
and deeper than ordinary ill-will. This makes me additionally wretched, especially as I cannot help thinking
that some mysterious cause enables her to frighten and
tyrannise over my poor father. I sometimes think he
absolutely detests her; yet, though fiery altercations en-
sue, he ultimately submits to this bad and cruel woman.
Oh, my dear Charles, you have no idea of the shocking,
or rather the terrifying, reproaches I have heard inter-

changed between them, as I accidently passed the room
where they were sitting—such terms as have sent me to
my room, feeling as if I were in a horrid dream, and
made me cry and tremble for hours after I got there.
. . . . . I see my father very seldom, and when I
do, he takes but little notice of me. . . . . . .
Poor Willett, you know, returned with me. She accom-
panies me in my walks, and is constantly dropping hints
about mademoiselle, from which I know not what to gather. . . . .

"I often fear that my father has some secret and
mortal ailment. He generally looks ill, and sometimes
quite *wretchedly*. He came twice lately to my room, I
think to speak to me on some matter of importance; but
he said only a sentence or two, and even these broken
and incoherent. He seemed unable to command spirits
for the interview; and, indeed, he grew so agitated and
strange, that I was alarmed, and felt greatly relieved
when he left me. . . . .

"I do not, you see, disguise my feelings, dear Charles;
I do not conceal from you the melancholy and anguish
of my present situation. How intensely I long for your
promised arrival. I have not a creature to whom I can
say one word in confidence, except poor Willett; who,
though very good-natured, and really dear to me, is yet
far from being a companion. I sometimes think my intense anxiety to see you here is almost selfish; for I
know you will feel as acutely as I do, the terrible change
observable everywhere. But I cannot help longing for
your return, dear Charles, and counting the days and the
very hours till you arrive. . . . .

"Be cautious, in writing to me, not to say anything
which you would not wish mademoiselle to see; for
Willett tells me that she *knows* that she often examines,
and even intercepts the letters that arrive; and, though
Willett may be mistaken, and I hope she is, yet it is better that you should be upon your guard. Ever since I
heard this, I have brought my letters to the post-office

myself, instead of leaving them with the rest upon the
hall table; and you know it is a long walk for me. . .

. . . .

"I go to church every Sunday, and take Willett along
with me.   No one from this seems to think of doing so
but ourselves.   I see the Mervyns there.   Mrs. Mervyn
is particularly kind; and I know that she wishes to
offer me an asylum at Newton Park; and you cannot
think with how much tenderness and delicacy she
conveys the wish.   But I dare not hint the subject to
my father; and, earnestly as I desire it, I could not but
feel that I should go there, not to visit, but to *reside*.
And so even in this, in many respects, delightful project, is mingled the bitter apprehension of dependence—
something so humiliating, that, kindly and delicately as
the offer is made, I could not bring myself to embrace it.
I have a great deal to say to you, and long to see you."

. . . .

These extracts will enable the reader to form a
tolerably accurate idea of the general state of affairs
at Gray Forest.   Some particulars must, however, be
added.

Marston continued to be the same gloomy and joyless
being as heretofore.   Sometimes moody and apathetic,
sometimes wayward and even savage, but never for a
moment at ease, never social—an isolated, disdainful,
ruined man.

One day as Rhoda sate and read under the shade of
some closely-interwoven evergreens, in a lonely and shel-
tered part of the neglected pleasure-grounds, with her
honest maid Willett in attendance, she was surprised
by the sudden appearance of her father, who stood unexpectedly before her.   Though his attitude for some
time was fixed, his countenance was troubled with

anxiety and pain, and his sunken eyes rested upon her with a fiery and fretted gaze. He seemed lost in thought for a while, and then, touching Willett sharply on the shoulder, said abruptly—

" Go ; I shall call you when you are wanted. Walk down that alley. And, as he spoke, he indicated with his walking-cane the course he desired her to take.

When the maid was sufficiently distant to be quite out of hearing, Marston sate down beside Rhoda upon the bench, and took her hand in silence. His grasp was cold, and alternately relaxed and contracted with an agitated uncertainty, while his eyes were fixed upon the ground, and he seemed meditating how to open the conversation. At last, as if suddenly awaking from a fearful reverie, he said—

" You correspond with Charles ?"

" Yes, sir," she replied, with the respectful formality prescribed by the usages of the time, " we correspond regularly."

" Ay, ay ; and, pray, when did you last hear from him ?" he continued.

" About a month since, sir," she replied.

" Ha !—and—and—was there nothing strange—nothing—nothing mysterious and menacing in his letter? Come, come, you know what I speak of." He stopped abruptly, and stared in her face with an agitated gaze.

" No, indeed, sir; there was not anything of the kind," she replied.

" I have been greatly shocked, I may say incensed," said Marston, excitedly, " by a passage in his last letter to me. Not that it says anything specific ; but—but it amazes me—it enrages me."

He again checked himself, and Rhoda, much surprised, and even shocked, said, stammeringly—

"I am sure, sir, that dear Charles would not intentionally say or do anything that could offend you.

"Ah, as to that, I believe so, too. But it is not with *him* I am indignant; no, no. Poor Charles! I believe he *is*, as you say, disposed to conduct himself as a son ought to do, respectfully and obediently. Yes, yes, Charles is very well; but I fear he is leading a bad life, notwithstanding—a very bad life. He is becoming subject to *influences* which never visit or torment the good; believe me, he is."

Marston shook his head, and muttered to himself, with a look of almost craven anxiety, and then whispered to his daughter—

"Just read this, and then tell me is it not so. Read it, read it, and pronounce."

As he thus spoke, he placed in her hand the letter of which he had spoken, and with the passage to which he invited her attention folded down. It was to the following effect :—

"I cannot tell you how shocked I have been by a piece of scandal, as I must believe it, conveyed to me in an anonymous letter, and which is of so very delicate a nature, that without your special command I should hesitate to pain you by its recital. I trust it may be utterly false. Indeed I assume it to be so. It is enough to say that it is of a very distressing nature, and affects the lady (Mademoiselle de Barras) whom you have recently honoured with your hand."

"*Now* you see," cried Marston, with a shuddering fierceness, as she returned the letter with a blanched

cheek and trembling hand—"now you see it all.   Are
you stupid?—the stamp of the cloven hoof—eh ?"

Rhoda, unable to gather his meaning, but, at the same
time, with a heart full and trembling very much, stammered a few frightened words, and became silent.

"It is *he*, I tell you, that does it all; and if Charles
were not living an evil life, he could not have spread his
nets for him," said Marston, vehemently.   "He can't go
near anything good; but, like a scoundrel, he knows
where to find a congenial nature; and when he does, he
has skill enough to practise upon it.   I know him well,
and his arts and his smiles; ay, and his scowls and his
grins, too.   He goes, like his master, up and down, and
to and fro upon the earth, for ceaseless mischief.   There
is not a friend of mine he can get hold of, but he whispers in his ear some damned slander of me.   He is
drawing them all into a common understanding against
me; and he takes an actual pleasure in telling me how
the thing goes on—how, one after the other, he has converted my friends into conspirators and libellers, to blast
my character, and take my life, and now the monster
essays to lure my children into the hellish confedera-
tion."

"Who is he, father, who is he?" faltered Rhoda.

"You never saw him," retorted Marston, sternly.
"No, no; you can't have seen him, and you probably
never will; but if he *does* come here again, don't listen
to him.   He is half-fiend and half-idiot, and no good
comes of his mouthing and muttering.   Avoid him, I
warn you, avoid him.   Let me see: how shall I describe
him?   Let me see.   You remember—you remember
Berkley—Sir Wynston Berkley.   Well, he greatly re-

sembles that dead villain : he has all the same grins, and shrugs, and monkey airs, and his face and figure are like.   But *he* is a grimed, ragged, wasted piece of sin, little better than a beggar—a shrunken, malignant libel on the human shape.   Avoid him, I tell you, avoid him : he is steeped in lies and poison, like the very serpent that betrayed us.   Beware of him, I say; for if he once gains your ear, he will delude you, spite of all your vigilance ; he will make you his accomplice, and thenceforth, inevitably, there is nothing but mortal and implacable hatred between us !"

Frightened at this wild language, Rhoda did not answer, but looked up in his face in silence.   A fearful transformation was there—a scowl so livid and maniacal, that her very senses seemed leaving her with terror. Perhaps the sudden. alteration observable in her countenance, as this spectacle so unexpectedly encountered her, recalled him to himself; for he added, hurriedly, and in a tone of gentler meaning—

"Rhoda, Rhoda, watch and pray.   My daughter, my child ! keep your heart pure, and nothing bad can approach you for ill.   No, no ; you are good, and the good need not fear !"

Suddenly Marston burst into tears, as he ended this sentence, and wept long and convulsively.   She did not dare to speak, or even to move ; but after a while he ceased, appeared uneasy, half ashamed and half angry ; and looking with a horrified and bewildered glance into her face, he said—

"Rhoda, child, what—what have I said?   My God! what have I been saying ?   Did I—*do* I look ill ?   Oh, Rhoda, Rhoda, may you never feel this !"

He turned away from her without awaiting her answer, and walked away with the appearance of intense agitation, as if to leave her. He turned again, however, and with a face pallid and sunken as death, approached her slowly—

"Rhoda," said he, "don't tell what I have said to any one—don't, I conjure you, even to Charles. I speak too much at random, and say more than I mean—a foolish, rambling habit: so do not repeat one word of it, not one word to any living mortal. You and I, Rhoda, must have our little secrets."

He ended with an attempt at a smile, so obviously painful and fear-stricken, that as he walked hurriedly away, the astounded girl burst into a bitter flood of tears. What was, what could be, the meaning of the shocking scene she had then been forced to witness? She dared not answer the question. Yet one ghastly doubt haunted her like her shadow—a suspicion that the malign and hideous light of madness was already glaring upon his mind. As, leaning upon the arm of her astonished attendant, she retraced her steps, the trees, the flowers, the familiar hall-door, the echoing passages—every object that met her eye—seemed strange and unsubstantial, and she gliding on among them in a horrid dream.

Time passed on: there was no renewal of the painful scene which dwelt so sensibly in the affrighted imagination of Rhoda. Marston's manner was changed towards her; he seemed shy, cowed, and uneasy in her presence, and thenceforth she saw less than ever of him. Meanwhile the time approached which was to witness the long-expected, and, by Rhoda, the intensely prayed for arrival of her brother.

Some four or five days before this event, Mr. Marston, having, as he said, some business in Chester, and further designing to meet his son there, took his departure from Gray Forest, leaving poor Rhoda to the guardianship of her guilty stepmother; and although she had seen so little of her father, yet the very consciousness of his presence had given her a certain confidence and sense of security, which vanished at the moment of his departure. Fear-stricken and wretched as he had been, his removal, nevertheless, seemed to her to render the lonely and inauspicious mansion still more desolate and ominous than before.

She had, with a vague and instinctive antipathy, avoided all contact and intercourse with Mrs. Marston, or as, for distinctness sake, we shall continue to call her, " Mademoiselle," since her return; and she on her part had appeared to acquiesce with a sort of scornful nonchalance, in the tacit understanding that she and her former pupil should see and hear as little as might be of one another.

Meanwhile poor Willett, with her good-natured honesty and her inexhaustible gossip, endeavoured to amuse and re-assure her young mistress, and sometimes even with some partial success.

*　　*　　*　　*　　*　　*　　*

We must now follow Mr. Marston in his solitary expedition to Chester. When he took his place in the stage-coach he had the whole interior of the vehicle to himself, and thus continued to be its solitary occupant for several miles. The coach, however, was eventually hailed, brought to, and the door being opened, Dr. Danvers got in, and took his place opposite to the pas-

senger already established there. The worthy man was
so busied in directing the disposition of his luggage from
the window, and in arranging the sundry small parcels
with which he was charged, that he did not recognise
his companion until they were in motion. When he did
so it was with no very pleasurable feeling; and it is
probable that Marston, too, would have gladly escaped
the coincidence which thus reduced them once more to
the temporary necessity of a *tête-à-tête*. Embarrassing
as each felt the situation to be, there was, however, no
avoiding it, and, after a recognition and a few forced
attempts at conversation, they became, by mutual
consent, silent and uncommunicative.

The journey, though in point of space a mere
trifle, was, in those slow-coach days, a matter of fully
five hours' duration; and before it was completed the
sun had set, and darkness began to close. Whether it
was that the descending twilight dispelled the painful
constraint under which Marston had seemed to labour,
or that some more purely spiritual and genial influence
had gradually dissipated the repulsion and distrust with
which, at first, he had shrunk from a renewal of intercourse with Dr. Danvers, he suddenly accosted him
thus :—

" Dr. Danvers, I have been fifty times on the point of
speaking to you—confidentially of course—while sitting
here opposite to you, what I believe I could scarcely
bring myself to hint to any other man living; yet I must
tell it, and soon, too, or I fear it will have told itself."

Dr. Danvers intimated his readiness to hear and advise, if desired; and Marston resumed abruptly, after a
pause—

" Pray, Doctor Danvers, have you heard any stories
of an odd kind ; any surmises—I don't mean of a *moral*
sort, for *those* I hold very cheap—to my prejudice ?
Indeed I should hardly say to my *prejudice ;* I mean—I
ought to say—in short, have you heard people remark
upon any fancied eccentricities, or that sort of thing,
about me ?"

He put the question with obvious difficulty, and at
last seemed to overcome his own reluctance with a sort of
angry and excited self-contempt and impatience. Doctor
Danvers was a little puzzled by the interrogatory, and
admitted, in reply, that he did not comprehend its drift.

"Doctor Danvers," he resumed, sternly and dejectedly, " I told you, in the chance interview we had some
months ago, that I was haunted by a certain fear. I did
not define it, nor do I think you suspect its nature.   It
is a fear of nothing mortal, but of the immortal tenant
of this body.   My *mind*, sir, is beginning to play me
tricks ; my guide mocks and terrifies me."

.There was a perceptible tinge of horror in the look of
astonishment with which Dr. Danvers listened.

" You are a gentleman, sir, and a Christian clergyman ; what I have said and shall say is confided to your
honour; to be held sacred as the confession of misery,
and hidden from the coarse gaze of the world.   I have
become subject to a hideous delusion. It comes at intervals. I do not think any mortal suspects it, except,
maybe, my daughter Rhoda.   It comes and disappears,
and comes again.   I kept my pleasant secret for a long
time, but at last I let it slip, and committed myself,
fortunately, to but one person, and that my daughter ;
and, even so, I hardly think she understood me.   I

recollected myself before I had disclosed the grotesque and infernal chimera that haunts me."

Marston paused. He was stooped forward, and looking upon the floor of the vehicle, so that his companion could not see his countenance. A silence ensued, which was interrupted by Marston, who once more resumed.

"Sir," said he, "I know not *why*, but I *have* longed, intensely longed, for some trustworthy ear into which to pour this horrid secret ; *why*, I repeat, I cannot tell, for I expect no sympathy, and hate compassion. It is, I suppose, the restless nature of the devil that is in me ; but, be it what it may, I will speak to you, but to *you* only ; for the present, at least, to you alone."

Doctor Danvers again assured him that he might repose the most entire confidence in his secrecy.

"The human mind, I take it, must have either comfort in the past or hope in the future," he continued, "otherwise it is *in danger*. To me, sir, the past is intolerably repulsive ; one boundless, barren, and hideous Golgotha of dead hopes and murdered opportunities; the future, still blacker and more furious, peopled with dreadful features of horror and menace, and losing itself in utter darkness. Sir, I do not exaggerate. Between such a past and such a future I stand upon this miserable present ; and the only comfort I still am capable of feeling is, that no human being pities me ; that I stand aloof from the insults of compassion and the hypocrisies of sympathetic morality ; and that I can safely defy all the respectable scoundrels in Christendom to enhance, by one feather's weight, the load which I myself have accumulated, and which I myself hourly and unaided sustain."

Doctor Danvers here introduced a word or two in the direction of their former conversation.

"No, sir, there is no comfort from that quarter either," said Marston, bitterly; "you but cast your seeds, as the parable terms your teaching, upon the barren sea, in wasting them on me. My fate, be it what it may, is as irrevocably fixed, as though I were dead and judged a hundred years ago."

"This cursed dream," he resumed abruptly, "that every day enslaves me more and more, has reference to that—that *occurrence* about Wynston Berkley—he is the hero of the hellish illusion. At certain times, sir, it seems to me as if he, though dead, were still invested with a sort of spurious life; going about unrecognised, except by me, in squalor and contempt, and whispering away my fame and life; labouring with the malignant industry of a fiend to involve me in the meshes of that special perdition from which alone I shrink, and to which this emissary of hell seems to have predestined me. Sir, this is a monstrous and hideous extravagance, a delusion, but, after all, no more than a trick of the *imagination;* the reason, the judgment, is untouched. I cannot choose but *see* all the damned phantasmagoria, but I do not believe it real, and this is the difference between my case and—and—*madness!*"

They were now entering the suburbs of Chester, and Doctor Danvers, pained and shocked beyond measure by this unlooked-for disclosure, and not knowing what remark or comfort to offer, relieved his temporary embarrassment by looking from the window, as though attracted by the flash of the lamps, among which the vehicle was now moving. Marston, however, laid his hand upon his

T

arm, and thus recalled him, for a moment, to a forced attention.

"It must seem strange to you, Doctor, that I should trust this cursed secret to your keeping," he said ; and. truth to say, it seems so to myself. I cannot account for the impulse, the irresistible power of which has forced me to disclose the hateful mystery to you, but the fact is this, beginning like a speck, this one idea has gradually darkened and dilated, until it has filled my entire mind. The solitary consciousness of the gigantic mastery it has established there had grown intolerable ; I must have told it. The sense of solitude under this aggressive and tremendous delusion was agony, hourly death to my soul. That is the secret of my talkativeness ; my sole excuse for plaguing you with the dreams of a wretched hypochondriac."

Doctor Danvers assured him that no apologies were needed, and was only restrained from adding the expression of that pity which he really felt, by the fear of irritating a temper so full of bitterness, pride, and defiance. A few minutes more, and the coach having reached its destination, they bid one another farewell, and parted.

*　　　*　　　*　　　*　　　*　　　*　　　*

At that time there resided in a decent mansion about a mile from the town of Chester, a dapper little gentleman, whom we shall call Doctor Parkes. This gentleman was the proprietor and sole professional manager of a private asylum for the insane, and enjoyed a high reputation, and a proportionate amount of business, in his melancholy calling. It was about the second day after the conversation we have just sketched, that this little gentleman, having visited, according to his custom, all his domestic patients, was about to take his accustomed walk in his somewhat restricted pleasure-grounds, when his servant announced a visiter.

"A gentleman," he repeated; "you have seen him before—eh ?"

"No, sir," replied the man; "he is in the study, sir."

"Ha !—a *professional* call. Well, we shall see."

So saying, the little gentleman summoned his gravest look, and hastened to the chamber of audience.

On entering he found a man dressed well, but gravely, having in his air and manner something of high breeding. In countenance striking, dark-featured, and stern, furrowed with the lines of pain or thought, rather than of age, although his dark hairs were largely mingled with white.

The physician bowed, and requested the stranger to take a chair; he, however, nodded slightly and impatiently, as if to intimate an intolerance of ceremony, and, advancing a step or two, said abruptly—

"My name, sir, is Marston; I have come to give you a patient."

The doctor bowed with a still deeper inclination, and paused for a continuance of the communication thus auspiciously commenced.

"You are Dr. Parkes, I take it for granted," said Marston, in the same tone.

"Your most obedient, humble servant, sir," replied he, with the polite formality of the day, and another grave bow.

"Doctor," demanded Marston, fixing his eye upon him sternly, and significantly tapping his own forehead, "can you stay execution ?"

The physician looked puzzled, hesitated, and at last requested his visiter to be more explicit.

"Can you," said Marston, with the same slow and stern articulation, and after a considerable pause——"can you *prevent* the malady you profess to cure?——can you meet and defeat the enemy half-way?——can you scare away the spirit of madness *before* it takes actual possession, and while it is still only hovering about its threatened victim?"

"Sir," he replied, "in certain cases—in very many, indeed—the enemy, as you well call it, *may* thus be met, and effectually worsted at a distance. Timely interposition, in ninety cases out of a hundred, is *everything;* and, I assure you, I hear your question with much pleasure, inasmuch as I assume it to have reference to the case of the patient about whom you desire to consult me; and who is, therefore, I hope, as yet merely *menaced* with the misfortune from which you would save him."

"I, myself, am that patient, sir," said Marston, with an effort; "your surmise is right. I am not mad, but unequivocally menaced with madness; it is not to be mistaken. Sir, there is no misunderstanding the tremendous and intolerable signs that glare upon my mind."

"And pray, sir, have you consulted your friends or your family upon the course best to be pursued?" inquired Dr. Parkes, with grave interest.

"No, sir," he answered sharply, and almost fiercely; "I have no fancy to make myself the subject of a writ *de lunatico inquirendo;* I don't want to lose my liberty and my property at a blow. The course I mean to take

has been advised by no one but myself—is *known* to no
other. I now disclose it, and the causes of it, to you,
a gentleman, and my professional adviser, in the expectation that you will guard with the strictest secrecy my
spontaneous revelations; this you promise me?"

"Certainly, Mr. Marston; I have neither the disposition nor the right to withhold such a promise," answered the physician.

"Well, then, I will first tell you the arrangement I
propose, with your permission, to make, and then I
shall answer all your questions respecting my own
case," resumed Marston, gloomily. "I wish to place
myself under your care, to live under your roof, reserv-
ing my full liberty of action. I must be free to come and
to go as I will; and on the other hand, I undertake that
you shall find me an amenable and docile patient enough.
In addition, I stipulate that there shall be no attempt
whatever made to communicate with those who are connected with me: these terms agreed upon, I place myself in your hands. You will find in me, as I said
before, a deferential patient, and I trust not a troublesome one. I hope you will excuse my adding, that I
shall myself pay the charge of my sojourn here from
week to week, in advance."

The proposed arrangement was a strange one; and
although Dr. Parkes dimly foresaw some of the embarrassments which might possibly arise from his accepting
it, there was yet so much that was reasonable as well as
advantageous in the proposal, that he could not bring
himself to decline it.

The preliminary arrangement concluded, Dr. Parkes
proceeded to his more strictly professional investigation.

It is, of course, needless to recapitulate the details of Marston's tormenting fancies, with which the reader has indeed been already sufficiently acquainted. Doctor Parkes, having attentively listened to the narrative, and satisfied himself as to the physical health of his patient, was still sorely puzzled as to the probable issue of the awful struggle already but too obviously commenced between the mind and its destroyer in the strange case before him. One satisfactory symptom unquestionably was, the as yet transitory nature of the delusion, and the evident and energetic tenacity with which reason contended for her vital ascendancy. It was a case, however, which for many reasons sorely perplexed him, but of which, notwithstanding, he was disposed, whether rightly or wrongly the reader will speedily see, to take by no means a decidedly gloomy view.

Having disburthened his mind of this horrible secret, Marston felt for a time a sense of relief amounting almost to elation. With far less of apprehension and dismay than he had done so for months before, he that night repaired to his bedroom. There was nothing in his case, Doctor Parkes believed, to warrant his keeping any watch upon Marston's actions, and accordingly he bid him good-night, in the full confidence of meeting him, if not better, at least not worse, on the ensuing morning.

He miscalculated, however. Marston had probably himself been conscious of some coming crisis in his hideous malady, when he took the decisive step of placing himself under the care of Doctor Parkes. Certain it is, that upon that very night the disease broke forth in a new and appalling development. Doctor Parkes, whose bedroom was next to that occupied by Marston, was awakened in the dead of night by a howling, more like that of a beast than a human voice, and which gradually swelled into an absolute yell; then came some horrid laughter and entreaties, thick and frantic; then again the same unearthly howl. The practised ear of Doctor Parkes recognised but too surely the terrific import of those sounds. Springing from his bed, and seizing the candle which always burned in his chamber, in anticipation of such sudden and fearful emergencies, he hurried with a palpitating heart, and spite of his long habituation to such scenes as he expected, with a certain sense of horror, to the chamber of his aristocratic patient.

Late as it was, Marston had not yet gone to bed; his candle was still burning, and he himself, half dressed, stood in the centre of the floor, shaking and livid, his eyes burning with the preterhuman fires of insanity. As Doctor Parkes entered the chamber, another shout, or rather yell, thundered from the lips of this demoniac effigy; and the mad-doctor stood freezing with horror in the doorway, and yet exerting what remained to him of presence of mind, in the vain endeavour, in the flaring light of the candle, to catch and fix with his own practised eye the gaze of the maniac. Second after second, and minute after minute, he stood confronting this frightful slave of Satan, in the momentary expectation that he would close with and destroy him. On a sudden, however, this brief agony of suspense was terminated; a change like an awaking consciousness of realities, or rather like the withdrawal of some hideous and visible influence from within, passed over the tense and darkened features of the wretched being; a look of horrified perplexity, doubt, and inquiry, supervened, and he at last said, in a subdued and sullen tone, to Doctor Parkes—

"Who are you, sir? What do you want here? Who are you, sir, I say?"

"Who am I? Why, your physician, sir; Doctor Parkes, sir; the owner of this house, sir,"͵ replied he, with all the sternness he could command, and yet white as a spectre with agitation. "For shame, sir, for shame, to give way thus. What do you mean by creating this causeless alarm, and disturbing the whole household at so unseasonable an hour? For shame, sir; go to your bed; undress yourself this moment; for shame."

Doctor Parkes, as he spoke, was reassured by the arrival of one of his servants, alarmed by the unmistakeable sounds of violent frenzy; he signed, however, to the man not to enter, feeling confident, as he did, that͵ the paroxysm had spent itself.

"Ay, ay," muttered Marston, looking almost sheepishly; "Doctor Parkes, to be sure. What was I thinking of? how cursedly absurd! And *this*," he continued, glancing at his sword, which he threw impatiently upon a sofa as he spoke. "Folly—nonsense! A false alarm, as you say, doctor. I beg your pardon."

As Marston spoke, he proceeded with much agitation slowly to undress himself. He had, however, but commenced the process, when, turning abruptly to Doctor Parkes, he said, with a countenance of horror, and in a whisper—

"By ——, doctor, it has been upon me worse than ever. I would have sworn I had the villain with me for

hours—*hours*, sir—torturing me with his damned sneering threats; till, by ——, I could stand it no longer,
and took my sword. Oh, doctor, doctor, can't you save
me? can nothing be done for me?"

Pale, covered with the dews of horror, he uttered
these last words in accents of such imploring despair,
as might have borne across the dreadful gulf the prayer
of Dives for that one drop of water which never was to
cool his burning tongue.

*   *   *   *   *   *   *

When Rhoda learned that her father, on leaving
Gray Forest, had fixed no definite period for his return, she began to feel her situation at home so
painful and equivocal, that, having taken honest Willett
to counsel, she came at last to the resolution of accepting the often conveyed invitation of Mrs. Mervyn
and sojourning, at all events until her father's return, at
Newton Park.

"My dear young friend," said the kind lady, as soon
as she heard Rhoda's little speech to its close, "I
can scarcely describe the gratification with which I
see you here; the happiness with which I welcome you
to Newton Park; nor, indeed, the anxiety with which I
constantly contemplated your trying and painful position
at Gray Forest. Indeed I ought to be angry with you
for having refused me this happiness so long; but you
have made amends at last; though, indeed, it was impossible to have deferred it longer. You must not fancy,
however, that I will consent to lose you so soon as you
seem to have intended. No, no; I have found it too
hard to catch you, to let you take wing so easily; besides, I have others to consult as well as myself, and per-

sons, too, who are just as anxious as I am to make a
prisoner of you here."

The good Mrs. Mervyn accompanied these words with
looks so sly, and emphasis so significant, that Rhoda
was fain to look down, to hide her blushes ; and com-
passionating the confusion she herself had caused, the
kind old lady led her to the chamber which was henceforward, so long as she consented to remain, to be her
own apartment.

How that day was passed, and how fleetly its hours
sped away, it is needless to tell. Old Mervyn had his
gentle as well as his grim aspect ; and no welcome was
ever more cordial and tender than that with which he
greeted the unprotected child of his morose and repulsive neighbour. It would be impossible to convey any
idea of the countless assiduities and the secret delight
with which young Mervyn attended their rambles.

The party were assembled at supper. What a contrast did this cheerful, happy—unutterably happy—
gathering, present, in the mind of Rhoda, to the dull,
drear, fearful evenings which she had long been wont to
pass at Gray Forest.

As they sate together in cheerful and happy intercourse, a chaise drove up to the hall-door, and the knocking had hardly ceased to reverberate, when a well-known
voice was heard in the hall.

Young Mervyn started to his feet, and merrily ejacu-
lating, " Charles Marston ! this *is* delightful !" disappeared, and in an instant returned with Charles himself.

We pass over all the embraces of brother and sister ;
the tears and smiles of re-united affection. We omit
the cordial shaking of hands ; the kind looks ; the

questions and answers; all these, and all the little attentions of that good old-fashioned hospitality, which
was never weary of demonstrating the cordiality of its
welcome, we abandon to the imagination of the good-
natured reader.

Charles Marston, with the advice of his friend, Mr.
Mervyn, resolved to lose no time in proceeding to Chester, whither it was ascertained his father had gone,
with the declared intention of meeting and accompanying him home. He arrived in that town in the evening;
and having previously learned that Doctor Danvers had
been for some time in Chester, he at once sought him at
his usual lodgings, and found the worthy old gentleman
at his solitary " dish" of tea.

" My dear Charles," said he, greeting his young
friend with earnest warmth, " I am rejoiced beyond
measure to see you. Your father *is* in town, as you
supposed; and I have just had a note from him, which
has, I confess, not a little agitated me, referring, as it
does, to a subject of painful and horrible interest; one
with which, I suppose, you are familiar, but upon which
I myself have never yet spoken fully to any person, excepting your father only."

" And pray, my dear sir, what *is* this topic?" inquired Charles, with marked interest.

" Read this note," answered the clergyman, placing
one at the same time in his young visiter's hand.

Charles read as follows :—

" My dear Sir,—I have a singular communication
to make to you, but in the strictest privacy, with reference to a subject which, merely to name, is to awaken

feelings of doubt and horror; I mean the confession of Merton, with respect to the murder of Wynston Berkley. I will call upon you this evening after dark ; for I have certain reasons for not caring to meet old acquaintances about town; and if you can afford me half an hour, I promise to complete my intended disclosure within that time.   Let us be strictly private; this is my only pro- viso.   Yours with much respect,

"RICHARD MARSTON."

"Your father has been sorely troubled in mind," said Doctor Danvers, as soon as the young man had read this communication ; " he has told me as much ; it may be that the discovery he has now made may possibly have relieved him from certain galling anxieties. The fear that unjust suspicion should light upon himself, or those connected with him, has, I dare say, tormented him sorely.   God grant, that as the providential unfolding of all the details of this mysterious crime comes about, he may be brought to recognise, in the just and terrible process, the hand of heaven.   God grant, that at last his heart may be softened, and his spirit illuminated by the blessed influence he has so long and so sternly re- jected."

As the old man thus spake—as if in symbolic answer- ing to his prayer—a sudden glory from the setting sun streamed through the funereal pile of clouds which filled the western horizon, and flooded the chamber where they were.

After a silence, Charles Marston said, with some little embarrassment—" It may be a strange confession to make, though, indeed, hardly so to you—for you know but too well the gloomy reserve with which my father has uniformly treated me—that the exact nature of Merton's confession never reached my ears; and once or twice, when I approached the subject, in conversation with you, it seemed to me that the subject was one which, for some reason, it was painful to you to enter upon."

"And so it was, in truth, my young friend—so it was; for that confession left behind it many fearful doubts, proving, indeed, nothing but the one fact, that, *morally*, the wretched man was guilty of the murder."

Charles, urged by a feeling of the keenest interest, requested Dr. Danvers to detail to him the particulars of the dying man's narration.

"Willingly," answered Dr. Danvers, with a look of gloom, and heaving a profound sigh—"willingly, for you have now come to an age when you may safely be entrusted with secrets affecting your own family, and which, although, thank God, as I believe, they in no respect involve the honour of any one of its members, yet might deeply involve its peace and its security against the assaults of vague and horrible slander. Here, then, is the narrative : Merton, when he was conscious of the approach of death, qualified, by a circumstantial and detailed statement, the absolute confession of guilt which he had at first sullenly made. In this he declared that the guilt of design and intention only was his—that in the act itself he had been *anticipated*. He stated, that from the moment when Sir Wynston's servant had casually mentioned the circumstance of his master's usually sleeping with his watch and pocket-book under his pillow, the idea of robbing him had taken possession of his mind. With the idea of robbing him (under the peculiar circumstances, his servant sleeping in the apartment close by, and the slightest alarm being, in all probability, sufficient to call him to the spot) the idea of anticipating resistance by murder had associated itself. He had contended against these haunting and growing solicitations of Satan, with an earnest agony. He had intended to leave his place, and fly from the mysterious temptation which he felt he wanted power to combat, but accident or fate prevented him. In a state of ghastly excitement he had, on the memorable night of Sir Wynston's murder, proceeded, as had afterwards appeared in evidence, by the back stair to the baronet's chamber; he had softly stolen into it, and gone to the bed-side, with the weapon in his hand. He drew his breath for the decisive stroke, which was to bereave the (supposed) sleeping man of life, and when stretching his left hand under the clothes, it rested upon a dull, cold corpse, and, at the same moment, his right hand was immersed in a pool of blood. He dropped the knife, recoiled a pace or so. With a painful effort, however, he again grasped with his hand to recover the weapon he had suffered to escape, and secured, as it afterwards turned out, not the knife with which he had meditated the commission of his crime, but the dagger which was afterwards found where he had concealed it. He was now fully alive to the horror of his situation; he was compromised as fully as if he had in very deed driven home the weapon. To be found under such circumstances, would convict him as surely as if fifty eyes had seen him strike the blow. He had nothing now for it but flight; and in order to guard himself against the contingency of being surprised from the door opening upon the corridor, he bolted it; then groped under the murdered man's pillow for the booty which had so fatally fascinated his imagination. Here he was disappointed. What further happened you already know."

Charles listened with breathless attention to this recital, and, after a painful interval, said :—

"Then the actual murderer is, after all, unascertained. This is, indeed, horrible ; it was very natural that my father should have felt the danger to which such a disclosure would have exposed the reputation of our family, yet *I* should have preferred encountering it, were it ten times as great, to the equivocal prudence of suppressing the truth with respect to a murder committed under my o n roof."

" He has, however, it would seem, arrived at some new conclusions," said Dr. Danvers, " and is now prepared to throw some unanticipated light upon the whole transaction."

Even as they were talking, a knocking was heard at the hall-door, and after a brief and hurried consultation, it was agreed, that, considering the strict condition of privacy attached to this visit by Mr. Marston himself, as well as his reserved and wayward temper, it might be better for Charles to avoid presenting himself to his father on this occasion. A few seconds afterwards the door opened, and Mr. Marston entered the apartment. It was now dark, and the servant, unbidden, placed candles upon the table. Without answering one word to Dr. Danvers' greeting, Marston sat down, as it seemed, in agitated abstraction. Removing his hat suddenly (for he had not even made this slight homage

to the laws of courtesy), he looked round with a care-
worn, fiery eye, and a pale countenance, and said—

"We are quite alone, Dr. Danvers—no one anywhere
near?"

Dr. Danvers assured him that all was secure.

After a long and agitated pause, Marston said—

"You remember Merton's confession. He admitted
his *intention* to kill Berkley, but denied that he was the
actual murderer. He spoke truth—no one knew it
better than I ; for *I* am the murderer."

Dr. Danvers was so shocked and overwhelmed that
he was utterly unable to speak.

"Ay, sir, in point of law and of morals, literally and
honestly, the MURDERER of Wynston Berkley. I am resolved you shall know it all. Make what use of it you will
—I care for nothing now, but to get rid of the d——d,
unsustainable secret, and that is done. I did not intend
to kill the scoundrel when I went to his room ; but with
the just feelings of exasperation with which I regarded
him, it would have been wiser had I avoided the interview ; and I meant to have done so. But his candle
was burning ; I saw the light through the door, and
went in. It was his evil fortune to indulge in his old
strain of sardonic impertinence. He provoked me ; I
struck him—he struck me again—and with his own
dagger I stabbed him three times. I did not know what
I had done ; I could not believe it. I felt neither remorse nor sorrow—why should I ?—but the thing was
horrible, astounding. There he sat in the corner of his
cushioned chair, with the old fiendish smile on still.
Sir, I never thought that any human shape could look

so dreadful. I don't know how long I stayed there, freezing with horror and detestation, and yet unable to take my eyes from the face. Did you see it in the coffin? Sir, there was a sneer of triumph on it that was diabolic and prophetic."

Marston was fearfully agitated as he spoke, and repeatedly wiped from his face the cold sweat that gathered there.

" I could not leave the room by the back stairs," he resumed, " for the valet slept in the intervening chamber. I felt such an appalled antipathy to the body, that I could scarce muster courage to pass it. But, sir, I am not easily cowed—I mastered this repugnance in a few minutes—or, rather, I acted in spite of it, I knew not how; but instinctively it seemed to me that it was better to lay the body in the bed, than leave it where it was, shewing, as its position might, that the thing occurred in an altercation. So, sir, I raised it, and bore it softly across the room, and laid it in the bed; and, while I was carrying it, it swayed forward, the arms glided round my neck, and the head rested against my cheek—that *was* a parody upon a brotherly embrace!

" I do not know at what moment it was, but some time when I was carrying Wynston, or laying him in the bed," continued Marston, who spoke rather like one pursuing a horrible reverie, than as a man relating facts to a listener, " I heard a light tread, and soft breathing in the lobby. A thunder-clap would have stunned me less that minute. I moved softly, holding my breath, to the door. I believe, in moments of strong excitement, men

U

hear more acutely than at other times; but I thought I heard the rustling of a gown, going *from* the door again. I waited—it ceased; I waited until all was quiet. I then extinguished the candle, and groped my way to the door; there was a faint light in the corridor, and I thought I saw a head projected from the chamber-door, next to the Frenchwoman's—mademoiselle's. As I came on, it was softly withdrawn, and the door not quite noiselessly closed. I could not be absolutely certain, but I learned all afterward. And now, sir, you have the story of Sir Wynston's murder."

Dr. Danvers groaned in spirit, being wrung alike with fear and sorrow. With hands clasped, and head bowed down, in an exceeding bitter agony of soul, he murmured only the words of the Litany—"Lord, have mercy upon us; Christ, have mercy upon us; Lord, have mercy upon us."

Marston had recovered his usual lowering aspect and gloomy self-possession in a few moments, and was now standing erect and defiant before the humbled and afflicted minister of God. The contrast was terrible—almost sublime.

* * * * * * *

Doctor Danvers resolved to keep this dreadful secret, at least for a time, to himself. He could not make up his mind to inflict upon those whom he loved so well as Charles and Rhoda the shame and agony of such a disclosure; yet he was sorely troubled, for his was a conflict of duty and mercy, of love and justice.

He told Charles Marston, when urged with earnest inquiry, that what he had heard that evening was intended solely for his own ear, and gently but peremptorily declined telling, at least until some future time, the substance of his father's communication.

Charles now felt it necessary to see his father, for the purpose of letting him know the substance of the letter respecting "mademoiselle" and the late Sir Wynston which had reached him. Accordingly, he proceeded, accompanied by Doctor Danvers, on the next morning, to the hotel where Marston had intimated his intention of passing the night.

On their inquiring for him in the hall, the porter appeared much perplexed and disturbed, and as they pressed him with questions, his answers became conflicting and mysterious. Mr. Marston was there—he had slept there last night; he could not say whether or not he was then in the house; but he knew that no one could be admitted to see him. He would, if the gentlemen wished it, send their cards to (*not* Mr. Marston, but) the *proprietor*. And, finally, he concluded by begging that they would themselves see "the proprietor," and despatched a waiter to apprise him of the circumstances of the visit. There was something odd and even sinister in all this, which, along with the whispering and the curious glances of the waiters, who happened to hear the errand on which they came, inspired the two companions with vague misgivings, which they did not care mutually to disclose.

In a few moments they were shown into a small sitting-room up stairs, where the proprietor, a fussy little gentleman, and apparently very uneasy and frightened, received them.

"We have called here to see Mr. Marston," said Doctor Danvers, "and the porter has referred us to you."

"Yes, sir, exactly—precisely so," answered the little man, fidgeting excessively, and, as it seemed, growing paler every instant; "but—but, in fact, sir, there is, there has been—in short, have you not heard of the—the *accident* ?"

He wound up with a prodigious effort, and wiped his forehead when he had done.

"Pray, sir, be explicit: we are near friends of Mr. Marston; in fact, sir, this is his son," said Doctor Danvers, pointing to Charles Marston; "and we are both uneasy at the reserve with which our inquiries have been met. Do, I entreat of you, say what has happened ?"

"Why—why," hesitated the man, "I really—I would not for five hundred pounds it had happened in my house. The—the unhappy gentleman has, in short ——" He glanced at Charles, as if afraid of the effect of the disclosure he was on the point of making, and then hurriedly said—"He is *dead*, sir; he was found dead in his room, this morning, at eight o'clock. I assure you I have not been myself ever since."

Charles Marston was so stunned by this sudden blow, that he was upon the point of fainting. Rallying, however, with a strong effort, he demanded to be conducted to the chamber where the body lay. The man assented, but hesitated on reaching the door, and whispered something in the ear of Doctor Danvers, who, as he heard it raised his hands and eyes with a mute expression of horror, and turning to Charles, said—

"My dear young friend, remain where you are for a few moments. I will return to you immediately, and tell you whatever I have ascertained. You are in no condition for such a scene at present."

Charles, indeed, felt that the fact was so, and, sick and giddy, suffered Doctor Danvers, with gentle compulsion, to force him into a seat.

In silence the venerable clergyman followed his conductor. With a palpitating heart he advanced to the bedside, and twice essayed to draw the curtain, and twice lost courage; but gathering resolution at last, he pulled the drapery aside, and beheld all he was to see again of Richard Marston.

The bedclothes were drawn so as nearly to cover the mouth.

" *There* is the wound, sir," whispered the man, as with coarse officiousness he drew back the bedclothes from the throat of the corpse, and exhibited a gash, as it seemed, nearly severing the head from the body. With sickening horror Doctor Danvers turned away from the awful spectacle. He covered his face in his hands, and it seemed to him as if a soft, solemn voice whispered in his ear the mystic words, " Whoso sheddeth man's blood, by man shall his blood be shed."

The hand which, but a few years before, had, unsuspected, consigned a fellow-mortal to the grave, had itself avenged the murder—Marston had perished by his own hand.

*   *   *   *   *   *   *

Naturally ambitious and intriguing, the perilous tendencies of such a spirit in Mademoiselle de Barras had never been schooled by the mighty and benignant principles of religion. Of her accidental acquaintance at Rouen with Sir Wynston Berkley, and her subsequent introduction, in an evil hour, into the family at Gray Forest, it is unnecessary to speak. The unhappy terms on which she found Marston living with his wife, suggested, in their mutual alienation, the idea of founding a double influence in the household ; and to conceive the idea, and to act upon it, were, in her active mind, the same. Young, beautiful, fascinating, she well knew the power of her attractions, and determined, though probably without one thought of transgressing the limits of literal propriety, to bring them to bear upon the discontented, retired *roué*, for whom she cared absolutely nothing, except as the instrument, and in part the victim of her schemes. Thus yielding to the double instinct that swayed her, she gratified, at the same time, her love of intrigue and her love of power. At length, however, came the hour which demanded a sacrifice to the evil influence she had hitherto worshipped on such easy terms. She found that her power must now be secured by crime, and she fell. Then came the arrival of Sir Wynston—his murder—her elopement with Marston, and her guilty and joyless triumph. At last, however, came the blow, long suspended and terrific, which shattered all her hopes and schemes, and drove her once again upon the world. The catastrophe we have just described. After it she made her way to Paris. Arrived in the capital of France, she speedily dissipated whatever remained of the money and valuables which she had taken with her from Gray Forest; and Madame Marston, as she now styled herself, was glad to place herself once more as a governess in an aristocratic family. So far her good fortune had prevailed in averting the punishment but too well earned by her past life. But a day of reckoning was to come. A few years later France was involved in the uproar and conflagration of revolution. Noble families were scattered, beggared, decimated; and their dependants, often dragged along with them into the flaming abyss, in many instances suffered the last dire extremities of human ill. It was at this awful period that a retribution so frightful and extraordinary overtook Madame Marston, that we may hereafter venture to make it the subject of a separate narrative. Until then the reader will rest satisfied with what he already knows of her history; and meanwhile bid a long, and as it may possibly turn out, an eternal farewell to that beautiful embodiment of an evil and disastrous influence.

The concluding chapter in a novel is always brief, though seldom so short as the world would have it. In a tale like this, the "winding up" must be proportionably contracted. We have scarcely a claim to so many lines as the formal novelist may occupy pages, in the distribution of poetic justice, and the final grouping of his characters into that effective tableau upon which, at last, the curtain gracefully descends. We, too, may be all the briefer, inasmuch as the reader has doubtless anticipated the little we have to say. It amounts, then, to this:— Within two years after the fearful event which we have just recorded, an alliance had drawn together, in nearer and dearer union, the inmates of Gray Forest and Newton Park. Rhoda had given her hand to young Mervyn. Of ulterior consequences we say nothing—the nursery is above our province. And now, at length, after this Christmas journey through somewhat stern and gloomy scenery, in this long-deferred flood of golden sunshine we bid thee, gentle reader, a kind farewell.

THE END.

Dublin: Printed by EDWARD BULL, 6, Bachelor's-walk.

CPSIA information can be obtained at www.ICGtesting.com
Printed in the USA
LVOW08*1453171214

419283LV00004B/71/P